Transforming Rural China

Since the introduction of economic reforms in the late 1970s, rural China has undergone a profound and at times devastating transformation from a state-run economy and society to one of private ownership. In *Transforming Rural China*, Chen shows that this transformation has not necessarily taken the form of free market capitalism, as many believe, but in fact has assumed different forms in different parts of the country. Based on years of extensive research in villages in the Yangtze Delta region and southern Fujian, Chen provides shocking insight into the workings of China's local economy and society – how party officials have become entrepreneurs, building economic success on the backs of workers and peasants, and how and why entrepreneurs have been assimilated into the party. What emerges is a disturbing picture of property rights transformation lying far outside of the aims and control of the central government, and is wrapped in the utter disharmony of particular local institutions.

Chih-jou Jay Chen is Assistant Research Fellow, Institute of Sociology, Academia Sinica.

RoutledgeCurzon studies on China in transition
Series Editor: David S. G. Goodman

1 **The Democratisation of China**
   Baogang He

2 **Beyond Beijing**
   Dali Yang

3 **China's Enterprise Reform**
   Changing state/society relations after Mao
   You Ji

4 **Industrial Change in China**
   Economic restructuring and conflicting interests
   Kate Hannan

5 **The Entrepreneurial State in China**
   Real estate and commerce departments in reform era Tianjin
   Jane Duckett

6 **Tourism and Modernity in China**
   Tim Oakes

7 **Cities in Post-Mao China**
   Recipes for economic development in the reform era
   Jae Ho Chung

8 **China's Spatial Economic Development**
   Regional transformation in the Lower Yangtze Delta
   Andrew M. Marton

9 **Regional Development in China**
   States, globalization and inequality
   Yehua Dennis Wei

10 **Grassroots Charisma**
Four local leaders in China
Stephan Feuchtwang and Wang Mingming

11 **The Chinese Legal System**
Globalization and local legal culture
Pitman B. Potter

12 **Transforming Rural China**
How local institutions shape property rights in China
Chih-jou Jay Chen

13 **Negotiating Ethnicity in China**
Citizenship as a response to the state
Chih-yu Shih

14 **Manager Empowerment in China**
Political implications on rural industrialisation in the reform era
Ray Yep

15 **Cultural Nationalism in Contemporary China**
The search for national identity under reform
Yingjie Guo

16 **Elite Dualism and Leadership Selection in China**
Xiaowei Zang

17 **Chinese Intellectuals Between State and Market**
Edward Gu and Merle Goldman

18 **China, Sex and Prostitution**
Elaine Jeffreys

19 **The Development of China's Stockmarket, 1984–2002**
Equity politics and market institutions
Stephen Green

20 **China's Rational Entrepreneurs**
The development of the new private business sector
Barbara Krug

21 **China's Scientific Elite**
Cong Cao

Transforming Rural China
How local institutions shape property rights in China

Chih-jou Jay Chen

RoutledgeCurzon
Taylor & Francis Group
LONDON AND NEW YORK

First published 2004
by RoutledgeCurzon
2 Park Square, Milton Park, Abingdon, Oxon OX14 4RN

Simultaneously published in the USA and Canada
by RoutledgeCurzon
270 Madison Ave, New York, NY 10016

RoutledgeCurzon is an imprint of the Taylor & Francis Group

© 2004 Chih-jou Jay Chen

Typeset in Baskerville by Wearset Ltd, Boldon, Tyne and Wear
Printed and bound in Great Britain by MPG Books Ltd, Bodmin

All rights reserved. No part of this book may be reprinted or reproduced or utilized in any form or by any electronic, mechanical, or other means, now known or hereafter invented, including photocopying and recording, or in any information storage or retrieval system, without permission in writing from the publishers.

British Library Cataloguing in Publication Data
A catalogue record for this book is available from the British Library

Library of Congress Cataloging in Publication Data
A catalog record for this book has been requested

ISBN 0-415-19672-8

For Shuting and Yongguan

Contents

List of illustrations x
Acknowledgments xii
List of abbreviations xiv

   Introduction: notes from the field   1
1 Explaining property rights transformations   7

PART I
The Yangtze Delta property rights transformations   31

2 The Yangtze Delta in the reform era   33
3 The Yangtze Delta in the post-reform era   70
4 Shuang village: the case study   100

PART II
Southern Fujian property rights transformations   125

5 Southern Fujian under economic reforms   127
6 Hancun village: the case study   160
7 Conclusion: local institutions and the future of China   178

Notes 188
Bibliography 194
Index 208

Illustrations

Plates

4.1	Overlooking Shuang village industry	102
4.2	Roof of differential polyester chip factory in Shuang	109
4.3	Shuang village government office building	113
4.4	Entrepreneur and cadre residences in Shuang village	117
4.5	Farmland waiting to be turned into an industrial park	120
4.6	Peasant home in Shuang	122
6.1	Hancun village lineage hall	163
6.2	Garment factory in Shishi employing out-of-province workers	167
6.3	A Hancun village entrepreneur at home with a 30,000-yuan large-screen LCD TV behind him	168
6.4	A ship from Lin Xuiyan's fleet	171
6.5	Villagers' residences in Hancun's New Village area	176
6.6	Ocean dike around Hancun village built by Lin Wei	177

Maps

1.1	Map of China showing Jiangsu, Shanghai, and Fujian	21
1.2	Map of Jiangsu, Shanghai, and Fujian research sites	22

Tables

1.1	Per capita rural household net income and average annual growth	23
1.2	Per capita gross domestic products and average annual growth	24
1.3	Regional variation in shares of industrial output by ownership at mid-reform	26
1.4	Composition of gross social product, 1980	28
1.5	Industrial base in different regions	29
2.1	Growth of rural industry in Shanghai suburbs, 1978–2001	37

2.2	The ownership structure of rural industry in Shanghai suburbs, 1978–2001	38
2.3	Growth of rural industry in Wujiang, 1978–2001	40
2.4	The ownership structure of rural industry in Wujiang	41–42
2.5	The development of industrial enterprise in Shanghai sampled villages, 1987 and 1993	44
2.6	The ownership composition of village enterprises in Shanghai suburbs, 1987 and 1993	46
2.7	Jointly operated TVEs in southern Jiangsu, 1986	63
2.8	The joint operation of TVEs in Shanghai suburbs	64
2.9	The foreign funds absorbed in rural industry	66
3.1	Performance of TVEs in Shuang village, 1984–2001	76–78
3.2	Financial indicators for village enterprises in Shuang village, February 1998	85
3.3	Financial indicators for TVEs in Shuang village, 1998–2001	87
3.4	Changes of share divisions for TVEs in Shuang village, 1998–2002	88
3.5	Cadre and director posts in Shuang village, 1970s–2002	92
3.6	Average annual earnings in Shuang village, 1987–1999	95
3.7	The annual fees paid by the enterprises after privatization in Shuang village, 1998–297	97
5.1	The ownership structure of industrial output in Jinjiang and Shishi, 1970–1993	130
5.2	Basic data on field sites in southern Fujian, 1994	132
5.3	Ownership structure of rural enterprises in Jinjiang and China, 1984 and 1992	136
5.4	Household enterprises in Jinjiang, 1995	138
5.5	Receipts and expenditures of village governments in Jinjiang	153

Acknowledgments

This project began in 1995 with the fieldwork for my dissertation at Duke University. Over the course of eight years in the field, as well as in academia, I have incurred the debt of many who have helped me along the way, not the least so because this book has gone above and beyond what my dissertation started out as.

Nan Lin steered me into the China field as a first year Ph.D. student at Duke and has continued to encourage and advise me throughout this project and my career. He gave me what every graduate student needs but is not always so lucky to get: a mentor. His inclusion into my institute at Academia Sinica has meant that our relationship has only grown stronger since my graduation, from which I have benefited tremendously in learning and collaboration with him.

During my research trips to China, I incurred many debts to many people. My relationships with many of these contacts have spanned the better part of a decade. Ye Endian, of the Quanzhou Maritime Museum, opened many doors for me in the Jinjiang area. Lin Shuiqiang, a retired government official and well respected local gentry, welcomed me into his home when we first met and continued to accommodate me throughout my fieldwork for my dissertation and follow-up visits thereafter. Lu Hanlong, director of the Institute of Sociology at the Shanghai Academy of Social Sciences, cooperated with Nan Lin on a village survey in suburban Shanghai and arranged my field research in several Shanghai villages. Wang Yuhua, a non-traditional female scientist, bridged me into the village in Wujiang, and facilitated connections and information collection over the past several years.

Jean Oi and Andrew Walder offered valuable comments and criticism on a book chapter drawn from this study. This book has greatly benefited from their insights and expertise. Discussions on related issues in China studies and economic sociology with Xueguang Zhou also helped me through different stages of writing this book. Thanks also go to my past teachers and current colleagues at Academia Sinica, among whom Chih-Ming Ka and Ying-Hwa Chang are most representative and supportive. Thanks also go to my colleagues in the sociology institute at Academia

Sinica, the sociology department at National Taiwan University, and the Center for Contemporary China at National Tsing-Hua University.

Duke University provided generous scholarship for my graduate study and field research. The National Science Council and Academia Sinica in Taiwan offered research grants for later research.

Macabe Keliher's substantial and tactile contribution to this book, complimented by his unreserved commitment, helped me realize the book's completion in the critical last mile. A collaborative project with him is in the works, and promises to expand the importance of local institutions to its uncompromising ramifications in China.

Stanford University Press has kindly granted me permission to draw on a previously published material, which has been extensively revised and updated: "Local Institutions and Property Rights Transformations in Southern Fujian," pp. 49–70 in *Property Rights and Economic Reform in China*, edited by Jean C. Oi and Andrew G. Walder; © 1999 by the Board of Trustees of the Leland Stanford Jr. University.

Finally, I thank my family members for putting up with this project and my complete obsession with it for an unnecessarily long time. I dedicate this book to my wife, Shuting, and our newborn son, Yongguan.

Chih-jou Jay Chen
Taipei
October 2003

Abbreviations

DZDJ	*Dandai zhongguo de jiangsu* (Jiangsu in Modern China)
FDI	Foreign Direct Investment
FTN	*Fujian tongji nianjian* (Statistical Yearbook of Fujian)
FJN	*Fujian jingji nianjian* (Economic Yearbook of Fujian)
GVIO	Gross Value of Industrial Output
HDXW	*Huadong xinwen* (Eastern China News of People's Daily)
JSZ	*Jinjiang shi zhi* (Jinjiang Annals)
JGTZ	*Jinjiang xian guoming jingji tongji ziliao* (Statistical Material on National Economy in Jinjiang County)
JTN	*Jiangsu tongji nianjian* (Statistical Yearbook of Jiangsu)
JXQ	*Jiangsu sheng xiangzhen qiye tongji ziliao 1986* (Statistical Material on Rural Enterprises, Jiangsu Province 1986)
QGZH	*Quanguo gesheng zizhiqu zhixiashi lishi tongji ziliao huibian 1949–1989* (Historical Statistical Material on the Nation's Provinces, Autonomous Regions, and Municipalities, 1949–1989)
QSHZ	*Quanzhou shi huaqiao zhi* (Annals of Quanzhou's Overseas Chinese)
QSXQZ	*Quanzhou shi xiangzhen qiye zhi* (Annals of Quanzhou's township and village enterprises)
QZWB	*Quanzhou wanbao* (Quanzhou Evening News)
SJN	*Shanghai jiaoqu nianjian* (Almanac of Shanghai Suburbs)
SJTN	*Shanghai jiaoqu tongji nianjian* (Statistical Yearbook of Shanghai Suburbs)
SNTN	*Shanghai nongcun tongji nianjian* (Statistical Yearbook of Rural Shanghai)
STN	*Shanghai tongji nianjian* (Statistical Yearbook of Shanghai)
SUSJTZ	*Suzhou shi shehui jingji tongji ziliao 1949–1985* (Statistical Material on Society and Economy, Suzhou City, 1949–1985)
SUTN	*Suzhou tongji nianjian* (Statistical Yearbook of Suzhou)
TVES	Township and Village Enterprises
XSGTZ	*Xinshanghai gongye tongji ziliao 1949–1990* (Statistical Yearbook of New Shanghai's Industry 1949–1990)

XQZFX	*Xiangzhen qiye zhengce fagui xuanbian* (Selected Laws and Regulations Concerning Township-Village Enterprise)
ZGC	*Zhongguo guoqing congshu: baixiangshi jingji shehui diaocha, jinjiang juan* (A Series of China's National Information – One Hundred County and City Socioeconomic Survey: Jinjiang book part)
ZNN	*Zhongguo nongye nianjian* (Agricultural Yearbook of China)
ZSJN	*Zhongguo siying jingji nianjian* (Almanac of Chinese Private Economy)
ZTN	*Zhongguo tongji nianjian* (Statistical Yearbook of China)
ZXQN	*Zhongguo xiangzhen qiye nianjian* (Yearbook of Chinese Township and Village Enterprises)

Introduction
Notes from the field

I first came to Fujian as a Duke graduate student looking for a case study on which to base my sociology dissertation. Although I had grown up in Taiwan, where the closest I had gotten to China was peering 2 kilometers through binoculars everyday while stationed in Jinmen (Quemoy) during mandatory military service, I had an intuitive feeling that China's economic reforms were not only deceiving but also non-uniform. Sure these reforms have been touted the world over as a shift away from a command economy and towards free market capitalism, and the literature about the transition and its consequences swamp libraries, but it all struck me as disjointed, if not illusionary. If policies were uniform, why would peasant workers in Tianjin be striking while former peasants in Fujian were opening clothing manufacturing businesses in their living rooms? If the party was the protector of the people then why were lineage families in the southern coastal provinces responsible for village affairs, including infrastructure projects, while party secretaries in Shanghai got rich off large chemical factories? Indeed, was it even possible to talk about the reforms and their outcome – or even China for that matter – as a plenary constant?

My idea was to pick two diverse regions – Fujian and Jiangsu – and perform in-depth case studies, charting the past twenty years of development of these two areas since economic reforms. Such a study would, presumably, show how each region moved out from the umbrella of uniform state regulations at the end of the 1970s, to grow in drastically disparate ways over the next twenty years due to endemic factors.

While in Fujian on summer vacation in 1995 I happened upon a recently published lineage history of Hancun village, a coastal village about 120 kilometers north of Xiamen. It was meticulously compiled, charting the village and its inhabitants from its birth in the Ming Dynasty up until the present. I got in touch with the copy editor who agreed to introduce me to Lin Shuiqiang, the chief editor and initiator of the project and also the village elder. The editor said he would meet me at the Shishi bus station, just 3 kilometers southwest of Hancun, and take me to meet Lin.

I woke late on the said morning, and the muggy Fujian heat had already swarmed the city. My little apartment, which I rented by the week, was hot, making me torpid, and unwilling to change out of the shorts and T-shirt I had fallen asleep in the night before. So I only strapped on my money belt and headed to the Xiamen train station to flag down a minibus heading north to Shishi.

The bus drove around the city for an hour trying to fill the seats before it headed out of town. The driver's acolyte hanging out of the open folding door yelling at anyone and everyone walking down the sidewalk, as if they would suddenly become possessed by the urge to drop the day's activities in Xiamen and take a ride to Shishi. In this way we picked up a merchant in a cheap polyester western suit, another merchant in a western suit with the label still on the jacket sleeve, a poor peasant who took seasonal work in the city, and one or two local women. The peasant sat in the seat directly in front of me, a young dirty kid, dressed for hard labor in his western suit, who tried not to exist. We were finally on our way.

Going was slow and dirty. The road was under construction, reducing us to a slow crawl over dirt and gravel and dust, or long standstills in the putrid sun. All the windows were open and all the dust and pollution blew in to mix with the chronically smoking passengers. Furthermore, despite a cramped bus with people already sitting on wooden stools in the aisle, the driver and his abettor wanted to increase their earnings by stopping for anyone and everyone along the road and cramming them too into the bus. People got on, people got off. The dust stayed.

About an hour up the road we came to Jimei town, which has a historical reputation of being bandit infested. Just outside of the town, the driver pulled over and swung open the door for four suit-clad men. Before the bus could get back on the road they yelled at him to pull over. Whether the driver and the money collector were in cohorts with the bandits one can never know, but the suited men let them keep their ticket fares and instead pressed the cold blade of a three foot machete against the neck of the passenger in the first seat. They took the black bag the men dangle off their wrists, and in which they conceal all their earnings, transactions and cash. The highwaymen wanted the bags of every single passenger on the bus. The noisy chatter had suddenly become deathly silent.

With over $800 in US currency and 800 yuan in cash I was by far the most opulent on the bus. As the blade went around from neck to neck I resigned myself to the fact that all was lost. Oh well. Duke and my advisor would still have grant money to give. By the time the thieves had come within a few rows I had become more curious than startled; I was even excited. I had come to China to do fieldwork, and here an opportunity to observe wrinkles in the social system had jumped into my lap. I poked my head around to see how much they collected from each passenger; I threw a look of compliment if they happened upon a substantial score.

The blade went to the peasant's throat and he began to cry. "I am poor and worked for two months to take this money home. It's all I have."

His babbling got him a slap on the face and an insulting invective. How much money? Two months salary at 1,000 yuan. "You fool, why do you carry around so much cash," I said slapping him playfully on the back of the head.

The thieves were amused. I seemed just a baby faced insouciant kid with glasses and four big white characters, Xiamen University, plastered against my blue shirt. They took me for a student. They took me for a poor student with nothing to lose and nothing to gain; one who did not malign their acts nor deprecate their persons. One who took an interest and not a fear. The knife hesitated at my throat for a second before passing me by and touching the others around me. Then they left with their loot. I kept mine, and gave the poor peasant what he lost.

Five hours later, I got off, taking only the grime of the road with me. The editor was at the station and hurried me into the back of a three-wheeled two-stroke pickup truck, where we enjoyed a twenty-minute ride with twelve other men to Hancun village. A few Toyotas and minivans crawled the streets here, but most people rode the pickups or had motor scooters. Even the village party secretary drove himself around on a motor scooter he purchased himself. The streets were crowded and loud with horns blaring. Street girls crawled the blocks in between crowds of men and women rushing this way and that. Businessmen and merchants filled the sidewalks in their polyester western suits, some hawking their wares, some haggling for prices. Although I was a foreigner to these parts, not once did anyone look twice at me, nor wonder what I was doing in this village on the coast.

Here I met Lin Shuiqiang, who would become one of the key subjects of my eight-year long research project on China's local institutions. Lin was a former Quanzhou City deputy mayor and remained the village elder. He spoke Minnan, a southern dialect of Mandarin, which is as similar to Taiwanese as a Boston accent is to a Texas accent. I addressed him in my native Taiwanese tongue and he responded as if we were relatives, launching into an ecstatic tale of how he had been to Taiwan when he was eighteen years old, and how he had always felt close to Taiwan. I told him I had read his book and thought it one of the most important things to come out of Fujian. I told him I would take it to the US and to Taiwan and make sure all the libraries I visited had it on their shelves.

That night, over the round table at Lin's home, picking at his wife's home cooking with chopsticks, I told Lin I too was writing a book about Fujian. I told Lin I wanted to research his village. "You can stay as long as you want," he said. "You can come as often as you like, and you will stay in my home."

That was the summer of 1995. Although I would visit Shuang village in Sunan (southern Jiangsu) a few months later, it was not until 2002 – after seven years of interacting with the village and its people – that I was finally welcome as a personal friend, instead of a business guest, of the village; that I was finally able to stay in the village hotel and have a casual, instead of official, dinner with the village leaders. The whole Sunan experience was, in fact, vastly different from the Fujian one. It came to characterize my entire research project, weighing the two regions of China in adroit and disparate personal experiences.

While finding an appropriate case study in Fujian entailed making a direct call to the copy editor of a book I found fascinating, Sunan needed patience and a lot of time cultivating personal relationships. My dissertation advisor put me in touch with a former student of his at the sociology department at Nanjing University, Professor Song. Song had a student whose father was the party secretary of a township in Sunan. This was a good start, but we could not meet the secretary without an introduction from someone in a city government. Fortunately the chair had a classmate who was the deputy director of the policy research office in Suzhou City. This would do.

From Nanjing we rode the train two hours west to Suzhou, where the deputy director's driver picked us up in the office's black Santana VW and drove us an uneventful 40 minutes to Tuncun township to meet the party secretary, the father of Professor Song's student.

We had lunch with the secretary in a cold formal dining room that still had Cultural Revolution banners hanging in the corner. "Remember the bitterness of yesterday to know the sweetness of today," read one. I had to fill myself with enough rice wine to detoxify a Chinese hospital in order to get the meat down. There was plenty of alcohol and the party secretary loved to drink, especially when the bill went to the government. I told him I wanted to research economic development in Sunan. He told me I would be better off researching Mei township, the next town over, because it was doing better. Maybe it was, or maybe he just wanted to get me out of his district so he would have one less complication in the graft he ran, but he said he would put a call in for me that afternoon.

Prohibited from staying in the countryside, the driver took the professor and I to Wujiang City for a night in the city's best hotel; complete with two karaoke bars, three restaurants, and three waitresses for every customer, the only thing the place lacked was a swimming pool. Fellow travelers appeared to be officials from other parts of the country.

The next morning the driver came to pick us up for another uneventful 30-minute ride to Mei township, for another lunch with another party secretary, Huang Song. Again we drank, and again we ate, and again the officials were less than munificent with information, but happy to let the tax payers foot the bill. I asked about development in their town and how far they had come and what they hoped to see. Answers were laconic and everyone seemed happy when the party ended.

Having fulfilled his obligation, Professor Song felt my field work complete with more than enough information to go back to America and write my dissertation; the whole thing would have ended right there too if it had not been for two engineers who joined us for lunch: Wang Hua and Li Dong. They were from Tianjin, and had come to the village to help develop chemical fibers. Educated, and with less vested personal interest in the village and its web of personal relationships, they were outsiders like me. And they were college educated, unlike anyone else in the village who rarely even had a middle school education. They had come to the village in 1987 but still sparked the curiosity of the residents when out and about town. There were no bustling markets here, no street girls or motor scooters. If Hancun was dirty, crowded and noisy, Shuang was clean, empty and quiet. No one that did not live here traveled here, there was no reason to; there was hardly any transportation. Residents walked or rode bicycles. Officials rode in chauffeured sedans.

I rode with the chair out of the village that afternoon in our chauffeured sedan speeding along down the new asphalt. I let the badgered Song believe that I had achieved what I needed and dropped him back in his office at Nanjing. But over the next three months I would make the trip to Wujiang at least five times. I would stay in that ostentatious hotel and place a call to Wang Hua, asking if she could come down and meet me. It was here that I began to learn about the operations of a village in Sunan and its industry. Wang teased my curiosity with details of the collectives breaking out from central control and developing their own industries; of the party control over all finances and profits; and strict sensors placed on private entrepreneurs. I also heard the story of how Wang and Li were cheated out of promised stock options and bonus, and how the village leaders stocked the industries with their people, keeping profits among the elite circle.

Throughout the 1990s, I was never trusted or fully accepted in the village. Wang brought me for a tour a few times, but only for half a day. I kept alert to possible troubles while poking around and asking questions, and I could never stay the night without incurring suspicion. In fact, I was taking a risk by not applying to the city governments for permission to research the countryside. Regulations stipulated that anyone not doing business had to report to authorities with their purpose of travel and inquiry. Such regulation brought with it constraint of movement, and thus limited access. I had decided to go without official approval and take my chances by cultivating advantageous relationships. It involved a bit of clandestine, for if anyone become unhappy with me and reported me I could have been deported and blacklisted. China does not encourage such research. In Fujian, these problems felt almost nonexistent; in Sunan suspicions were easier provoked. Indeed, if Fujian was the libertine, then Sunan was the chaste prude.

Then, in 2002, the government handed down directions, commanding Sunan to privatize and promote foreign investment. I was suddenly welcome with open arms. Huang Song, the party secretary, visited me in Taipei, asking for help in finding Taiwanese investors for his township and village. When I went to visit them in Shuang I was treated like royalty with all expenses paid. I stayed in the village hotel and ate everyday in the village restaurant reserved for party officials. "Dr. Chen, just tell us what you need and we will get it for you," Huang said to me when I arrived. I told him I wanted to look at the transfer of ownership contracts. He told the accountants to give me whatever I needed, to copy for me whatever I wanted to take with me. And there was my reward. After seven years trying to piece this village puzzle together I finally held between my fingers everything that had made it go round over the past 20 years. I had just been handed the secrets of China's economic reforms; the corruption, the nepotism, the contradictions, and the evidence of the wealth grabbed by the elites at the expenses of the people.

1 Explaining property rights transformations

Economists were not nonplussed when China opened its markets in the 1980s and its economy took off in double-digit annual growth rates. Free market capitalism at work, economists said. As reforms quickened in the early 1990s, annual GDP growth rose in double digits. Still, China watchers and scholars held that this was a historical trend. The USSR had collapsed, after all, and Eastern Europe was now posting strong growth under a free market economy.

China is not Eastern Europe, however. In fact, China is not even a free market economy, no matter how many special characteristics the country's leaders make up. Although the central government enacted economic reforms beginning in the late 1970s that were a step away from the centrally controlled economy imposed upon the entire country, the market was far from free. In fact it was coming under the control of local institutions that could vary widely in shape, size and power, from one end of the great country to the other. Because of the sometimes rigid control of these local institutions, which allowed them to be flexible to central policy in their own right, the local, and thus national, economy changed and grew. In particular, China's rural economy developed under a variety of local institutions.

The figures are enough to raise eyebrows. Gross value of industrial output of rural nonagricultural enterprises (township and village enterprises – TVEs) jumped from 9.8 percent of the country's total in 1980 to 47 percent in 2000. In the mid-1990s TVEs already employed 34 percent of the country, up from 9.4 percent in 1980, and accounted for nearly half of the country's exports (ZXQN 1997: 3–9). This means that nearly half of China's economy was built on the industrialized countryside; an unprecedented phenomena in the history of modern economics.

How did China's countryside transform in such a monumental way? Central to the analysis and understanding of China's rural reforms lies the question of the types of institutions that have undergone changes and the ways in which they have changed. Village party secretaries, for example, who were once loyal communist party ideologues, have become profit driven capitalist bosses, who have affected, and will continue to affect

8 *Explaining property rights transformations*

China's economic development. In fact, there exists a wide variety of paths for local development based on different property rights relations in the localities – these range from the local government-controlled collective economy to the predominance of private businesses.

These observations on Chinese rural reforms and consequent developments lead to the question of how this all came about. What are the specific property rights arrangements of rural enterprises in Chinese reforms? How should we understand the variations of property rights relations across regions in both the reform and post-reform era? Why did rural industries take off in a post-communist society with its political institutions largely intact and property rights and incentive structure poorly defined? Who have exercised property rights over assets, and how were these rights enforced? How do property rights arrangements vary across regions and how (and why) do they evolve through time? If transfers of the collective property rights are carried out thoroughly in pro-collective regions, what are the ramifications for the socialist nature of China's rural economy?

This study takes these issues as both a starting point and a central focus, and seeks to offer a sociological explanation of the Chinese-style market transformations over the past two decades that have played a pivotal role in China's economic growth. It aims to understand the social institutional foundations of the successful developing Chinese economies and account for the mechanisms underlying developmental progress.

Contending explanations of Chinese reforms

Studies of China's economy have painted different pictures of the economic institutions in rural China and the property rights relations that define them. Some studies argue that the driving force behind economic reforms comes from the private sector, in which individual entrepreneurs have continued to push for economic change. This is the Market Transition Account. The other side holds that local bureaucratic organs drive rural economic reform by using village collectives as money making entities – this is to say, the local governments play the role of the entrepreneur, even throughout the privatization process. This is the Local State Corporatism Account.

The Market Transition Account

The Market Transition Account is a line of thinking about market reform in state socialist countries inspired by Kornai (1986), first developed by Szelenyi (1978), and later elaborated into the arresting "market transition theory" by Nee (1989, 1991, 1996). The theory suggests that China's reforms can best be understood as a transition from a redistributive command system to a market system. Under this theory, market reforms drive enterprises to focus on supply and demand in the market, and to achieve cost-effectiveness and competitiveness, thus leading to hard budget constraints. This means that power will shift from "redistributors" (i.e., cadres) to the "direct producers" (i.e., entrepreneurs). As this happens, human capital becomes more salient than political capital in seizing economic gains, and thus inequality of opportunity and rewards will be reduced. This argument predicts a decline in the power of cadres, a corresponding gain in the power of producers, and the lessening inequality in the distribution of resources and rewards.

This perspective assumes that the existence of well-defined private property rights is a basic precondition to the proper functioning of a market economy. Without true private ownership, problems associated with the soft budget syndrome tend to arise since there are no clearly identified owners to pay for mistakes. (Someone else, usually the state, pays (Kornai 1992).) Therefore, the economy tends to perform relatively badly if ownership arrangements remain ambiguous or unstable (Alchian and Demsetz 1972).

The market transition account draws on a dichotomous framework of planned economy versus free market, which can be delineated by such dichotomies as centralization versus decentralization, regulation versus deregulation, vertical ties versus horizontal linkage, and bureaucratic command versus market transaction. The reform process focuses on the transition between two extreme points on a continuum, from the command system to the market system.

According to Nee, as the source of power shifts from hierarchies to the market, economic transactions will be embedded more in societal networks between buyers and sellers and less in political networks dominated by officials (Nee 1989: 663). Private entrepreneurs, by forging horizontal ties on the market, create resources that lie outside of the discretionary powers of officials. This in turn obviates the need for entrepreneurs to cultivate *guanxi* (personal connections; network) with officials (i.e., creates vertical ties), and erodes the patron–client ties that form the basis of the political order in socialist societies. The advantage of cadre status for entrepreneurial pursuits diminishes in the course of market transition because stronger market institutions reduce the strategic value of redistributive control over the movement of goods and services.

The market transition account has certain affinities with the logic espoused by a group of economists who Wing Thye Woo (1999) has termed "the Convergence school," who, among other recommendations, advised post-communist regimes to make a clean break with such past arrangements as government ownership. This group attributes China's remarkable economic performance since 1978 to market forces, including the increasing liberalization, internationalization, and privatization of economic activities. As to the interpretation of rural reforms, this school argues that the collective ownership of TVEs, which is a typical

10 *Explaining property rights transformations*

non-capitalist institution, has been proven to be unsuccessful and should evolve toward private entities (Wu 1998; Shirley and Galal 1994). It holds the assumption that a normal economy is characterized by market-based transactions between private agents. Therefore, faster privatization of collective TVEs in a transparent and equitable manner and more sweeping industrial and trade deregulation will produce faster growth. For this group, any half measures in a reforming post-communist economy would be ineffective compromises, and alternative non-western-style institutions would be wishful thinking (Sachs 1993, Peck and Richardson 1992). In short, this perspective highlights a universal and necessary role played by market forces that can bring transitional economy onto a development track heading toward capitalist market economy.

Local state corporatism and market-bureaucracy interaction account

In contrast to the Market Transition Account, the second perspective, local state corporatism and market-bureaucracy interaction, or Local State Corporatism Account, emphasizes the pivotal role played by local governments in engineering rapid economic growth in rural China. Local bureaucratic organs substitute for the private sector, which is traditionally identified as the vanguard of entrepreneurial effort. This view criticizes the market transition account for ignoring the fact that much of China's post-Mao rapid rural industrialization – at least for most of the 1980s and 1990s – was due to the collective enterprises owned and managed by local governments. Reforms transferred power from the central government to the local governments, allowing local cadres to not only preserve their power by controlling resource allocation and redistribution, but also increase it by playing a predominant role in economic decision making (Oi 1995, 1999; Walder 1995a; Blecher and Shue 1996, 2001).

This account also examines how the course of economic reforms has been shaped by political institutions in the localities. Fiscal decentralization has altered incentives for political actors in local governments; officials seek to promote extensive economic growth as a means to increase government revenues (Wong 1992; Oi 1992). Strong economic performance of rural industry in the reforms can therefore be explained in terms of the greater capacity local governments now wield to monitor and to draw income from township and village firms (Walder 1995a; Oi 1992). This perspective questions the commonplace assumption that public bureaucrats cannot behave as efficiently as private entrepreneurs in the capitalist market economy (Oi 1995).

One important theme of this account is Oi's "local state corporatism," which draws an analogy between local community governments and profit-seeking corporations, in which local governments act as the headquarters of large corporations (Oi 1995, 1999). Contrary to some scholars who stress the financial predatory behavior of local governments, this view argues that "mutual dependence rather than predation is a more apt description of the relationship" between local governments and local enterprises (Oi 1999: 98). This view claims that while the reforms decentralized power to the regions and localities, cadres not only retained power by controlling resource allocation and redistribution, but also dominated in the symbiotic and clientelist ties between local state officials and private entrepreneurs. Access to resources for societal actors is embedded in the cultivation of personal-instrumental ties with the officials in the administrative hierarchy. Clientelism not only existed under the Mao era, but also still persisted under the reform period (Oi 1986, 1989; Walder 1986; Wank 1999). Oi (1999) argues that institutional change has led local governments to act more as principals than as agents, thus gaining autonomy within their jurisdiction. The clients of local government, comprised mostly of private entrepreneurs and peasants, seek patrons in the bureaucracy for political protection as well as for commercial advantage, and thus strengthen local cadres' positional advantage (Wank 1999).

This view diverges sharply from the market transition account in arguing that there is not necessarily a correspondence between the emergence of markets and the decline of patron–client relations. The vision of a future China held by this group is close to a society of "clientelist capitalism."

The limitations of an economic paradigm

Each of the above perspectives presents incomplete conceptualizations of the transition process, while creating empirical inconsistencies. How did rural industries get from collectively owned to privately owned? And why do profitable privately run small businesses in Fujian exist at the same time as do profitable collective enterprises in Sunan? Studies in rural China have found that China's TVE sector demonstrated a remarkable degree of local and regional diversity in areas such as ownership structure, property rights relations, local policies toward TVEs, and the level of development and industrialization (Byrd and Lin 1990; Sen 1990; Zhou and Zhang 1991; Putterman 1993: 51–81; Ma *et al.* 1994; Oi and Walder 1999; Ronnas 1993; Whiting 2001; Hsu 1999; Liu 1992; Chen 2001a, 2001b). Different regions reflect different degrees of market penetration and local state corporatism. That is, regional variation in the degree of market infusion does not necessarily correlate to the decline in redistributive power. Some rich and industrialized littoral locales in Fujian and Guangdong – both located in South China – boast a laissez-faire style of economic activity and local development (Chen 1999; Nee 1996; Long 1994; Shieh 2000), while southern Jiangsu, suburban Shanghai, and suburban Tianjin all display strong corporatist arrangements characterized by a collective economy (Byrd and Lin 1990; Lin and Chen 1999; Lin 1995; Kung 1999; Whiting 2001).

12 Explaining property rights transformations

The simultaneous presence of various local economic arrangements cannot be explained away either by central government policies or by any of the theoretical propositions discussed above. The market transition account loses its empirical basis when viewed against the privileged position and advantages enjoyed by cadres or former cadres which have persisted throughout the reform and post-reform era. The alternative view, local state corporatism, also cannot explain thriving private enterprises in China's countryside, where individual entrepreneurs play a predominant role in economic activities with limited bureaucratic intervention. Since the mid-1990s, the expanding private sector and rapid privatization of collectively owned TVEs in once pro-collective regions signals a need to observe newly developing trends in the grassroots political economy in order to modify original hypotheses of local state corporatism.

In addition to providing insufficient explanations of empirical phenomena appearing across the country, both the market transition account and the local state corporatism approaches are essentially based on, or have certain "affinities" with, an economic paradigm (Lin 1995), and lack the ability to explain empirical variations that may be caused either by market infusion or by local state structure. The market transition account focuses on the extent to which a market institution has been established and how market forces and market mechanisms affect economic organizations and sociopolitical structure (e.g., inequality, social stratification, and power structure). Likewise, the analysis of local state corporatism also begins with an economic premise – revenue incentives in fiscal reform, despite its focus being on the functioning of local state government, acts as the major agent of change and reform. This view highlights the predominant role of political institution that characterizes the emerging market economy. Note that both adopt an economic paradigm: overly stressing either the role of market institutions or political institutions. By building on the premise of an economic paradigm and by concentrating on market institutions and political institutions, these perspectives may have overlooked the role of local social institutional arrangements that have been critical in shaping various local development models.

Since the mid-1990s, scholars moved beyond an economic paradigm and called for greater attention to be paid to concrete institutional arrangements and local social structure in order to identify distinct paths toward differently structured market economies in the localities (Lin 1995; Walder 1995b, 1996; Nee and Matthews 1996; Fligstein 1996; Parish and Michelson 1996). Although local social structures – such as cliques of firms in local production markets, local corporatist arrangements in rural communities, and personal ties to the cadres – have been taken into account in some studies (Oi 1995; Nee and Matthews 1996), it is still not clear how features of local social structure and institutional contexts combine to both limit and facilitate the emergence of various kinds of local economic organizations. Each local economic organizational feature seems to have emerged from local roots and each seems to be thriving on its own terms (Lin 1995). Therefore, a careful specification of local social structure and institutional arrangements could lead to an improved understanding of the enormous variation in modes of market transition and local corporatism at the local level. For example, local corporatist arrangements appear to be dominant in southern Jiangsu while private entrepreneurship dominates Wenzhou and southern Fujian. These differences very well account for the enduring features of local institutions and the economic and political legacies in the localities.

Economic activity embedded in social institutions

This study builds on an institutional approach favored in "new economic sociology" (Swedberg and Granovetter 1992; Smelser and Swedberg 1994), and focuses on the social context in localities and social networks in which business relations are embedded. This section first points out the essence of sociological institutional explanation by comparing it with the traditional rational choice, utility driven economic models, before turning to the embeddedness issue. It stresses the influence of social networks on economic activities and organizational features. It also refers to the network-centered approach in the studies of East Asian economies, showing that social networks and local institutions play a predominant role in many aspects of economic activities in the non-western market economies.

Most sociological approaches to institutional analysis agree on the idea that economic organizations are embedded in a wider socio-political context (DiMaggio and Powell 1991a; Scott 1995: 16–62). This approach goes beyond politics and economy to find institutions rooted in society. It suggests that economic action is socially situated and cannot be fully explained only by reference to individual motives. Economic institutions are "socially constructed" (Berger and Luckmann 1966). An actor's action in a certain situation is mostly determined by a "rule of appropriateness," which is internalized through socialization and learning. This view echoes the central theme of Durkheim's *The Division of Labor in Society*, which emphasizes that

> even where society rests wholly upon the division of labor, it does not resolve itself into a myriad of atoms juxtaposed together, between which only external and transitory contact can be established. The members are linked by ties that extend well beyond the very brief moment when the act of exchange is being accomplished.
> (Durkheim [1893] 1984: 173)

Institutional analysis has also been applied to the study of state socialist and post-socialist countries in Eastern Europe and China. Stark and

14 *Explaining property rights transformations*

Bruszt's study on transforming politics and property in East Central Europe argues that under conditions of uncertain transformation, where the lack of central policy and legal networks creates ambiguous market conditions, networks and relations between enterprises become the fundamentals for economic development, blurring the boundaries of public and private, and yielding distinctive patterns of interorganizational ownership. Their study demonstrates the benefits of informal institutions which offer alternatives to traditional markets and hierarchies. In post-socialist reforms, strengthening markets and strengthening states require recognizing and facilitating coordination between economic actors that are neither market nor hierarchy (Stark and Bruszt 1998). Likewise, in opposition to the earlier theoretical models of totalitarianism and modernization, many scholars aim to understand patterns of institutional regularity which can explain how the mechanism of the economy operates in reality; how a post-socialist economy is moving away from a command economy (see Stark and Nee 1989; Nee 1996; Walder 1996).

The distinction between economic and sociological paradigms

The differences between institutional analyses in economics and sociology can be illustrated from three perspectives: the definition of institution, the view of individual choice, and the dependence and efficiency of institutions.

For economists and rational choice adherents, an institution is defined as "the rules that provide a set of incentives and disincentives for individuals," or "any form of constraint that human being devise to shape human interaction," including formal and informal ones (North 1986: 231; 1990: 4). For North, "informal constraints," however, are extensions, modifications, and qualifications of formal rules commonly referred to as tradition, culture, custom, or routines (North 1991). The sociological approach allows for a complex view of institutions as more than a focus on rules; the institution can be seen as "an organized and established procedure" or "those social patterns that, when chronically reproduced, owe their survival to relatively self-activating social processes" (Jepperson 1991). The economic approach emphasizes that institutions "have a legalistic aspect and rely on a relatively clear structure of enforcement" (Levi 1990), and that "informal constraints" are at best "extensions" and "modifications" of the formal rules. For sociologists, institutions do not depend primarily on explicit rules and enforcement machinery, but more importantly on subtle and shared beliefs and meaning systems encompassing cognitive and normative elements (Scott 1994, 1995).

The underlying assumptions about institutions lead to the second set of differences: the answers to the question of whether or not institutions reflect individual preference. In general, economic institutionalists of rational choice view institutions as the product of *a priori* rational decision makers' political strategies and interests. While the sociologically oriented institutional approach does not assume that institutions are necessarily the products of conscious design, they are certainly the results of human activities (DiMaggio and Powell 1991a). The sociological institutional approach is skeptical of the rational-actor model of organizations, and suggests that individuals do not choose freely among institutions, customs, social norms, or legal procedures which are "always associated with certain situations by rules of appropriateness" (March and Olsen, 1984: 741). Individuals make choices by reference to standards of obligation absorbed through socialization, education, or acquiescence to convention. People have mixtures of motives and consequently act in ways difficult to describe in terms of pure self-interest. The sociological institutional approach has expanded on this point by addressing how particular kinds of social relations drive behaviors which diverge from the narrowly instrumental considerations (Granovetter 2002).

A third difference between the two approaches is the notion of efficiency, the central theme of new institutional economics. For institutional economists, an institution or organization exists because it is efficient, and efficiency is central to the choice of one organizational form rather than another.

> Efficient organization entails the establishment of institutional arrangements and property rights that create an incentive to channel individual economic effort into activities that bring the private rate of return close to the social rate of return.
> (North and Thomas 1973: 1)

Sociologists claim, however, that the notion of efficiency cannot be used to explain the existing institutions in the economy or elsewhere (Granovetter 1985; Oberschall and Leifer 1986; Bradach and Eccles 1989). Perrow (1986) points out that power considerations usually override efficiency principles. Two other factors also lead to additional skepticism about the efficiency-centered theme: the ambiguous goal of an organization and the fact that choice is not only rational but also influenced by existing norms, rules, and culture (Oberschall and Leifer 1986; Nelson and Winter 1982).

In brief, studies based on an economic paradigm emphasize the economic features of the institutions in which actors' behaviors are studied. The concept of institution refers to the result of human design in economic structure, and the establishment and change of institution is viewed as referring to the functional needs of economic mechanisms. In contrast, the sociological institutional approach emphasizes the social and cultural aspects of people's behavior, on the phenomenological (that is, taken for granted character of relationship and action) and cognitive feature of institutions, and on the complexity of settings and changing of institutions

(DiMaggio and Powell 1991a; Swedberg and Granovetter 1992; Guillen *et al.* 2002).

Embeddedness and social networks: the East Asian model

A neoclassical economic approach views business networking as rational or instrumental only if it aims at and achieves clear economic goals. Businesspeople as individuals are described in the economic model as being those who fearlessly enter unfamiliar territory, and seek advice and resources from whoever might be willing to provide them. Businesspeople view social networks as a means of obtaining access to information and resources with exchange value, which could be used to enhance upward mobility, to maximize profits, or to obtain technological know-how. In this sense, networks and business relations are seen as the marketplace in which information is traded. Economic actors (e.g., entrepreneurs and managers) build social networks and business relations pragmatically on an efficiency account, selecting and discarding members based on their perceived contributions and changing business needs. For most economists, networks are thus transitory, pragmatic, and held together by the narrow economic calculations of individual actors, without much attention being paid to social norms or convention. To the extent that social ties are infused with notions of equity, loyalty, and tradition, they may be viewed, from this perspective, as constraints on efficient exchange.

By contrast, a social embeddedness approach argues that an analysis of economic activities cannot be separated from an understanding of the social context in which business relations are embedded (Granovetter 1985; Powell and Smith-Doerr 1994). Embeddedness refers to the process by which social relations shape economic actions. Some economic schemes overlook or misspecify this process because they assume that social ties affect economic behavior only minimally or even reduce efficiency. From the embeddedness perspective, economic actors behave rationally and instrumentally if they conduct their economic activities through personal networks, because all economic actions are infused with social motives and because economic actors are never wholly atomized in economic life. The key unit in analyzing economic exchange is social relations, which involve recurrent transactions, rather than individual actors or isolated transactions (Baker 1990; Swedberg 1994). Exchange may begin in an impersonal way, but often develops "noneconomic contents as people try actively to prevent economic and noneconomic aspects of their lives from being separated" (Granovetter 1992: 26).

Studies of East Asian economies done by a group of economic sociologists provide a typical example of applying the social embeddedness approach in analyzing economic organizations and activities in Chinese reforms. Using a firm survey data collected in two metropolitan cities, Zhou *et al.* (2003) find economic relations in China's transitional economy are deeply embedded in social relations and social institutions; social relations, institutional links, and regulatory environments play distinct roles in initiating contractual partners and different forms of contracts in the marketplace. Redding and Whitley (1990) argue that Anglo-Saxon conceptions of the legally bounded firm as the basic unit of economic action are inadequate to explain the economic actions and structure of Asian business organizations which, like Chinese family businesses, have complex extra-firm linkages influencing decision making and resource distribution. Biggart and Hamilton (1990) suggest that East Asia's success depends on a fit between institutional environment and business structure. Asian economies have worked so well because they have created organizational arrangements and management practices that suit their social arrangements, and therefore give them a competitive advantage. Other institutions given emphasis include village and family, which also help define acceptable "ways of doing" things. In Hong Kong and Taiwan, for example, the Chinese family business is related to "economic familism," which derives from Imperial China under which the state supervises moral order, but "leaves the people at rest" regarding economic activities and family life (Hamilton and Biggart 1988). Chinese enterprises tend to form business networks and subcontacting systems in order to enhance flexibility and coordination, showing their strength in entrepreneurship rather than management (Wong 1988a, 1988b). Wong (1985, 1996) highlights the positive role played by Chinese cultural values – including familism, pragmatism, autonomy, and personal trust – in facilitating economic development in Chinese societies, including Hong Kong, Taiwan, and post-communist China. Unger and Chan (1995) suggest that the East Asian states have shared a cultural bias favorable to corporatist structure, and China's trends of "corporatism" is displayed both at national and regional levels of organization. They emphasize that harmony, regardless of being truly consensual or imposed from above, is key to a corporatist system. This stands in contrast to the divisive competition and conflict entailed by pluralist interest-group models of organization. Thus, for institutionalists, the business structures of East Asian capitalism are explained by institutional environments – a legacy of institutions and ideas which determine that the organization enacts behavioral patterns understood and accepted by its constituents.

Local institutions in rural China: research issues

The social embeddedness and network-centered approach in economic sociology provides a perspective to explain the organizational features in rural China by examining how economic activities are embedded in social institutional arrangements in the localities. This study extends the work on market mechanisms and local state corporatism by focusing on the critical role of local institutions in shaping different patterns of property

18 *Explaining property rights transformations*

rights relations. It argues that central and local government policies set a contextual condition that constrains or facilitates the emergence of certain types of local institutions. Yet an analysis of state policies and bureaucratic institutions is not sufficient to explain local economic development, particularly local diversity in development patterns. It is inadequate to follow the theme of North and Thomas's account (1973) of economic development which assumes that if the state creates right institutions, and avoids too much rent seeking, sooner or later local development is inevitable.

Local institutions are formed around both local social networks and personal ties in which entrepreneurs' economic activities and resource mobilization are embedded. While acknowledging the infusion of the market mechanisms and the persistent authority of local governments, this study argues that these elements are interacting with, and are increasingly superseded by, leadership and institutions formed around local networks and ties. Consequently, the features of economic organizations, represented by various types of property rights arrangements, are characterized by the local institutional arrangements.

This study argues that as economic reforms proceed, local officials in different regions adapt national policies to local social and economic realities. Local actors are constrained by the conditions of local resource endowment, and thus cannot fully implement policies passed on from above. On the other hand, open-door policies and market forces indeed promote economic production and market transactions, but these factors operate within local institutional arrangements in bounded rural communities in which different forms of economic activities are constituted. Overlooking the particular characteristics of local institutions in each area likely results in the exaggeration of the initiative of market forces and overstating the effects of central policies, leading to a misunderstanding of the reforms' transformation mechanisms. Market transition and bureaucratic corporatism alone, therefore, are not enough to characterize and coordinate economies in rural China. This study shows that the operation and legacies of native institutional arrangements play an important role in regional development in the same way – if not greater – that market mechanisms and state institutions do – by shaping cost and choices for local cadres and entrepreneurs – and that such local institutions can be critical for ultimate outcomes and the trajectory of change.

Institutions bounded by locality

China's revolutionary history is distinguished by the principal role played by the rural villages and townships that were the loci of grassroots communist organizations and revolutionary power. Through collectivization in the 1950s, villages and townships also became the basic units of ownership of land and other means of production. The permanence and immobility of their constituent populations were ensured by the extraordinary household registration system enforced from the late 1950s on. China's rigid household registration system ties the jobs, residences, and social interactions of peasants to where they are registered to live. Most people born into a rural community stay there for their entire lives, and their children belong to the same community. The villages are the basic units of organization for the undertaking of massive efforts in farming irrigation, public health, and education, which in turn leads to the expansion and consolidation of the village administrative apparatus. All these institutional arrangements give grassroots communities a role in rural change that is exceptional from the standpoint of both developing and socialist countries. In the reform era, in some localities, under the twin stimuli of increased local autonomy and market incentives, the collectives (villages and townships) became the primary units for rural industrialization and retained the cohesiveness of the communities. Although local governments and officials in China are part of the administrative apparatus, they are also "distinct entities apart from the central state and society, with their own agendas and increasingly with their own resources." (Oi 1999: 9). In some other localities, the coherence of rural communities have been tied and consolidated by socio-cultural forces such as local dialects, kinship and clan institutions, and religious rituals shared by community members. Whether the community cohesiveness is maintained by bureaucratic or societal mechanism reveals the particular institutional arrangements embodied in the locality.

This study argues that while the economic policies at the national level initiated the process of reforms, variation in social and political institutions in each locality dictates variation in economic organization and property rights relations. The political institutions in the locality, represented by the local state's ability to control local economic affairs and decision making, act as a contextual condition that constrains or facilitates the arrangements of local social institutions. In the historically well-endowed localities, local governments have had sufficient resources at their disposal, and have maintained strong incentives to control local economic affairs. As a result, there exists a mighty administrative apparatus; thus the local social institutional arrangements, represented by entrepreneurs' resource mobilization through social networks, are dominated by bureaucratic coordination under which the patterns of social relations are characterized by patron–client ties and vertical relations in the bureaucratic system. In a locality with limited resources, the local government's weakened role as a redistributor provides an opportunity for potential arrangements such as kinship and family coordination to develop and take control. Local social institutions are examined through the entrepreneurs' mobilization of resources through activities embedded in local community networks, as well as external networks out of the locale. The features of economic organizations, represented by the bundles of property rights relations, can be adequately explained by the arrangements of local political and social institutions.

Design of the study: comparing the Yangtze Delta region and southern Fujian

This study is a comparative case study based on survey data, interviews, and archival research. It aims to identify and explain particular patterns that have emerged in property rights transformations and local institutional arrangements. The study was designed to achieve theoretical leverage by comparing local variation in empirical relationships among the variables of interest. The two regions selected, the Yangtze Delta region and southern Fujian, exemplify the economically successful corporatist and littoral patterns in China's rural transformation in the reform era. The research in the Yangtze Delta region was done primarily on the villages in suburban counties of Shanghai, and in Wujiang of Suzhou. In southern Fujian, research was done in villages in Jinjiang and Shishi, now county-level cities under the jurisdiction of Quanzhou prefecture. Data collection and field research began in 1995, with intensive interviews conducted in 1995–1996 and 2000–2002.[1]

The Yangtze Delta region, with Shanghai as its center, has become the most dynamic market region in China today, perhaps even in all of East Asia – a remarkable gain from a decade ago when Shanghai's bureaucratic structure was seeped a rigid command economy under central control. This region accommodates the greatest amount of foreign investment in China in the early 2000s, and is seen as the fastest developmental showcase of Chinese reforms. In the early 1980s, when the reform was just launched, the region housed China's major state-owned industrial base, and its rural development was entitled the "Sunan Model" (southern Jiangsu model). Historically termed the "fish and rice country," this region was also one of the richest areas for China's production of agricultural commodities, including grain, cotton, and edible oil.

Jinjiang and Shishi are located in southeastern Fujian, south of the estuary of the Jin River, which empties into Quanzhou Bay, an inlet of the Taiwan Strait. Quanzhou, a port city about 100 kilometers north of Xiamen, was Marco Polo's Zaitan, which he considered the world's greatest port in the thirteenth century. Before it was renamed Quanzhou prefecture in 1984, Jinjiang prefecture included today's Quanzhou, Jinjiang, and Shishi City. Shishi (Stone Lion) used to be one of Jinjiang's 18 townships before it was amalgamated with three nearby townships to establish Shishi City in 1989. Although the administrative boundaries were redrawn several times, the region of Jinjiang has long been known as today's Jinjiang City (consisting of 14 townships) and Shishi City (consisting of four townships), with a land area of 903 square kilometers and a population of

1.3 million in 2002. This region, famous for its "Jinjiang Model" in the early reform era, is the hometown for many overseas Chinese in Taiwan and Southeast Asia. Culturally, Jinjiang is part of the Minnan (southern Fujian) dialect region that contains three prefectures – Quanzhou, Zhangzhou, and Xiamen. Minnan dialect is also used among overseas Chinese communities in the Philippines, Singapore, and Malaysia, and is also spoken by 75 percent of the people in Taiwan, whose ancestors came from southern Fujian beginning in the seventeenth century.[2]

These two regions under study are among the richest and most developed areas in eastern China. In a 2002 county-level economic competitiveness evaluation, Jinjiang and Wujiang were respectively ranked the sixth and tenth among the nation's 2,861 county-level units (Zhongguo xianyu jingjiwang 2002). In 2001, per capita incomes of rural populations in the Shanghai suburbs (5,850 yuan), Wujiang (5,651 yuan), and Jinjiang and Shishi (6,234 yuan) were as much as 2.5 times the national average (2,366 yuan). In 2002, per capita gross domestic product (GDP) in the region of Jinjiang and Shishi combined reached 33,548 yuan, similar to that of Wujiang's 30,378 yuan but a little lower than the Shanghai

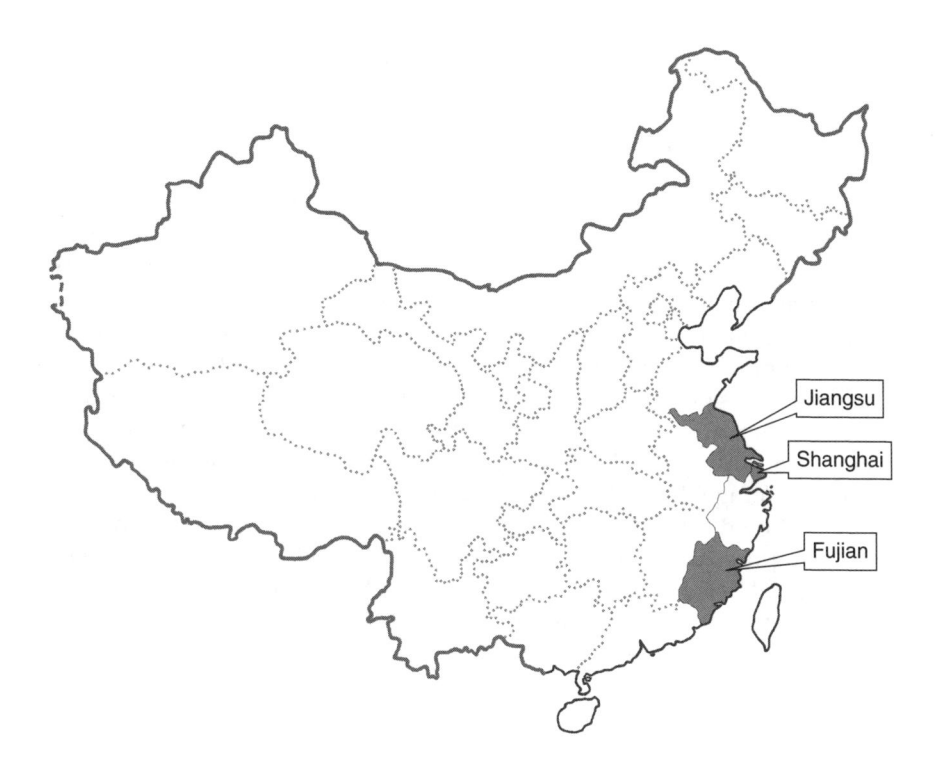

Map 1.1 Map of China showing Jiangsu, Shanghai, and Fujian.

Map 1.2 Map of Jiangsu, Shanghai, and Fujian research sites.

suburbs' 40,597 yuan. The GDP per capita of all these regions were far ahead of the national average of 8,023 yuan in 2002.

Their prosperity today does not mean that they were well-to-do in the old days. In the early 1980s, Jinjiang's economic performance lagged behind the national average. Its per capita rural income in 1980 (129 yuan) was much lower than the national average of 191 yuan. In 1985, however, Jinjiang overtook the national average in per capita rural income, and since then the gap has increased rapidly (Table 1.1). The trend was the same for GDP. In the pre-reform 1978, Jinjiang's per capita GDP of 95 yuan was less than one third of the national average (379 yuan). Not until 1990 did Jinjiang per capita GDP begin to outpace the national average. Shanghai suburbs and Wujiang are situated in a region more endowed, with rural income and economic production already overshadowing the entire country in the late 1970s and early 1980s. In 1980, rural household per capita income in Shanghai suburbs (402 yuan) and Wujiang (230 yuan) exceeded the national average (191 yuan), and the difference among their per capita GDP were similar, with Shanghai suburbs (2,738 yuan) posting a big lead over the national average (460 yuan) (Table 1.2).

Table 1.1 Per capita rural household net income and average annual growth

Region	Year (yuan; current prices)						Average annual percentage change (%)				
	1978	1980	1985	1990	1995	2001	1978–1980	1980–1985	1985–1990	1990–1995	1995–2001
National[a]	134	191	398	686	1,578	2,366	20	16	12	18	7
Jiangsu[b]	152	218	493	959	2,457	3,785	20	18	14	21	7
Fujian[c]	135	172	396	764	2,049	3,381	13	18	14	22	9
Shanghai[d]	281	402	806	1,665	4,246	5,850	20	15	16	21	5
Wujiang[e]	173	230	665	1,176	4,204	5,651	15	24	12	29	5
Jinjiang and Shishi[f]	107	129	525	1,015	4,279	6,234	10	33	14	33	6

Notes

a ZXQN 1994: 21; ZXQN 1993: 458; ZTN 1999: 339; ZXQN 1993: 458; ZTN 1998: 346; ZTN 2002: 344.
b ZXQN 1993: 458; ZTN 1992: 308; ZTN 1998: 346; ZTN 2002: 344.
c ZXQN 1993: 458; ZTN 1999: 339; ZTN 1998: 346; FTN 2002: 113.
d STN 1994: 21; STN 2002: 6.
e WTN 1995: 182; STN 1991: 315; WTN 1995: 15; SUTN 2002: 543.
f Jinjiang: ZGC 1992: 42; FTN 1991: 504; FTN 1996: 432; FTN 2002: 385.
Shishi: Shishi shi jianshi yilai zhuyao jingji zhibiao (Main Economic Indicators of Shishi City since its establishment) Online. Available HTTP: http://stats.shishi.gov.cn/sj.asp?fg_id=3 (accessed October 10, 2003).

Table 1.2 Per capita gross domestic products and average annual growth

Region	Year (yuan; current prices)						Average annual percentage change (%)					
	1978	1980	1985	1990	1995	2002	1978–1980	1980–1985	1985–1990	1990–1995	1990–1995	1995–2002
National[a]	379	460	855	1,634	4,854	8,023	10	13	14	14	24	7
Jiangsu[b]	430	541	1,053	2,103	7,299	14,397	12	14	15	15	28	10
Fujian[c]	273	348	737	1,763	6,787	13,610	13	16	19	18	31	10
Shanghai[d]	2,498	2,738	3,855	5,910	18,943	40,597	5	7	9	8	26	12
Wujiang[e]	482	630	1,412	3,204	17,032	30,378	14	18	18	18	40	9
Jinjiang and Shishi[f]	153	257	716	1,666	16,384	33,548	30	23	18	21	58	11

Notes

a ZTN 2001: 49; for 2002, Online. Available HTTP: http://www.people.com.cn/GB/shizheng/19/20030320/948401.html (accessed October 27, 2003).
b JTN 1998: 49; for 2002, Online. Available HTTP: http://www.jssb.gov.cn/sjzl/sjzl.htm (accessed October 27, 2003).
c FTN 1999: 31; for 2002, Online. Available HTTP: http://www.fjnj.net/fj/all119.htm (accessed October 27, 2003).
d STN 1996: 27; for 2002, Online. Available HTTP: http://jiansuo.jfdaily.com (accessed October 27, 2003)
e WTN 1995: 174; for 2002, Online. Available HTTP: http://www.qsjournal.com.cn/qs/20030201/BIG5/qs%5E352%5E0%5E26.htm (accessed October 27, 2003).
f Jinjiang: ZGC 1992: 53; JSZ: 1428.
  Shishi: Shishi shi zhuyao jingji zhibiao (Main Economic Indicators of Shishi City) Online. Available HTTP: http://stats.qz.fj.cn/qzhome/qztjsj/qx50/qzqx50.html#30 (accessed October 11, 2003); for 1980, JGTZ 1986: 1 (Statistical Material on National Economy in Jinjiang County 1986) (for 1980, per capital national income).

Regional variations of property rights arrangements

Rural firms of various ownership types drove the economy in the Yangtze Delta region and southern Fujian throughout the reform era. In the reform era, the Yangtze Delta region's township- and village-run enterprises dominated the regional economy, while in southern Fujian the rural economy was concentrated at the village and household level. Although village-run enterprises occupied significant positions in these two regions, they still displayed very different styles of organizational features and property rights relations. As of 1994, the mid-period of China's reform, the share of rural non-state enterprises in China's total national gross value of industrial output (GVIO) reached 44 percent; those in Shanghai suburbs, Wujiang, and Jinjiang all accounted for more than 80 percent of total GVIO in their localities. In terms of ownership forms, Shanghai suburbs and Suzhou displayed a pattern different with that in Jinjiang. State-owned enterprises accounted for 15 percent and 9 percent of GVIO in rural Shanghai and Wujiang respectively, but only constituted 2 percent of GVIO in Jinjiang, where 82 percent of GVIO was drawn from village-run enterprises and "below-village enterprises" (namely, joint-household or individual enterprises). On the other hand, the combined shares of township-run and state-owned enterprises in Shanghai suburbs and Wujiang were 64 percent and 60 percent of GVIO, respectively, compared with a mere 3 percent in Jinjiang. Within the rural non-state sector, township-run enterprises dominated in Shanghai suburbs and Wujiang, accounting for 49 percent and 51 percent of GVIO respectively; village-run enterprises stood out in Jinjiang, however, constituting 53 percent of GVIO. The "below-village enterprises," joint and individual household firms, seized 29 percent of GVIO in Jinjiang, while their counterparts only occupied a thin slice of GVIO in Shanghai suburbs (less than 3 percent) and Wujiang (1 percent) (Table 1.3). The figures show that, at mid-reform period, township governments in the Yangtze Delta region possessed a greater proportion of economic entities than any other sector, implying the dominance of local governments in economic affairs and highlighting the characteristic type of "publicly-owned" enterprises in this region. Village-run enterprises were also far more developed in the Yangtze Delta region and southern Fujian than in other areas in China.

In theory, collective enterprises belong to a collective, a group of individuals who hold joint ownership over property. Accordingly, state enterprises belong to the whole people, township-run enterprises belong to the people of the township, and so on down the line to private enterprises. As applied in rural China, collective enterprises are properties jointly owned by local residents within an administrative territory (i.e., township or village), who are represented and governed by the local state and the local party. Therefore, theoretically speaking, local governments, on behalf of

26 *Explaining property rights transformations*

Table 1.3 Regional variation in shares of industrial output by ownership at mid-reform (%)

	All China 1994	Shanghai suburbs 1994	Suzhou Wujiang 1994	Jinjiang 1993
State-owned enterprises	34	15	9	2[a]
Township-run enterprises	15	49	51	1
Village-run enterprises	16	33	32	53
Rural joint and individual enterprises	13	–	1	29
City–town joint and individual enterprises	8	3	0	6
Other (foreign invested, etc.)	14	–	7	10
of which, township- and village-run enterprises	31	82	83	54
of which, rural non-state enterprises	44	83[b]	84	82
of which, township and above	49	64	60	3
of which, village and below	29	35[c]	33	6

Sources: ZTN 1995; SJTN 1995; SUTN 1995; FTN 1994.

Notes
a Estimated from data in previous years. In 1991, state-owned enterprises accounted for 4 percent of industrial output in Jinjiang.
b Since data for industrial output of rural joint and individual enterprises are not available, an estimated mean value (1.5) of the residual is applied.
c Ibid.

local people, are entitled to exercise the property rights of use, return, and alienation associated with a collective enterprise.

However, the statistics tell only half of the story regarding the property rights arrangements of rural enterprises in Chinese reforms. One single ownership category (e.g., village-run enterprise) may denote a variety of property rights configurations and different organizational features. The various ownership forms are so mixed that the true identity of establishments cannot be ascertained from their nominal status. To suggest that local governments controlled the variety of property rights pertaining to collective enterprises assumes that the ownership of Chinese collective enterprises was well defined and adequately enforced. As this study will articulate in detail, however, it does not necessarily entail cadre involvement and government intervention for the enterprises registered as being township- or village-run. It remains to be seen as to how the bundles of property rights in collective enterprises have been arranged, perceived, and implemented. Since the property rights of China's rural enterprises had been ill-defined, confused and sometimes falsely recorded during the reform period, the property rights transformation deserves a closer examination.

Two major institutional arrangements directly led to the confusion of property rights over collective enterprises: the contract responsibility system and false registration. Following the "contract management responsibility system" introduced in the mid-1980s to reform state-owned enterprises, local governments adopted various kinds of contract responsibility arrangements (*chengbao zeren zhi*) to manage collective enterprises. In practice, the collective enterprises were contracted or leased either to individuals, or management teams. The terms of the contracts, as well as the labels adopted, varied within and across regions. For example, one extreme, usually called "collective unified management" (*jiti tongyi jingying*) practiced in rural Shanghai, denoted a comprehensive "contract of responsibility" with local cadres either intervening in or themselves directly controlling the day-to-day management of enterprises. In many instances the contractors were local cadres. The other extreme, individual contracting (*geren chengbao*), involved a complete autonomy of the lessee in management and profit distribution, with fixed rent paid to the government "owner" of the enterprise. As a result, contracting and leasing prompted the division of the bundle of property rights over collective enterprises and in some cases served as a prelude to the transformation of property rights relations.

At the same time, in the 1980s and 1990s, a large number of rural enterprises listed as collective were, in fact, private, although they were often attached to an administrative organ. They simply used the collective flag to help overcome remaining difficulties and the stigma attached to private enterprises given that the private sector had not yet received sufficient official support and recognition. These nominally collective but actually private firms were not exceptional, yet were quite popular in certain regions in Chinese countryside during the reform period (Luo 1990; Liu 1992; Parris 1993; Nolan and Dong 1990; Chen 1999, 2001a, 2001b; Unger and Chan 1999).

Local legacies in the early reform era

The regions under study bear different local legacies in the pre-reform and early reform era, a fact which also had significant implications for their institutional transformations later on. The Yangtze Delta region, distinguished by its historically prosperous and rewarding environments, the so-called "fish and rich country," initially had a fairly strong industrial base in commune and brigade industries. Even before 1949, the Yangtze Delta had been one of the most advanced areas of China, both in terms of agricultural and industrial development (Huang 1990: 323). During the period of the Great Leap Forward (1958–1960), many handicraft cooperatives were established in the countryside, although most of the investments turned out to be wasteful.[3] Rural enterprises developed rapidly after 1978, when the central government's policy shifted toward diversified economic development in rural areas. The proximity to state-owned enterprises in nearby Shanghai also provided local enterprises with the

28 *Explaining property rights transformations*

advantage of obtaining technology, information, machinery, and raw materials.

Fujian, conversely, had no industry. Its mountainous terrain, deficiency in natural resources, and limited arable land characterized its backwardness and shortage before the reforms. Fujian's location as the front-line in any potential conflict with Taiwan further resulted in the withdrawal of central government investment in the three decades before the reforms. As a defensive response to the threat posed by Taiwan, the industrial plants built by the government had been located in western interior counties and the traditional coastal commercial towns were left underdeveloped.

Table 1.4 compares the composition of gross social product in these two regions in the early reform period. As early as 1980, nonagricultural activities had already overridden agriculture in the Shanghai suburbs and in Wujiang, whose agricultural production accounted for only 34 percent and 24 percent of total production, respectively. In comparison, industry and construction accounted for more than 60 percent of total social product in this region. At the same time, the shift from agricultural to nonagricultural sectors was not clearly seen in Jinjiang in the early reform era – agriculture and industry accounted for 43 percent and 40 percent of total social product respectively (Table 1.4). Furthermore, the legacies of industrialization in these two regions differed, which also cast implications for their industrial development in the reform era. The Yangtze Delta region had outperformed southern Fujian largely in the level of industrialization. For example, as of 1980, the GVIO per capita of either Shanghai suburbs (945 yuan) or Wujiang (968 yuan) was nearly five times as large as that in Jinjiang (191 yuan) (Table 1.5).

The data demonstrate that the two locales covered by this study had very different economic endowments, industrial bases, and financial situations. The relative strength of resources in local industries in southern Jiangsu and Shanghai contrasted sharply with the relative paucity of such

Table 1.4 Composition of gross social product, 1980

	Shanghai suburbs	Wujiang	Jinjiang
Total (10,000 yuan)	558,244	109,715	42,581
Percent of total	100	100	100
Agriculture	34	24	43
Industry	51	63	40
Construction	11	5	6
Transport	2	1	3
Commerce	3	6	8

Sources: Calculated from data in SJN 1994: 599; SUSJTZ 1986: 5; FTN 1995: 367–373.

Note
Prices for Shanghai suburbs are in original prices, and for Suzhou and Jinjiang are in 1980 prices.

Table 1.5 Industrial base in different regions

	Population (10,000)	GVIO (millions of yuan)	GVIO (per capita)
Shanghai suburbs			
1970	492.32	93,497	190
1975	519.67	248,615	478
1980	545.23	514,982	945
Wujiang			
1970	74.00	14,991	228
1975	69.31	23,752	343
1980	71.61	69,321	968
Jinjiang			
1970	76.06	4,590	60
1975	87.80	6,084	69
1980	96.81	18,962	196

Sources: Calculated from data in SJN 1994; SUSJTZ 1986; SUTN 1989; JSZ 1994.

Note
The data are in current prices for Shanghai suburbs and in 1980 prices for Wujiang and Jinjiang.

resources in southern Fujian before and in the beginning of the reform era. Despite their comparable economic prosperity in the 1990s, these two locales actually grew out of diverse local legacies, with one well endowed and the other relatively backward.

Structure of the book

This chapter has outlined the theoretical background and methodological framework of this study. The rest of the book is divided into two parts: Sunan and Fujian. Chapters 2, 3 and 4 deal exclusively with Sunan, while Chapters 5 and 6 deal exclusively with Fujian. Each of the two parts leads with an academic discussion and analysis of the said region's development, and how the local institutions have shaped, and continue to shape, economic development. The final chapter of each part is a narrative case study of the area.

The narrative style of Chapters 4 and 6 is meant to be an engaging and enlightening read, not only bringing these two diverse regions to life, but also emphasizing their variations, and the influence of local actors.

The book's conclusion takes up the academic debate again to explore the empirical and theoretical implications of this study. It highlights the implications of regional variation and local institutional arrangements, which have not been fully examined in previous research. It also discusses how the empirical findings of this study extend the perspective of current studies in economic sociology by showing the impact and operations of social embeddedness in a post-reform socialist economy.

Part I

The Yangtze Delta property rights transformations

2 The Yangtze Delta in the reform era

The Yangtze Delta region arose as a model of rural industrial development in the 1980s and mid-1990s. Here, in the greater Shanghai and southern Jiangsu regions, the countryside not only underwent enough economic growth to become the industrial center of China, but saw the unique development of the economy and the party in an anomalous integral fashion. The Sunan model, as it has become known, refers to the collective ownership of TVEs, the dominant role of the local government and party cadres in rural industrialization, and social services provided by local governments. Under the control of local governments and officials, the TVE were the priority asset of the local economy and the main revenue generator.[1]

The Sunan model followed the trends of the national economy. In the early 1990s, collective TVEs throughout China began to overtake state-owned players and soon overwhelmed their private counterparts, then still underdeveloped in rural China. In 1994, rural enterprises accounted for 44 percent of the country's industrial gross output, while the contribution of the state-owned firms dropped to a record low of 34 percent (calculated from ZTN 1995). Sunan was one of the leading areas driving this growth.

The collective TVEs did encounter difficulties that hindered their fast-paced growth, however. Since the mid-1990s, the country's economic growth tapered off and rural firms output and profits have dwindled. The GDP grew at an annual average change of 24 percent from 1990 to 1995, for example, but averaged only 7 percent from 1995 to 2002 (Table 1.2). Likewise, rural household net income increased yearly at around 18 percent between 1990 and 1995, but only 7 percent yearly from 1995 to 2001 (Table 1.1). Accordingly, the central government no longer applauded the so-called Chinese socialist model of rural development, and reports and commentaries in state-monitored media and academic journals started to question the orthodox position of the Sunan model.

This economic slowdown put pressure on the collectives around the country, and in Sunan, leading to highly leveraged village run companies. In order to alleviate the state from near crushing debt, the central government pushed privatization. Local cadres began to loosen their control over collective enterprises, and allowed them to be owned by private individuals and become more subject to market forces. This policy of "changing the institution" (*gaizhi*) for public enterprises had profound effects on property rights transformation and direct consequences for collective TVEs in the traditionally pro-collective region.

By 2003, the traditional socialist collectives and enterprises were a thing of the past. The near decade-long process of privatization had caused the prominent and glorious Sunan model of community and government-owned TVEs to completely vanish. What grew up in place of this now extinct communist economic system was a new set of firms including private, shareholding and foreign joint ventures.

The changes that occurred in TVE property rights and management also demonstrate the pervasiveness of the social consequences that occurred in this region. Whereas peasants used to be guaranteed a job and social services as co-owners of the collectives, they became wage laborers, expendable at the whim of the new private owners. Unequal distribution of resources and wealth has ballooned since the mid-1990s, inciting unrest throughout the country.

The present and following chapters explore the nature, process, and consequences of the property rights transformation of the Sunan model. This chapter focuses on the reform era up to the mid-1990s, whereas the subsequent chapter will discuss the latest post-reform development in the late 1990s and after. These chapters draw on empirical evidence from village surveys and in-depth case studies, which will help to address some lingering questions in the literature about the transformation of property rights and local institutions at the grassroots level. Also, to explain the organizational features of the TVEs, this study examines the nature of entrepreneurship in the TVEs and the context under which entrepreneurship emerges. The economic activities in rural China – such as establishing new firms, developing new products, and seizing market channels – actually demonstrate the level of entrepreneurship in a post-centrally planned economy. A study of these entrepreneurial activities and the contextual conditions that produce them will help us to better understand the regional differences of institutional arrangements in rural China, and thereby account for the variation of economic organizations in the localities.

To provide the necessary institutional background, this chapter opens with a description of rural industries under different ownerships over the past two decades, and how their development differed throughout Shanghai suburban countryside and southern Jiangsu. It shows that as reform proceeded, a variety of ownership arrangements emerged under the same terminology of collective ownership. Local institutional forms evolved with high flexibility, and adapted to newly emerging changes in macro economic and political environment. The following chapter explores the background, process, and social implications of TVEs' privatization in the post-reform period. An in-depth examination of a village's TVE property rights transformation over the past three decades shows that the privatization process not only involved a market mechanism but also intimately implicated grassroots social and political institutions.

Two decades of reform-era collectives

A comparison of the development of rural enterprises in this region shows a number of interesting trends indicating the supreme contribution of TVEs to local development. First of all, the growth of the rural industry between the late 1970s and early 1990s was spectacular, whether measured by enterprise numbers, employment, output, or profits. In the Shanghai suburbs, TVEs' nominal gross industrial output value increased at a double-digit growth up until the early 1990s. In 1995, two separate sets of statistics showed similar trends to varying degrees.[2] Figures from Shanghai's Statistics Bureau show negative growth of output value from 1995–2000 in the TVE sector – negative 4 percent annual change in township enterprises, and negative 6 percent in village enterprises. They did recover in 2000–2001, with 11 percent and 15 percent respectively. Whereas, figures from the Agricultural Bureau show significant decline but no negative growth in 1995–2000 (Table 2.1).

The general statistics for Shanghai's rural enterprises compare the four sectors under different jurisdictions; charting their level of growth shows that through most of the reform era up until the mid-1990s, township and village enterprises grew much faster than county or state enterprises. In 1985–1990, for instance, the industrial output value of township and village enterprises grew 28 and 23 percent, respectively. Conversely, county enterprises only grew 3 percent in the same period. Later in 1991–1995, township and village enterprises reported average annual output growth of 33 and 42 percent respectively, whereas country enterprises' output climbed only 22 percent annually. The period of 1995–2000, following the onset of Beijing's soft landing for overheated national economy, saw an unusual turnaround, with county firms maintaining steady growth; but TVEs declined or experienced negative growth. The recovery in 2000, however, did not include the county-owned state enterprises; but TVEs returned to double-digit growth (Table 2.1).

The industrial output of private and foreign enterprises (indicated as "others" in the statistics) experienced tremendous growth throughout the 1980s and 1990s. Prior to 1995, private enterprise did see double-digit growth, but still not as high as TVEs. After this period, however, their output continued to grow – whereas state and TVE sectors declined – growing at an average rate of 70 percent (Table 2.1).

The employment of peasant workers in the region's rural industry over these 20 years also had remarkable growth, particularly between 1978–1985, but started to slow down in the late 1980s. Beginning in 1991, however, the number of rural workers began to decline in the state and TVE sectors, while the private sector continued to grow – 54 percent in 1995–1997. This indicates a shift of the labor force from public to private sectors, and the need for peasants to find non-farm jobs away from their homes (Table 2.1).

Moreover, a tremendous number of new enterprises has been created in the private sector since the mid-1990s. After 1995, public sector growth went into significant decline, meaning that more state and TVE firms were closing than opening. Conversely, in the same period the private sector grew tremendously – 80 percent in 1995–1997 – indicating that growth of industry began to rely more and more on the private sector. In terms of profits earned, county-run state enterprises were the only firms to lose money – beginning in 1985–1990 – while TVEs posted substantial earnings throughout the 1980s and 1990s. However, after 1995 the private sector posted the most rapid profit growth: 55 percent annually in 1995–1997

Ownership composition of rural industry

A comparison of different ownership sectors as a percentage of the total rural industry shows the importance of TVEs in the local economy, and reveals that the private sector, while showing tremendous growth, still has only a minor role in rural industry.

In 1978 county enterprises accounted for 40 percent of industrial output, compared to 31 percent of township enterprises and 18 percent of village enterprises. But after the reforms were up and running, the TVEs took over to become the main actor in the rural economy. Throughout the 1980s, township enterprises accounted for 30–40 percent of output of the rural sector in Shanghai suburbs by themselves. In the 1990s, that percentage continued to grow to 40–50 percent. Likewise, village enterprises grew from under 20 percent in 1978, to 20–30 percent in the 1980s, and over 30 percent in the 1990s. Conversely, county enterprises continued to decline in the region's industrial output. From their dominance in the pre-reform era, falling to under 30 percent in the 1980s, and then less than 20 percent in the 1990s (Table 2.2).

In this light, the private sector, although growing by leaps and bounds year on year, did not improve its percentage of output by a similar amount. From 1980 to 1995, its share of the rural industrial output was less than 10 percent. By 1997 it increased to 14 percent. A gain, to be sure, but still a minor role in the rural economy. Likewise, in employment, although the private sector's hiring exploded in the 1990s and the TVEs fell, the TVEs continued to employ 73 percent of the rural labor force, whereas the private sector only raised its position from under 10 percent to 16 percent in 1997. This shows that although the number of private enterprises grew at over 60 percent in the 1990s, their contribution

Table 2.1 Growth of rural industry in Shanghai suburbs, 1978–2001

Annual average percentage change

	1978–1980	1981–1985	1985–1990	1991–1995	1995–1997	1995–2000[a]	1995–2000[b]	1997–2000	2000–2001
Number of enterprises	6	10	9	2	26	–	–	–	–
County enterprises	2	17	–	12	–11	–8	–8	–6	–11
Township enterprises	14	9	11	6	–7	–7	–10	–7	–4
Village enterprises	3	11	10	3	–9	–10	–14	–12	–12
Others	–	–3	–	–5	85	–	–	–	–
Number of workers	14	8	5	–2	–2	–	–	–	–
County enterprises	5	8	–	4	–11	–10	–10	–10	–13
Township enterprises	19	9	11	–1	–6	–8	–11	–10	–4
Village enterprises	15	8	1	0	–7	–9	–13	–10	–10
Others	1	4	–1	–18	54	–	–	–	–
Gross output value[c]	22	17	20	33	15	–	–	–	–
County enterprises	8	15	3	22	5	9	7	12	–9
Township enterprises	34	15	28	33	9	1	–4	–4	11
Village enterprises	34	25	23	42	14	1	–6	–7	15
Others	13	12	11	14	71	–	–	–	–
Total after tax profit[d]	21	12	8		12	5		–	6
County enterprises	2	12	–10		–10	1		10	30
Township enterprises	30	12	11		10	10		10	1
Village enterprises	33	13	12		7	5		4	8
Others	–	–	–		55	–		–	–

Sources: 1 For 1978–1980, 1981–1985, 1985–1990, calculated from XSGTZ 1949–1990. 2 For 1990–1995, 1995–2000,[a] 2000–2001, calculated from SJTN, various years. 3 For 1995–1997, 1995–2000,[b] 1997–2000, calculated from SNTN, various years.

Notes
a Figures calculated from SNTN, various years.
b Figures calculated from SJTN, various years.
c For 1970–1980, in 1970 prices; for 1981–1990, in 1980 prices; for 1990–1997, in 1990 prices.
d Figures for 1978–1990 are total profits; figures for 1991–2001 are total after tax profits.

Table 2.2 The ownership structure of rural industry in Shanghai suburbs, 1978–2001

Shanghai	1978 No.	%	1980 No.	%	1981 No.	%	1985 No.	%	1990 No.	%	1991 No.	%	1995[b] No.	%	1995[c] No.	%	1997 No.	%	2000[c] No.	%	2001 No.	%
Number of enterprises	5,615	–	6,255	–	6,928	–	10,258	–	15,816	–	23,617	–	25,436	–	22,288	–	35,433	–	–	–	–	–
County enterprises	578	10	606	10	720	10	1,350	13	1,374	9	1,421	6	2,232	9	2,232	10	1,786	5	1,477	–	1,309	15
Township enterprises	1,382	25	1,789	29	2,030	29	2,844	28	4,792	30	4,482	19	5,677	22	4,741	21	4,142	12	3,364	34	3,238	36
Village enterprises	3,394	60	3,597	58	3,869	56	5,796	57	9,376	59	9,696	41	11,033	43	8,821	40	7,378	21	5,069	51	4,469	50
Others[a]	261	5	263	4	309	4	268	3	274	2	8,018	34	6,494	26	6,494	29	22,127	62	–	–	–	–
Number of workers (10,000 yuan)	69.0	–	89.1	–	97.4	–	133.1	–	171.3	–	176.8	–	166.2	–	145.6	–	138.9	–	–	–	–	–
County enterprises	10.1	15	11.1	12	11.2	11	15.2	11	15.1	9	17.3	10	20.5	12	20.5	14	16.3	12	12.0	14	10.4	13
Township enterprises	20.7	30	29.3	33	34.0	35	48.5	36	82.9	48	77.7	44	75.8	46	66.3	46	58.4	42	42.8	50	41.1	52
Village enterprises	32.8	47	43.2	48	46.1	47	62.2	47	66.5	39	61.7	35	60.9	37	49.7	34	42.7	31	31.0	36	27.8	35
Others[a]	5.4	8	5.6	6	6.2	6	7.2	5	6.8	4	20.1	11	9.1	5	9.1	6	21.6	16	–	–	–	–
Gross output value[d] (10 million yuan)	34.6	–	51.7	–	61.6	–	115.7	–	292.3	–	510.7	–	1,597.9	–	1,221.9	–	1,611.1	–	–	–	–	–
County enterprises	13.7	40	16.1	31	17.1	28	30.0	26	35.6	12	74.5	15	166.5	10	150.2	12	165.7	10	231.7	18	211.8	15
Township enterprises	10.8	31	19.4	38	25.3	41	44.1	38	150.4	51	241.5	47	761.4	48	586.1	48	690.4	43	613.4	48	682.5	49
Village enterprises	6.3	18	11.3	22	13.7	22	33.0	29	92.0	31	141.7	28	581.6	36	409.2	33	530.9	33	429.2	34	492.6	36
Others[a]	3.8	11	4.9	9	5.5	9	8.5	7	14.3	5	53.0	10	88.4	6	76.4	6	224.2	14	–	–	–	–
Total after tax profits[e] (10 million yuan)	7.0	–	10.3	–	10.9	–	17.2	–	25.5	–	32.1	–	67.9	–	95.1	–	119.6	–	–	–	–	–
County enterprises	1.9	27	2.0	19	1.8	16	2.8	16	1.6	6	2.3	7	4.2	6	9.3	10	7.5	6	9.9	8	12.9	10
Township enterprises	2.6	37	4.4	43	4.9	45	7.6	44	12.8	50	14.7	46	26.6	39	39.9	42	48.1	40	63.3	53	63.7	50
Village enterprises	1.8	26	3.2	31	3.5	32	5.7	33	9.8	39	11.5	36	30.5	45	36.6	38	41.7	35	46.5	39	50.3	40
Others[a]	0.8	11	0.8	7	0.7	6	1.2	7	1.3	5	1.6	5	6.6	10	9.3	10	22.3	19	–	–	–	–

Sources: XSGTZ 1949–1990: 193–197; SJTN 1993: 119–121; SJTN 1996: 97; SNTN 1997: 100–101; SNTN 1998: 88–89; SJTN 2002: 80; SNTN 2001: 90–91; SJTN 2002: 80.

Notes
a Figures of "Others" are calculated from the residue of total.
b Figures calculated from SJTN, various years.
c Figures calculated from SNTN, various years.
d For 1970–1980, in 1970 prices; for 1981–1990, in 1980 prices; for 1990–1997, in 1990 prices.
e Figures for 1978–1995 are total profits; Figures for 1995–2001 are total after tax profits.

to local economy and labor market still remained marginal, while the TVEs, although their growth declined, still remained the main actor (Table 2.2).

A similar trend in nearby Wujiang

Table 2.3 presents the growth of number and output of industrial enterprises in Wujiang county in Suzhou. A comparison of sectors shows the same developments as suburban Shanghai: despite showing a strong growing pattern in output in 1990–1995, the number of TVEs has steadily dropped since 1990. From 1995 to 1997, township enterprises had no growth in output while village enterprises grew only 10 percent annually, whereas private enterprises reported an annual average growth of 139 percent (Table 2.3). Although TVEs showed no or marginal growth in output after 1995, they still maintained their dominant role in the local economy, accounting for 84 percent and 78 percent of total output in 1995 and 1997, respectively. The private sector accounted for 56 percent of rural enterprises in number in 1995, before jumping to 85 percent in 1997. It contributed a minor 2 percent of output in 1995, but grew rapidly to 8 percent in 1997 (Table 2.4).

Beginning in 1998, statistics are no longer compiled by industrial production and ownership structure, but rather by industrial size and ownership structure. Thus, in 1998–2001 an overwhelming majority of rural industrial enterprises in Wujiang, about 97 to 98 percent, were small and medium enterprises with an annual sales income lower than 5 million yuan. The number of large rural industrial enterprises remained at around 300, or 2 to 3 percent of total rural enterprises, yet contributed 46 percent of total output value in 2001 (Table 2.4).

Collective property rights through the early 1990s

The continuing importance and contribution of township and village enterprises in the region, as illustrated in the previous section, shows how village enterprises still play a significant role in the local economy. Such a phenomenon speaks volumes about how property rights in Sunan are embedded in local institutions, and facilitates a better and more complete understanding of how the TVE sector as a whole actually functions.

At face value, it appeared that the TVE sector boomed throughout the reform era, yet institutional and organizational structures were constantly changing, which gave new meaning to the terms "village enterprise" or "village-owned enterprises" depending on the region, the period and the organization. That is to say, to identify village-owned enterprises as some kind of "collectively owned enterprises" with Chinese-socialism characteristics, misleads and oversimplifies.

This section draws data from a survey of 30 villages in the Shanghai

Table 2.3 Growth of rural industry in Wujiang, 1978–2001

Wujiang	Annual average percentage change				
	1978–1980	1980–1985	1985–1990	1990–1995	1995–1997
Number of enterprises				11	58
Township enterprises	13	3	4	−4	−5
Village enterprises	10	6	0	−1	−5
Partnership or individual enterprises					
Number of staff and workers					
Township enterprises	19	16			
Village enterprises	17	18			
Partnership or individual enterprises					
Gross output value (1980 prices)	30	23	23		
Township enterprises	49	31	39		
Village enterprises	65	32	23		
Partnership or individual enterprises					
Gross output value (1990 prices)				30	7
Township enterprises				35	0
Village enterprises				33	10
Partnership or individual enterprises				80	139
Profits					
Township enterprises	60	6			
Village enterprises	73	−1			
Partnership or individual enterprises					

	1998–2001
Number of enterprises	2
Large scale industrial enterprises	4
Number of state-owned industrial enterprises	−16
Collective-owned industrial enterprises	−12
Others	19
Number of rural industrial enterprises	4
Small and medium scale industrial enterprises	2
Gross output value (1990 prices)	9
Gross output value (current prices)	9
Large scale industrial enterprises	18
Number of state-owned industrial enterprises	11
Collective-owned industrial enterprises	−2
Others	43
Number of rural industrial enterprises	16
Small and medium scale industrial enterprises	−2

Sources: Calculated from data in SUSJTZ 1986; SUTN 1991, 1996, 1998, 1999, 2002.

Note
Large scale industrial enterprises refers to those with more than 5 million yuan in annual sales income; small and medium enterprises refer to those with less than 5 million yuan in annual sales income.

Table 2.4 The ownership structure of rural industry in Wujiang

	1978 No.	1978 %	1980 No.	1980 %	1985 No.	1985 %	1990 No.	1990 %	1995 No.	1995 %	1997 No.	1997 %
Number of enterprises							3,163		5,386		13,520	
Township enterprises	238		302		344		419	13	349	6	318	2
Village enterprises	1,120		1,362		1,860		1,865	59	1,809	34	1,631	12
Partnership or individual enterprises							601	19	3,000	56	11,429	85
Number of staff and workers							223,424					
Township enterprises	16,543		23,272		48,296		145,798					
Village enterprises	27,079		37,156		85,637		75,612					
Partnership or individual enterprises							2,014					
Gross output value (1980 prices; 10,000 yuan)	41,244		69,321		191,4511		544,490					
Township enterprises	5,953	14	13,238	19	50,944	27	261,247	48				
Village enterprises	4,661	11	12,703	18	50,030	26	138,120	25				
Partnership or individual enterprises							1,769					
Gross output value (1990 prices; 10,000 yuan)							739,815		2,716,889		3,126,055	
Township enterprises							341,813	46	1,530,228	56	1,518,810	49
Village enterprises							183,712	25	755,276	28	906,505	29
Partnership or individual enterprises							2,354		44,612	2	255,058	8
Profits												
Township enterprises	1,084		2,778		3,756							
Village enterprises	746		2,235		2,106							
Partnership or individual enterprises												

continued

Table 2.4 Continued

	1998		1999		2000		2001	
	No.	%	No.	%	No.	%	No.	%
Number of enterprises (units)	14,999		16,035		15,777		16,140	
Large scale industrial enterprises	379	3	380	2	394	2	426	3
Number of state-owned industrial enterprises	42	0	40	0	31	0	25	0
Collective-owned industrial enterprises	170	1	164	1	141	1	117	1
Others	167	1	176	1	222	1	284	2
Number of rural industrial enterprises	299	2	290	2	299	2	339	2
Small and medium scale industrial enterprises	14,620	97	15,655	98	15,383	98	15,714	97
Gross output value (1990 prices; 10,000 yuan)	3,468,981		3,628,822		3,980,329		4,443,987	
Gross output value (current prices; 10,000 yuan)	3,551,356		3,731,020		4,131,972		4,55,0114	
Large scale industrial enterprises	1,665,121	47	1,876,460	50	2,318,918	56	2,765,147	61
Number of state-owned industrial enterprises	248,210	7	257,670	7	297,757	7	336,342	7
Collective-owned industrial enterprises	860,513	24	910,660	24	1,024,689	25	810,143	18
Others	556,398	16	708,130	19	996,472	24	1,618,662	36
Number of rural industrial enterprises	1,336,113	38	1,419,304	38	1,684,735	41	2,105,036	46
Small and medium scale industrial enterprises	1,886,235	53	1,854,560	50	1,813,054	44	1,784,967	39

Sources: SUSJTZ 1949–1985: 85,148–149, 151, 154; SUTN 1991: 54–56; SUTN 1996: 134–135; SUTN 1998: 126–127; SUTN 1999: 130–131; SUTN 2000: 144–145; SUTN 2001: 152–155; SUTN 2002: 154–155.

suburbs, complimented with in-depth interviews from village cadres and managers, in order to provide a descriptive analysis of the development of property rights arrangements in the TVE sector during the reform era. It goes far beyond official terminology, investigating a variety of different property rights arrangements – even though they have one official label – and their paths of development in the reform era. The village survey was conducted in 1993–1994.[3] Despite a small sample size, a systematic sampling scheme was implemented in sample selection. Of each of the ten suburban counties (districts) in Shanghai, three townships were selected according to their economic development level, and then one village was selected from each of the selected townships.[4]

Shanghai village survey

Table 2.5 shows the key features of village enterprises in the Shanghai countryside. The number of village enterprises, their output, profits, and remittances to the village government was compared in 1987 and 1993, charting the growth and wealth of villages under reforms. Of the 30 villages surveyed, in 1987 each had an average of four enterprises, with 16 being the largest number in any one village. Roughly 70 percent of villages in 1987 had only one to three enterprises under their jurisdictions, with only 7 percent containing over ten enterprises. The village industry in Shanghai expanded quickly. In 1993, each village had an average of nine enterprises, with 44 being the largest number in any one village. By this time the percentage of villages with only one to three companies had dropped to 37 percent, and those with over ten enterprises had increased to 10 percent (Table 2.5).

Likewise, output value and profit increased correspondingly. In 1987, average output value was 3.85 million yuan with the lowest output value of any one village at 320,000 yuan, and the highest output value of any one village at 16.9 million yuan. By 1993, the average output value per village increased over ten times to nearly 30 million yuan, with the lowest at 150,000 yuan, and the highest at 196 million yuan. In 1987, 77 percent of villages had output value of less than 5 million yuan, but in 1993, that number had fallen to 33 percent, while 10 percent were producing over 100 million yuan.

Profits generated by village enterprises in 1987 averaged 340,000 yuan per village, with the lowest profits of any one village at zero. The maximum profit of any one village was 2.41 million yuan. In 1993, the average had climbed to 1.74 million yuan, with a minimum of 1,200 yuan and a maximum of 12.63 million yuan. In 1987, half of the villages made less than 100,000 yuan, and only 3 percent made over 1.5 million yuan. However, the figures grew significantly. In 1993, 20 percent of total villages made less than 100,000 yuan, and over one third made over 1.5 million yuan.

Table 2.5 The development of industrial enterprise in Shanghai sampled villages, 1987 and 1993

Indicators of village enterprises	1987 No.	%	1993 No.	%
Number of enterprises	30	–	30	–
1–3	21	70	11	37
4–6	6	20	11	37
7–9	1	3	5	17
10 and more	2	7	3	10
Mean	4	–	6	–
Max.	16	–	44	–
Min.	0	–	1	–
Gross output value (10,000 yuan)	30	–	30	–
500 or less	23	77	10	33
500–1,000	3	10	5	17
1,000–5,000	4	13	10	33
5,000–10,000	0	0	2	7
10,000 and more	0	0	3	10
Mean	385	–	2,959	–
Max.	1,687	–	19,589	–
Min.	32	–	15	–
Profits (10,000 yuan)	30	–	30	–
10 or less	15	50	6	20
10–50	9	30	8	27
50–100	3	10	5	17
100–150	2	7	1	3
150 and more	1	3	10	33
Mean	34	–	174	–
Max.	241	–	1,263	–
Min.	0	–	0	–
Number of workers	30	–	30	–
100 or less	7	23	5	16
100–200	4	13	6	20
200–300	7	23	6	20
300–400	3	10	2	7
400 and more	9	30	11	37
Mean	316	–	405	–
Max.	954	–	2,290	–
Min.	0	–	30	–
Remittances to the village administration (10,000 yuan)	30	–	30	–
10 or less	22	73	14	47
10–20	4	13	2	7
20–30	2	7	2	7
30–40	0	0	4	13
40 and more	2	7	8	27
Mean	9	–	43	–
Max.	50	–	404	–
Min.	0	–	0	–

Source: Author's fieldwork, 1995.

The Yangtze Delta in the reform era   45

The objective of village enterprises was not entirely profit oriented; they also fulfilled social needs to solve villagers' employment problems. In 1987, on average each village had 316 workers working in their village enterprises; the number climbed to 405 in 1993. In 1987, approximately 40 percent of Shanghai's villages hired more than 300 peasant workers, and only one fourth of total villages failed to absorb more than 100 workers in their village enterprises. In 1993, 37 percent of villages employed more than 400 workers in their village enterprises, with the highest number at 2,290 and the lowest number at 30.

Among all the considerations, remittances submitted to village coffers played a crucial role for the incentives and motivations of village government leaders to establish and manage village enterprises. In Shanghai suburbs, remittances submitted by village enterprises to each village government averaged 90,000 yuan in 1987, and increased to 430,000 yuan in 1993. Even though there were villages receiving zero remittance from village enterprises, both in 1987 and 1993, the highest remittance received amounted to 500,000 yuan in 1987, and 4 million yuan in 1993. In 1993, more than half of Shanghai's village governments received more than 100,000 yuan annually from their village enterprises.

A variety of village-owned arrangements

Within the sector of village enterprises, there existed different kinds of property rights arrangements. In addition to enterprises in the private sector (i.e., individual enterprises, private enterprises, and foreign joint ventures), the survey broke down the collective category of "village-run enterprise" into four categories: collective unified management (*jiti tongyi jingying*), collective contracting (*jiti chengbao jingying*), individual contracting, and shareholding. Table 2.6 shows that in 1987 collective unified management dominated in village industry, contributing 94 percent of gross output, 90 percent of profits, 100 percent of remittances submitted to villages, and employing 76 percent of village workers. In 1993, shareholding and foreign joint-venture arose as new forms of property rights, producing 11 percent and 8 percent of total gross output, respectively, and reducing the contribution of collective unified management to 76 percent of total gross output by all village enterprises. Likewise, the number of enterprises, profits, employed workers, and remittances to villages contributed by shareholding and foreign joint ventures all increased significantly between 1987 and 1993 (Table 2.6).

Survey data also shows that these three ownership arrangements were evenly distributed across villages of different development levels, implying that there was no correlation between ownership arrangements and economic development in the villages. Finally, individual firms and private enterprises played a minor role in local economy in this region. Between 1987 and 1993, despite constituting about 20 percent of total village

Table 2.6 The ownership composition of village enterprises in Shanghai suburbs, 1987 and 1993

Type	Number of enterprises 1987 No.	%	1993 No.	%	Gross output value (10,000 yuan) 1987 No.	%	1993 No.	%	Profits (10,000 yuan) 1987 No.	%	1993 No.	%	Number of workers 1987 No.	%	1993 No.	%	Remittance to the village administration (10,000 yuan) 1987 No.	%	1993 No.	%
Collective unified managed (jiti tongyi jingying)	110	75.9	172	59.7	11,793.2	94.1	74,426.4	75.7	3,214.1	90.1	4,862.2	58.8	8,381	85.5	8,898	75.8	3,225.8	99.6	1,763.9	77.5
Collective contracting (jiti chengbao jingying)	5	3.4	8	2.8	430.2	3.4	1,765	1.8	344.4	9.7	178	2.2	900	9.2	370	3.2	10.2	0.3	45	2
Individual contracting (geren chengbao jingying)	3	2.1	17	5.9	207.8	1.7	1,815.4	1.8	6.4	0.2	100.2	1.2	97	1	418	3.6	4.5	0.1	61.9	2.7
Shareholding (gufengzhi jingying)	0	0	4	1.4	0	0	11,231.8	11.4	0	0	814.8	9.8	0	0	756	6.4	0	0	124.8	5.5
Individual management (geti jingying)	23	15.9	73	25.3	49.7	0.4	334.7	0.3	2.5	0.1	22.2	0.3	34	0.3	163	1.4	0	0	1	0
Private enterprise (siying qiye)	4	2.8	6	2.1	487	0.4	628	0.6	1	0	27.8	0.3	391	4	106	0.9	0	0	1.5	0.1
Foreign joint-venture (sanzi qiye)	0	0	8	2.8	0	0	8,176.2	8.3	0	0	2,270.4	27.4	0	0	1,033	8.8	0	0	277	12.2

Source: Author's fieldwork, 1995.

enterprises, individual and private enterprises combined to contribute less than 1 percent of industrial output produced by all village enterprises in Shanghai.

The essence of the so-called collective unified management (*jiti tongyi jingying*) is the dominant role of village government in the management of village-run enterprises.[5] Under this system, most villages in the Yangtze Delta in the reform era had adopted some form of contract responsibility management, in which the management of the enterprises was contracted to individuals, to small groups of individuals, or to enterprise managers representing the enterprises. The contract defined the contractor's power, responsibilities, and rewards; it did not have to be in the form of a formal document, and sometimes it was reached through verbal agreement or mutual consensus. In addition to a contract between the enterprise and the village government, another contract system was also implemented to regulate the relationship between township and village governments. In Shanghai villages, collective unified management included the appointment of enterprise managers by the village government and the direct involvement of village cadres in the day-to-day management of village-run enterprises. These cadres were usually enterprise directors. In effect, the entrepreneurs who sought out the opportunities, initiated the new projects, managed the production and investment, and allocated annual profits were the village cadres.

The manager contract responsibility system had been implemented with the following characteristics: clear responsibilities, remuneration tied to performance, and above-quota profits shared. Responsibilities of the economic targets (e.g., gross output, sale income, tax, profit, and remittance) were assigned to the enterprise; of these, the most important were profit and remittance. The salary level of the enterprise manager, along with bonus were linked to the enterprise's performance relative to assigned targets. A share of the above-quota profit was usually distributed among the village, the manager, the workers' wage bonus, and the enterprise fund (see also Ho 1994: 105–109). In theory, the township government had the authority to issue rewards or penalties to the village cadres if exceeding or not achieving the annual economic targets assigned to the village. In practice, however, villages were consulted on what targets they were capable of achieving before they were finalized.

Some small village enterprises with fewer than eight workers were contracted by individuals and called "individual contracting" (*geren chengbao*), under which the contractor paid the collective a fixed annual remittance and absorbed all remaining profits or losses. In effect, the contractor was paying a fixed rent for the use of village-owned assets, and thus, in theory, bore all the risk of operating the enterprise. In practice, however, the collective shared some of the risk and might not be able to collect the full fixed remittance if the contracted enterprise performed poorly and the contractor failed to pay the rent.

Shareholding system during the reforms

The shareholding system in the rural economy developed in the mid-1980s, and was applied rather loosely to a wide range of enterprise organizations.[6] In southern Fujian, for example, a business partnership between two people was termed shareholding. Likewise a collective enterprise in the Yangtze Delta, owned by a village, a state firm, or by the village and the township was also called shareholding. In this way numerous forms of shareholding firms coexisted and varied enormously in management and property rights relations across China.

In the Shanghai survey, shareholding firms emerged in the early 1990s, which was much later than other regions due to the rigidity of collective orientated policy. In 1991, Shanghai reported only eight rural enterprises managed by shareholding, whereas in the same time a national survey found that shareholding enterprises accounted for 3 percent of township-run enterprises, 13 percent of village-run enterprises, and 33 percent of individual and joint enterprises (Wang *et al.* 1997: 18).

Deng Xiaoping's southern tour and speeches in 1992 re-affirmed variations in enterprise forms and further fueled enthusiasm for shareholding. Then, following the guidelines of Deng's speeches, the Shanghai government requested each township to select one or two show-case enterprises for shareholding management. By the end of 1992, 593 enterprises were entitled to take a shareholding arrangement, accounting for a mere 4 percent of total rural enterprises (Xie and Ling 1994: 67). This study's village survey found that, in 1993, shareholding enterprises had produced 12 percent of industrial output, making nearly 10 percent of profits, hiring 6 percent of peasant workers in Shanghai suburbs (Table 2.6). In the mid-to-late-1990s, however, shareholding became an important form of organization in the TVE sector, and actually acted as a transitional mechanism from a command economy to a private ownership economy during the privatization process in the post-reform period (Lin and Chen 1999; Lin and Ye 1998).

Shareholding enterprises in the Shanghai TVE sector were established through an incentive to expand the enterprise's original assets with outside investment, so that more funds could be channeled into the firms, particularly during periods of tight credit. Financial investments drew from employees, legal entities (enterprises and public organs), and individuals. A shareholding enterprise might have contained only several collective entities like state firms, local collective enterprises or administrative organs, without any role by independent individuals.

In general, four types of shareholders were identified in the Yangtze Delta region: collective holders, enterprise holders, worker holders, and social holders. The collective holders represented the initial investments from a village or township. Enterprise holders came from two sources: the original investment of a village or township in an enterprise, and the enterprise's subsequent accumulation. Worker shares were developed by either cash investments or labor investments on the part of the workers. Social holders included any legal entity or individual external to the enterprise. Finally, in some occasions there was a category called "shadow" shares (or contribution shares), which converted surplus profit into shares and distributed to employees according to their seniority and contributions. In most circumstances, these shares were used to earn bonuses, and could not be transferred to others, with few exceptions for big stock listed TVEs whose shares were open to the general public and traded in the stock exchanges. While the shares might be owned by individuals, most shares belonged to the collectives in the reform period. In 1992, for instance, 54 percent of the shares among shareholding rural enterprises in suburban Shanghai belonged to the collectives (and enterprises), 12 percent belonged to legal entities, and 35 percent to workers and individuals (Xie and Ling, 1994: 71). Despite all the fuss over shareholding, before the late 1990s, the local economy in the Yangtze Delta still remained collective oriented without any sign of privatization.

Case studies of pro-collective villages in suburban Shanghai

In order to elaborate property rights arrangements and organizational features of TVEs in this region, this section presents four representative case studies showing the development of Shanghai's rural industry. These cases show clearly who are in control of the enterprises and the property rights and by what means they have come into control of these rights.

The data are drawn from a series of in-depth studies conducted among the Shanghai villages during 1995–1996 and 2001–2002. The first two examples, both located in the inner circle of Shanghai City, represent many of today's "quasi-urban" villages, which rely on their locational advantage and land assets to bring in rent income. Their leadership and organizations reflect many of China's glorious one-man-run villages that saw their administration and enterprises fully merged and come under the control of a super power leader. The third and fourth example also started with a leader-run model in village administration, but in village enterprises they adopted a shareholding system in the early 1990s – much earlier than their counterparts in this region.

Case study 1: from village collective to corporation

Kang village in Baoshan District, the north part of Shanghai municipality, represents one of Shanghai's booming upstart villages in the reform era. Among Shanghai's some 2,700 odd villages, Kang has been among the top since the mid-1980s. In a "top 100 village ranking" (*zonghe shili baiqiang cun*), a government designed scale comprised of various economic and social indicators, Kang peaked at number three among all Shanghai villages in 1993, then dropped to 27th in 1997, climbed back to 10th in 1999 before finally moving to 48th in 2001 and 53rd in 2002 (Shanghai Statistics Bureau 2003). Unlike traditional agricultural countryside with green fields and ponds, Kang has been urbanized with a sense of metropolitan Shanghai with six-lane boulevards and seven-story apartment buildings; factories, shops, supermarkets and a four-star hotel stand orderly on the village's territory of 2,600 mu (173 hectare). Another part of the village land supports a large residential area covering by about 500 two-story villager-owned houses, built in 1992–1998 under a village-endorsed project; the residential area is well equipped with village-provided tap water, gas, heat, and recreational facilities.

The Dakang multifunctional recreation center stood out as the leading money-maker over 60 enterprises in Kang in 2000, combining a four-star hotel and various recreation facilities including bowling, swimming, KTV, and playgrounds. It was managed by Dakang Real Estate Company, another village-run enterprise that supervises all of the village's real estate. Also in the service sector was Dakang Taxi Company, which was started in 1993, owned 60 cabs and employed 200 people by 2001. The village's industrial sector included garment manufacturers, makers of compressor and freezer equipment, and cosmetics manufacturing, of which a joint Sino-American venture, Glyn Cosmetics Company, played a leading role.

Kang's success today cannot simply be attributed to its geographical location near Shanghai. Back to the 1970s, Kang was poor and miserable, lagging behind other villages due to its bad location where the outbound transportation was impeded by an airport runway. Its later success was built on a traditional leader-run model, tightly connected with a key leader, Zhu Genrong, the village's party secretary for 25 years. Born in a poor farming family, Zhu started farm work when he was 15, and then became one of the village's production team leaders in the brigade. Between 1971 and 1975, he left home serving in the Army, which he significantly benefited in accumulating personal experiences and extending social networks. In 1976, as a demobilized solider, he was appointed the village party secretary.

Zhu took advantage of the village's proximity to urban Shanghai and started a business in agricultural sideline production. The village established several ranches to raise cows, chickens and hogs, and set up a vegetable farm of 550 mu (37 hectares). At the time, the agricultural commodity market was still strictly restricted by the bureaucratic distribution, and thus outlawed direct trade between buyers and producers. To open the market channel, Zhu reached a deal with the Agricultural Supply Company of the district (then the county) government through the township government and one of his fellow army veterans working in the district administration. The village supplied agricultural products (vegetables, milk, chicken, pork, eggs, etc.) to the Agricultural Supply Company that had direct market channels in Shanghai.

Zhu's development strategy was to first develop the village's industry as processing factories for nearby state firms, and utilize the village's locational advantage to build premises and warehouses for rent. Joint-ventures were established in a way that the village contributed land and labor management in exchange for rental income and villagers' employment. In nonagricultural activities, a village-run factory was first established in 1981 to repair farming equipment. It made an annual profit of 52,800 yuan.

Between 1981 and 1986, Kang jumped ahead and gradually outshone its counterparts. The village's economic achievement in 1987 beat other sample villages in the Shanghai village survey; it had 18 village-run enterprises, including 13 in industrial manufacturing, three in agriculture, and two in the service sector. Its industrial output reached 16.86 million yuan, making 1.07 million yuan in profit plus a remittance of 500,000 yuan submitted to the village administration. To acquire technology and skills, the village arranged and supported several middle school graduates to study in a technical school in Shanghai, and also sent workers to work as trainees in Shanghai state firms. These human resources helped the village's enterprises to rapidly develop. Zhu formed the Dakang Company in 1987 to organize all the village enterprises into a corporation, which expanded to a total of 53 enterprises in 1993, including 44 industrial factories, making 12 million yuan in profit and contributing 4 million yuan to the village coffers.

Throughout the 1980s and 1990s, the village's political and administrative organizations were completely merged with the corporation, which also housed the party office and the villagers' committee. The villager's official documents and announcements (e.g., the regulations of shareholding system for village enterprises) were underwritten by a stamp consisting of two titles: Kang Villagers' Committee and the Dakang Corporation.

The chief managers of the corporation were concurrently village cadres. The key man Zhu Genrong, the village's long-time party secretary since 1976, was also the chief executive officer (CEO) of the corporation in the 1980s and 1990s. Meanwhile Ms. Cao was the chief accountant for the village and also for the corporation. The CEOs of the three branch companies also served as members of the villagers' committee.

The corporation was organized as a three-layer multi-responsibility system. The corporation assigned responsibilities to the branch companies under which enterprises were responsible for the bottom line of output, benefits, and remittance to the village. The annual benefit surpluses of each enterprise was divided among the corporation, the supervisory branch company, and the enterprise. However, the corporation, commanded by Zhu, retained the principal policy-making power over each branch company and sometimes down to the enterprises. The corporation appointed the enterprises' director, deputy director, and accountant, and decided their workers' wages and bonuses at the end of the year. This type of organizational structure – a village corporation under a monolithic leadership combining party, government and enterprise authority – was quite common in rural China in the 1990s, particularly in well developed pro-collective coastal provinces like Shandong and southern Jiangsu (Wong *et al.* 1995; Chen 1998a, 1998b). A number of super-rich villages emerging in Chinese reforms, such as Daqiuzhuang in Tianjin and Huaxi in Wuxi, have revealed parallel organizational features and drawn much interest from the media and scholars (Lin 1995; Lin and Chen 1994, Lin and Ye 1998).

By the end of 1994, following a regulation from the upper district government, Kang village began to implement a shareholding system in all its village-run enterprises except eight agricultural farms. The first step was to return villagers' cash contribution made in the early agricultural collective period, with an interest rate of 400 percent. Then the village recalculated the assets and debts of each enterprise, allocating 10 percent of the cash deposit preparing for non-performing loans. The next step was to transform assets of each enterprise into shares, of which 40 percent were collective shares held by the village corporation and 60 percent as individual shares to be sold and awarded to individuals. The division of individual shares followed a detailed guideline that specifies the qualification and quantity of shares each individual was entitled to purchase or receive according to his/her position, seniority, and place of birth. As a result, senior cadres and managers received as much as twenty times the shares received by ordinary workers. From then on, the employees' income was drawn from basic wages and bonuses earned from shares they held. The collective shares of each enterprise were entitled to the village-corporation, i.e. the Dakang Corporation, which was under the party secretary's command. Between 1995 and 2000, a proportion of the village shares were gradually sold to enterprise managers and village cadres, but the village administration as the collective's representative still held the largest part of the assets and levied the biggest share of the income generated.

Case study 2: running the village by shareholding and joint ventures

Gao village's development is due to its location in Shanghai's Pudong New Area, established in 1990 and designated as an open economic zone for export processing, foreign trade and finance, and high technology. In 2000, the village had 1,858 residents in 710 households, occupying a small area of 1.7 square kilometers. As of 1993, the village had 15 enterprises, including two shareholding enterprises, three foreign joint ventures, and 10 village-run collective enterprises. All the enterprises were organized under the Xinguang General Company, under the leadership of Zhang Guomin, the CEO of the company and the village party secretary between 1983 and 2001. The industrial output of the village enterprises reached 84.84 million yuan in 1993, bringing in a remittance totaling 1.76 million yuan for the village. The village's backbone enterprise, Gaonan Steel Rolling Factory, established in 1984, had been managed in the form of a village collective until it was changed into a shareholding system in 1993. It created 62.68 million yuan in output and 1.50 million yuan in profit in 1993. The Xinguang Garment Factory, the village's oldest enterprise established in 1979 by Zhang, also initiated its shareholding arrangement in 1993. Under the shareholding arrangement, the factory's director was selected by the board of the factory. However, the board of the factory was merged with the General Company's board, with Mr. Zhang serving as the CEO. The village was not involved in the production and management of the three foreign joint ventures, but received annual payment for the use of land and factory buildings. One of the foreign joint ventures was a printing factory cooperated with a Hong Kong company, and its annual remittance was 20 percent of the factory's net profit. The other two joint-ventures paid fixed rents to the village, with a 2–4 percent annual increment. For example, the village received 180,000 yuan and 280,000 yuan respectively in 1993 from these two foreign joint ventures. As for the 10 village collective enterprises, six of them were set up in 1992–1993, under the arrangement of joint management with outside parties, such as state-owned and collective enterprises, who paid rent in return for the land, the buildings, the workers, and the service the village provided.

Case study 3: shareholding system for profit distribution

Songjiang enamel factory, the backbone enterprise in Huaqiao village in Songjiang County, became one of Shanghai's demonstration enterprises for a shareholding system in May 1992. The factory, and the village as well, had been under the leadership of Zhu Liangcai, the founder and director of the factory, and the village head for the past 15 years. In 1993, the factory's output reached 33 million yuan, and made a profit of 4.14 million yuan, making itself one of the top three ceramic factories in the country. Since 1992, the shareholding system had been operated as follows. The collective (the factory and the village) owned 70 percent of the shares, while individual shares accounted for the remaining 30 percent. All shares were worth 9 million yuan, with individual shares totaling 2.7 million yuan. Each individual share cost 500 yuan and earned a fixed 30 percent annual return. Zhu, the holder of the largest number of shares, invested 300,000 yuan, yielding a dividend of 90,000 yuan annually. Shares could be traded or sold among fellow villagers, but few had been transacted. The villagers held 70 percent of the individual shares; the remaining 30 percent were sold to township people (mostly township officials and enterprise managers). The collective shares were under the control of the board of the factory, whose chairman was Zhu's eldest son.

Case study 4: shareholding by collective investment

Shanghai Sifang Agriculture-Industry-Commerce Company, registered as a shareholding enterprise with assets totaling 1.5 million yuan, was established by Xincun village in Jinshang County in 1993. It combined investment from four governmental organs: 400,000 yuan from the Bureau of Agriculture of Shanghai City; 300,000 yuan from the Songjiang Agricultural Vocational School; 50,000 yuan from the Bureau of Agriculture of Jinshang County; and 700,000 yuan from Xincun village itself. Meng Hailin, the village party secretary and the general manager of the company, has engaged the company in real estate and trade business. Major investment projects up to 1995 were to build storage and commercial buildings in the village and to place them for sale or rent. The profits were distributed among the collective investors according to the capital contributed by each party. In this case, there were no individual shares involved.

Local institutions in the Yangtze River delta

This section explains how local institutions facilitate property rights transformations in the Yangtze Delta region throughout the reform era. It provides historical context and institutional arrangements in which economic behaviors and organizational configurations have been embedded. Historically, the Yangtze Delta region is distinguished by its prosperous environment, and even before 1949 it had been one of the most advanced areas of China in terms of agricultural and industrial development. Yet this factor is not sufficient to explain the stellar economic growth during the reform era, nor provide an answer of why collective property rights arose.

In response to common state policies and particular local legacies, the approaches to reform adopted by local governments have varied sharply across China. This section highlights the dynamic roles played by local governments and local cadres, and the process of resource mobilization initiated by bureaucratic connections and social networks. It first presents local state approaches in Shanghai suburbs and southern Jiangsu during the reform era, and then examines entrepreneurial activities in local and external networks that led to TVE development.

Local state approaches since the 1970s

In the early 1970s, the Yangtze Delta saw a revival of agricultural production and small industries. In southern Jiangsu, before the political environment became more permissive after the downfall of the ultra-leftist Gang of Four in 1976, local government initiatives for developing rural industry concentrated mainly on the commune and brigade levels (later the township and village levels). For example, in the early and mid-1970s, a number of rural factories in southern Jiangsu were "surreptitiously run," meaning they did not notify nor obtain approval from authorities at higher levels (Fei 1984: 45, 1989: 113; DZDJ 1989: 428).

In Wuxi, however, the most well-endowed county of southern Jiangsu, county authorities resisted to close down non-farm commune- and brigade-enterprises (CBEs) to concentrate on agriculture, even though the priority of grain production was stressed in political campaigns and sometimes rural collective enterprisers were at a risk of being attacked as "the tails of capitalism" (Mo 1987: 123–146; Svejnar and Woo 1990: 75). In 1976, CBEs in Jiangsu began to receive supportive policies from the province, including tax breaks and reductions, capital access and interest-free loans, and supply of raw materials. Province authorities convinced county officials to devote their efforts to the development of CBEs, and to move away from the restriction of "city for industry; countryside for agriculture" (Mo 1987: 147–154; DZDJ 1989: 605). Despite a national debate on the role of rural enterprise in 1979–1980, the Jiangsu provincial party committee continued to convene meetings and issue documents calling for support for CBEs in terms of funds, equipment, technology, and raw materials. The government called on local officials to "emancipate the mind" (*jiefang sixiang*), moving bravely from the planned economy toward market-oriented activities and expanding cooperation between CBEs and urban state-owned firms and research institutes (Mo 1987: 172–178; DZDJ 1989: 427–429).

At the same time, team-run enterprises were discouraged from operating independent of the senior bureaucratic units, although they were not severely restricted by provincial policy (Mo 1987: 185).[7] In Wuxi, for example, no production team was allowed to engage in factory production of its own (Luo 1990: 149). The commune (latterly the township) stood at the head of the local economy, and the brigade (latterly the village) and the production team were actually under its strict control.[8] The commune directly appointed top managers of enterprises at both the commune and sometimes brigade levels. In fact, brigade officials were often concurrently managers of the brigade's enterprises. In the early 1980s, southern Jiangsu still retained solid integration of the three levels of community institutions in economic life, in which peasant workers of CBEs were not paid directly by the factory but by the production teams from which they came. The production team pooled income from factories and from farming and paid each member according to the work-points they contributed. In this way, CBEs were responsible for subsidizing farming and balancing local income distribution (DZDJ 1989: 427–429).

More importantly, the revenue-sharing arrangements first introduced in Jiangsu in 1977 produced a real revenue imperative facing local officials. In 1977, Jiangsu led the nation in decentralizing the fiscal system to subprovincial regions, and over the years continued to decentralize revenue and expenditure responsibilities (DZDJ 1989: 611). The profits

56 *The Yangtze Delta property rights transformations*

earned and taxes paid by the township and village enterprises (formerly CBEs) furnished the bulk of local revenue and constituted the only source of funds for some items of government expenditures. Local peasants depended mainly on income earned by working in local firms from which township and village government officials drew resources and benefits. As such, since the late 1970s, the strong endowment in collective assets, the extreme dependence of the local government on rural enterprise for revenue source, and the consequent close financial ties between collective firms and the local government, all account for the heavy involvement of local officials in collective enterprises in the early reform period. The local officials in the Sunan region responded to the power and interest incentives by committing themselves to promoting township- and village-run enterprises, and, on the other hand, by resisting the development of joint-household or individual level firms.

Local cadres initiatives and local endowment

In addition to a supportive and leading role played by local governments, production factors were equally important, if not more important. As illustrated in the previous section, few of the village enterprises in Shanghai suburbs had been owned and managed by private entrepreneurs through the reform period. The village governments assumed a firm leadership in local economy with the predominant form of "collective unified management." The question is: who initiated these village enterprises, when, and by what means? This study's village survey in Shanghai suburbs reveals that it was village cadres who played a vital role in spearheading the village's market-oriented activities. Of the 30 sample villages, 23 villages (77 percent) saw their first village factories directly established by village cadres,[9] of which 14 were party secretaries and the rest party branch leaders or production team leaders. In addition to those founded by local cadres, four were set up by fellow villagers and three by outsiders from nearby villages or urban Shanghai. In market-oriented non-farm activities, the survey also finds that half of the village factories were established before 1975, during the decade of the Cultural Revolution (1966–1976); another 13 were set up between 1976 and 1980; only four of the 30 came into being after 1980.[10]

The sources of financial capital for village enterprises in this region mainly drew from community surplus and local financial institutions. In particular, the start-up capital for village firms during the pre-reform or early reform period mostly relied on community surplus, then under the control of the brigade (now the village). In the lower Yangtze Delta region, as early as 1970, industry had exceeded agriculture in rural gross output, and hence the community surplus was generated not only from agricultural accumulation but from industrial production as well. For example, in 1970, industry and agriculture contributed 935 million yuan and 871 million yuan in Shanghai suburbs respectively. In the same year, in Suzhou, the industrial output value of 1,746 million yuan far exceeded the agricultural output value of 1,289 million yuan (SJN 1992: 599; SUSJTZ 1986: 5).

The rural credit, provided by the Agricultural Bank and the Rural Credit Cooperatives under its direct supervision, did not become an essential source of funds for rural enterprises until the mid-1980s, when the central government openly encouraged state banks to help rural communities develop township and village enterprises. Since then, bank loans have gradually replaced government allocations for investment capital in the country's rising economy. As the Agricultural Bank and the Rural Credit Cooperatives assumed majority of banking transactions in the countryside, they became a key source of development capital for rural enterprises. Since 1979, the value of loans that each financial institution could make in a region had been linked to the amount of deposits it generated. Therefore, the level of lending by financial institutions to local enterprises was largely determined by the level of local deposits. In southern Jiangsu, the ratio of locally self-financed investments (i.e., reinvestment of local enterprises and new investments endorsed by local governments) to investments financed by bank loans declined from 4:1 in 1983 to 1:1 in 1988 (Shen 1991: 53–54). For Suzhou alone, bank loans and collective funds (including investment from community governments and retained profits saved by the collective enterprises) accounted for 34 and 56 percent of the fixed asset investment for rural enterprises in 1988, respectively.

Cadre entrepreneurship and bureaucratic connections

Despite the important role played by start-up capital, it is noteworthy that capital shortage was common throughout all China in the early 1970s. As such, the role of financial capital should not be overstated in the initial stages of village enterprises, particularly during the pre-reform period. The mobilization of start-up funds solved only one part of the investment problem. During the early stages of reform, markets were underdeveloped and highly imperfect, with poor transportation and inadequate communication channels. Thus, it was equally important for new enterprises to locate machinery and raw material supply, and acquire technical and management know-how. Looking beyond the economic production factors, such as start-up and development capital, information, and technological base (broadly defined, including human resources, machinery, and equipment), the way the cadre entrepreneurs in the Yangtze Delta region mobilized resources through a locally embedded bureaucratic networks is key to understanding the whole picture of TVEs' development.

In the 1970s and the early 1980s, the most useful strategy to set up village factories was for the village cadres to take the initiative in exploiting the comparative advantages of their localities and to seek assistance and mobilize resources from higher levels of governments. The motives for senior units (e.g., township and county governments) to offer bureaucratic support for the establishment and running of village enterprises lay in financial as well as political concerns. On the one hand, the interests of community enterprises were identical to those of their township and county governments, which relied on local enterprises for tax revenues and extrabudgetary income. On the other hand, the development of the industrial sector was the most useful means to relieve the employment pressure of surplus labor in the countryside and also served to expand income sources for the peasants. Usually, the villages arranged, through personal contacts and connections, to seize business opportunities outside the community and then turned to local governments for necessary bureaucratic support, such as business licenses and access to raw materials and market channels.

Another important piece of bureaucratic assistance provided by township and county governments was the acquisition of enterprise capital, which mainly came from collective funds (i.e., government coffers and retained profits of the collective enterprises) and local financial institutions. These two sources in Suzhou, for example, accounted for 90 percent of fixed asset investment for rural enterprises in 1988 (SUTN 1989). In many cases, the bureaucratic organs, including government bureaus, institutes (hospitals, schools, etc.), and collective enterprises, employed their own funds to invest in rural enterprises (in the form of shareholding or loans) to generate more returns. Township governments in the Shanghai suburbs and southern Jiangsu took the view that local bank funds form part of the community capital base, and thus the political interference on the part of the township governments played an important role in lending decisions. Local banks and rural credit cooperatives were not allowed to lend money freely outside the township, making their funds considered community capital. In theory, lending decisions were made independently, rationally, and efficiently on the part of local banks, considering a number of financial criteria of the firms and the qualification of the guarantors and collateral. In practice, local governments (particularly township and county governments) acted as intermediaries and guarantors in the loan acquisition process and functioned as risk bearers and loss absorbers.

For example, village government in many cases explicitly or implicitly served as a guarantor for bank borrowings by village-run enterprises under its jurisdiction. In case of overdue loans, the guarantors – mostly the village administrations – would take over the responsibility for repaying debts. As a result, in the Yangtze Delta region, in the pro-collective reform period, those who successfully obtained capital from other bureaucratic units or local financial institutions rarely bypassed the bureaucratic system, whose well-endowed resources and political authority played a key role in generating business opportunities and funds for community enterprises.

The following descriptions of entrepreneurial activities utilizing bureaucratic privilege and connections give additional details to illustrate the resource mobilization process in the Yangtze Delta area.

Case study 5: bureaucratic assistance in building up a village firm

Jinze in Qingpu County was one of the most backward villages in Shanghai suburbs in the early 1990s. In 1993, its industrial output value (830,000 yuan) and net profits (7,700 yuan) were both ranked 27th of the 30 sample villages. However, Jinze had a prosperous past. Between 1976 and 1980, it had been ranked the number one village both in output value and profits in the township, and had maintained its good days until the early 1990s. In 1975, due to certain strategic considerations, an arms factory under the jurisdiction of the Bureau of Light Industry in Shanghai decided to move to suburban Jinze, taking over a sizable field from the village's land. According to government regulations, the arms factory would employ 40 workers from the village in return for the villagers' loss of farmland. But the village cadres were not satisfied with the compensation and thought the city government was taking advantage of the peasants and sacrificed the collective's interest. They protested against this project to the township and county governments, and rejected any solutions except that the Bureau help the village build a village-run enterprise. As a result, the Bureau extended one of the production lines of its Second Machinery Plant into the village and built a village-run factory, manufacturing sports equipment like shot-put ball and dumb-bell. The state-owned plant was responsible for providing the village factory with raw materials, machinery, and technology, and, more importantly, buying the factory's products so that the marketing channel was guaranteed.

The turning point for this profit-generating village-run factory came in 1992, when the state-owned Shanghai plant got caught in a financial squeeze and nearly bankrupted. The plant ceased production and consequently put the once-winning village factory in suspended animation. To make matters worse, in 1989, the village had failed in an investment project that planned to build another village-run factory and as a result got into a debt of one million yuan from the local banks. Since then, Jinze's good days were gone and the village experienced a laggard development in the early 1990s.

Case study 6: capital formation based on collective funds and bank loans

As described in the previous section, the shareholding village-run enterprise, Shanghai Sifang Agriculture-Industry-Commerce Company in Xincun village, was established with a combined investment from four governmental organs. Meng Hailin, the village party secretary and the general manager of the company, started his cadre career as the brigade head and the deputy party branch secretary in 1985. In 1986, through connections of the director (a native villager) at a township-run textile enterprise, Meng acquired 24 used spinning- and weaving-machines from a state-owned factory in Suzhou and established a village-run silk mill, which turned out to be the first profit-generating factory in the village. After being promoted to party secretary in 1987, Meng started to mobilize his social resources in the agricultural system. Meng's father worked in the Bureau of Agriculture in the Shanghai City government, and his brother was the party secretary of the Bureau of Agriculture in the Jinshang County government. These kinship connections successfully helped Meng to locate adequate funds from related bureaucratic units and establish the shareholding Sifang Company.

Sent-down workers and returned villagers

In addition to bureaucratic resources and support, social networks also played a role in resource mobilization. Shanghai and southern Jiangsu belong to the "Wu" language group. This language affinity helps bind the Shanghai and southern Jiangsu together, facilitating flows of personnel, technology, information, and finance (Jacobs and Hong 1994). Specifically, TVEs in the Yangtze Delta region derived much of their initial technical strength and human resources from sent-down urban workers and youths during the early 1960s and the Cultural Revolution.[11] During the Cultural Revolution, in particular, many urban factories advocated "ceasing work and seizing revolution," forcing large numbers of workers who had been working in big city enterprises to return to their native villages. Meanwhile, urban youths were also sent to the countryside for re-education (Fei 1989: 57–135; Song 1994; Tao 1988: 24–30). Between 1961 and 1965, Suzhou Prefecture sent 43,820 urban workers to its rural villages (Du 1987: 151). In 1962 alone, more than 50,000 workers in Shanghai's factories were sent down to nearby Jiangsu (Shen and Tong 1992: 186).

The army of "sent-down" people brought with them not only their technical skills and experiences but also their networks of social connections, which were essential in obtaining technical support and other assistance in later years. During the pre-reform and early reform era, since capital goods were still largely controlled and allocated by a clumsy bureaucracy, it was almost impossible for villages to purchase new machinery and equipment, even when they had the funds. Since the market function was severely restricted, it was even more difficult for the manufactured products, if any, to gain access to buyers without an adequate middleman. Under these circumstances, rural factories were generally able to acquire only old machinery and equipment no longer needed by state and large collective enterprises, and what they were able to handle was to rely primarily on subcontracting or processing work from urban enterprises. As such, the sent-down people were put in a position to play the role of "nodes" (people who maintained ties to their families, work units, and neighborhoods in the cities). Through these ties, the village cadres entered into social networks, making it possible to access information, technology, materials, and talent heretofore unavailable. These "bridges," connecting the urban nodes with the rural villages, secured information as to what products were needed in the urban centers, where equipment could be obtained (by purchasing, subcontracting, or bartering), how necessary materials could be found (by banqueting or bribing), and how manufactured products could be channeled to the market. The following two examples further illustrate the resource mobilization channeled through sent-down workers in the early 1970s.

Case study 7: learning and connecting from urban enterprises

Songjiang Enamel Factory in Huaqiao village, one of the examples provided in the previous section, was founded by a "talented villager" through his entrepreneurship and social resources in urban factories. Zhu Liangcai, born in 1941, started off as the village's statistician and the party secretary of the youth league before he joined a township factory as an electrical technician in 1971. In 1978, when the reform first took place, Zhu was hired as a contract worker in a state-owned chemical machinery plant in Suzhou. During his work, he found that one kind of enamel cap widely used in chemical, plastic, and metal industry was in short supply and none of the rural factories was able to produce such "high-tech" products. Because this kind of product was not controlled by the state's allocation system and belonged to the category of easily consumed goods, its market channel would be smoother and freer for rural factories, Zhu thought. Zhu quit his job in the state-owned enterprise and returned to Huaqiao, starting a series of testing, designing, and manufacturing. In 1980, after one year of hard work, combining "do-it-my-own-way" and "asking around through connections" approaches, he successfully worked out the production method of the enamel cap, and, as anticipated, received a very good reward on the market. Zhu was not satisfied with this achievement, and in 1986, through a cooperation with Shanghai Welding Second Plant and Shanghai Research Institute of Shipbuilding, the village factory began to manufacture the machinery for producing enamel caps. Since then, the factory's profits have skyrocketed and Zhu's leadership in the village has consolidated.

Case study 8: village factories initiated by sent-down workers

Both Zhounan village in Nanhui County and Xunjian village in Pudong District saw their first village factories initiated by workers sent down from state-owned enterprises in Shanghai in the early 1970s. As of 1993, these two villages were among the advanced villages in Shanghai suburbs: Zhounan had a GVIO of nearly 74 million yuan, with a profit of 1.6 million yuan; Xunjian had a GVIO of 29 million yuan, with a profit of 2.2 million yuan. The sole village enterprise in Zhounan was an aluminum-smelting plant established in 1974, when one of its sent-down workers from an aluminum-smelting plant in Shanghai succeeded in smelting aluminum trash and sediment for aluminum ingots. Since then, the village appointed a competent villager to be the factory director, organized a team to collect waste metals around the country, and refined them for aluminum ingots. In a similar pattern, the first two village factories in Xunjian were set up by a sent-down worker from Shanghai. In 1970, through the connections of the sent-down worker and his former work unit, the village built up a leather-ball factory to take processing works from that state-owned enterprise in Shanghai. Two years later, through the same contact, the village set up another shoe factory for the processing works for another Shanghai shoe enterprise. These two early-established factories provided the village with satisfactory earnings and significantly solved the problem of a surplus labor force in the early reform period.

External resources through urban–rural linkages

This section extends the previous section's focus to analyze resource mobilization through connections outside the locales. The cultivation of locality-centered networks was often insufficient to mobilize adequate resources and to promote the interest of local economy. Therefore, reliance on external resources, such as state-owned enterprises and research institutes in the municipalities and foreign direct investment from abroad, have been vital for the success of economic development in a locality. The distinction between "local" and "outside" resources are more or less arbitrarily made and mainly used for the convenience of comparison and analysis. Market-oriented activities all involve utilizing resources outside of a particular community; the distinction to be emphasized here is whether the outside resource providers play a crucial role in fulfilling the business tasks.

In the reform era, external resources for the development of rural enterprises in the region came mainly from two sources: urban–rural cooperation and foreign direct investment. The former characterizes the institutional arrangements of the Sunan model since the early 1980s, while the latter started to play a significant role in local economy since the early 1990s when this region got the green light for a re-opening to the outside world.

In the reform era, the various links of cooperation between rural enterprises and urban units in the Yangtze Delta region were usually referred to as "lateral linkage" (*hengxiang lianhe*). Of the various lateral linkages, the most common and effective type for transferring resources to rural enterprises is the so-called joint management or joint operation (*lianying*). These are rural enterprises that are operated in cooperation with other (mostly urban) big enterprises or bureaucratic units (e.g., technical schools or research institutes). This type of relationship, established among governmental, technological, and enterprise units, usually lasted for an extended period of time, and was very intimate and interactive, bringing long-term benefits to rural enterprises.

Table 2.7 presents the available data on jointly operated township and village enterprises (TVEs) in southern Jiangsu in the early reform period. In 1986, joint operation in TVEs numbered nearly 1,687, employed 283,339 workers, and produced 3,974 million yuan in gross output. Of these jointly operated TVEs, almost 80 percent were in partnership with an urban enterprise, while 66 percent with a state enterprise and 14 percent with an urban collective enterprise. Only 6 percent of the joint-operation arrangements were made among rural enterprises themselves, usually involving a more developed and a less developed one. Unlike in southern Fujian, where foreign participation in rural enterprises was common in the early reform period, only 1 percent of rural

Table 2.7 Jointly operated TVEs in southern Jiangsu, 1986[a]

| | Jointly operated TVEs ||||||
| | Number || Employees || Gross output value[b] ||
	No.	%	No.	%	No.	%
Total	1,687		283,339		3,974	
By partner type						
State enterprises	1,113	66	203,129	72	2,868	72
Urban collective	243	14	36,369	13	562	14
Other TVEs	107	6	13,610	5	174	4
Foreign enterprise	13	1	1,223	0	14	0
Other units	207	13	29,009	10	356	9
By type of relation						
Joint production	394	23	73,075	26	1,085	27
Joint marketing	405	24	75,607	27	1,014	26
Joint equity	394	23	65,346	23	926	23
Technology	272	16	40,000	14	591	15
Other	221	13	29,311	10	358	9

Source: Calculated from data in JXQ 1987.

Notes
TVEs: Township and village enterprises.
a Includes Suzhou, Wuxi, Nantong, and Changzhou.
b Million yuan in 1980 constant prices.

enterprises in southern Jiangsu had foreign partners in 1986. In terms of labor employment and gross output value, more than 85 percent of labor force and production output in joint operation were associated with urban enterprises. Another source reveals that in 1985 the gross output value contributed by rural enterprises with "lateral linkages" with other collective units in Suzhou amounted to 3,420 million yuan, accounting for 18 percent of the area's total industrial output (Tao 1988: 90).

Joint operations primarily took on the form of joint production, joint marketing, joint equity, and technology transfer, together accounting for nearly 90 percent of the joint relations. In most cases, joint production referred to subcontracting and processing, meaning that the urban units supplied part of raw materials, components, or semi-finished goods to the rural enterprises to process or assemble for a fee. Joint marketing occurred when a rural enterprise marketed its output jointly with a commercial unit in the city. A common arrangement was for the rural enterprise to supply working capital to a retail outlet in exchange for a special counter at the store to sell its products. Another arrangement involved rural enterprises and commercial units pooling their resources and developing new retail outlets. Joint equity usually took on the form of equity investment in which the outside units provided machinery, technology, raw materials, and market channels, while the local enterprise contributed land, factory buildings, and labor forces. Under such an arrangement, profits were usually shared in proportion to the capital each side contributed.

In Shanghai suburbs, joint management between rural and urban units had also been a popular arrangement. The jointly operated TVEs' share of industrial output in Shanghai suburbs had increased sharply in the reform period, from 20 percent in 1985 to 45 percent in 1992 (Table 2.8). In the 1980s, the joint operations were mostly in the form of technology

Table 2.8 The joint operation of TVEs in Shanghai suburbs

Year	TVEs GVIO	Joint operated TVEs GVIO	% of TVEs
1985	84	17	20
1986	103	26	25
1987	132	42	32
1988	189	62	33
1989	209	73	35
1990	235	93	39
1991	377	170	45
1992	514	230	45

Sources: SJTN, various years.

cooperation and joint production, while equity investment began to become a popular type in the early 1990s (Xie and Ling 1994: 86–99).

The 1989 Tiananmen event also played an indirect role in promoting joint operation between TVEs and state-owned enterprises. In the aftermath of the Tiananmen event, there was strong pressure in China to slow down the economic reform process, re-emphasizing the socialist planning and constraining the growth of the non-state sector. Some party leaders openly called for "closing township and village enterprises and supporting state-owned enterprises" (ZXQN 1990: 19–20). As a result, in order to protect existing rural enterprises, Jiangsu and Shanghai governments asked TVEs to enhance joint operation with state-owned enterprises. The policy effects are clearly expressed in the sharp increase of joint operation of TVEs in Shanghai suburbs during 1990–1991 (Table 2.8).

The following example shows the extent and methods of how joint operations were implemented in the countryside.

Case study 9: Fei's study of small towns in southern Jiangsu

Fei Hsiao-tung (Xiaotong), the best known and widely admired Chinese sociologist and anthropologist, together with his research groups undertook a series of "investigation tours" in Jiangsu's small towns during 1983–1984 (Fei 1984, 1989). The preliminary study of rural enterprises in southern Jiangsu reveals that the urban–rural connections played a vital role in the revival of local economy in the early 1980s. For example, among more than 2,000 rural factories in Wuxi County, 709 were linked up with major plants in Shanghai, Wuxi, and Suzhou. In Tangquio township, in the early 1980s, 11 of the 24 commune-run factories had established technical cooperation with vocational colleges and research institutes in Suzhou and Shanghai. The township's computer chip factory, for example, formed a group of 18 technical advisors who were research fellows or engineers in universities and research institutes across the country, including Qinghua University in Beijing, Nanjing University, and a research institute under the Science and Technology Commission for National Defense. These advisors, mostly computer specialists, provided guidance in technology, business, and information, and since then had trained a group of local experts. Another township chemical fiber textile mill took the same road: it invited 48 retired technicians and skilled workers from the Wuxi No. 2 Sate-run Cotton Mill to serve for two years and pass on their know-how to help train workers. In Pinwang, a prosperous township close to Shanghai and Suzhou, connections with state-run enterprises took on several forms. In 1981, the township-run Wujiang Agricultural Machinery Plant became the No. 3 branch factory of Shanghai Sewing-Machine Plant, of which the Wujiang plant contributed 56 percent of the investment and the Shanghai plant 44 percent. The provision of raw material and other production factors, and marketing responsibilities were all included in the Shanghai plant's plan system, and the two plants shared profits according to the investment each contributed.

The influx of foreign resources in the 1990s

Since the early 1990s, foreign direct investment has been increasing sharply in the Yangtze Delta region. The most ambitious and paramount undertaking came in April 1990 with the establishment of the state-designed Pudong New Area of Shanghai.[12] Foreign investment in rural economy had also sprung up in the countryside of Shanghai suburbs and southern Jiangsu since the early 1990s. The biggest jump occurred during 1991–1992, during which the foreign funds absorbed in rural industry in Shanghai suburbs and in Suzhou increased by more than six fold. Later in 1992–1994, rural industry in Shanghai and Suzhou reported an annual growth of 79 percent and 59 percent respectively (Table 2.9). In 1994, the number of enterprises with foreign funds approved in Shanghai suburbs reached 1,530, accounting for 40 percent of those approved in the whole municipality; foreign funds received reached $2.69 billion, accounting for 27 percent of those received by the whole municipality. Between 1992 and 1994, the number of enterprises with foreign funds in Shanghai suburbs increased by 8.19 times the total sum in past years, and the foreign funds absorbed increased by 15 times (Economic Yearbook of Shanghai Editorial Board 1995: 120).

In sum, outside resources, such as the provision of technology, information, raw materials, and marketing channels, had played a critical role in the development of rural economy in the Yangtze Delta region. As soon as the reforms began, these resources were channeled from various urban

Table 2.9 The foreign funds absorbed in rural industry

Year	Shanghai suburbs		Suzhou	
	Foreign funds (US$10,000)	*Increase (%)*	*Foreign funds (US$10,000)*	*Increase (%)*
1986	1,165	–	–	–
1987	1,611	38	–	–
1988	4,316	168	–	–
1989	2,721	−37	–	–
1990	6,290	131	–	–
1991	11,789	87	11,862	–
1992	83,968	612	85,973	625
1993	180,000	114	150,899	76
1994	268,899	49	217,661	44

Sources: SJN 1995: 672; Economic Yearbook of Shanghai Editorial Board 1995: 93; SUTN 1995: 310.

units (e.g., state-owned enterprises, research institutes, etc.) to rural enterprises, mostly in the form of joint operation or personnel transfers. The links were made possible by mobilizing social relations through bureaucratic connections in the command system, not atomized exchange relations in the markets. Since the early 1990s, thanks to its advantageous location around Shanghai, foreign direct investment increased rapidly in this region. Again, the collectives (township and village governments), relying on their control rights over various kinds of property (enterprise assets, land, and even labor forces) in the locality, played a predominant role in the Sino-foreign cooperation projects.

Case study 10: developing the village enterprises by reaching out

The development history of Gao village in Shanghai suburbs serves as a good example of the process of reaching out for foreign resources. The Tianyi Garment Factory in Gao village was originally set up in 1983 to produce children's garments. At that time, exports went only through the government department in charge of foreign trade. So the village cadres approached the County Foreign Trade Bureau proposing a joint venture through the County's Foreign Trade Corporation. The joint venture was launched in 1985, with the participation of three parties. The township government invested 200,000 yuan, and the County Foreign Trade Corporation and the village's garment factory each invested 180,000 yuan. Dividends would be drawn according to each member's share of equity capital. After several years of cooperation, Zhang Guomin, the village's party secretary, found that another Shanghai state-run enterprise had access to a stable supply of raw materials and a guaranteed quota under the state plan. It also had the right to direct export with plenty of orders from foreign buyers. Zhang therefore approached the Shanghai enterprise for an arrangement to process their semi-finished goods. In 1989, the village factory signed a joint venture agreement with the Shanghai enterprise, which invested 250,000 yuan and became the fourth party of the joint venture. Since then, the new joint venture had implemented the production and supply plan drawn up by the Shanghai enterprise. In turn, the Shanghai enterprise purchased the venture's products, helped with technical training, and developed new products for export markets. With increases in marketing channels, the joint venture was eager to expand its production capacity. Then two factories run by neighboring villages became its processing workshops. The joint venture provided each village workshop with an interest-free loan of 30,000 yuan for the purchase of sewing machines and other equipment. It also supplied raw materials, design and production technology to the workshops for processing assignments. These two workshops received processing fees from the joint venture. By 1992 the joint venture had rapidly expanded its export markets. However, it conducted its exports through foreign trade corporations in the governments, which received most of the trade profits. To have a higher share of profits for itself, the joint venture decided to establish direct export channels. Through the township government, the village reached an agreement with a Hong Kong company on establishing an equity joint venture with a registered capital of $300,000 yuan. The village invested $150,000 in factory buildings, equipment and the land-use rights, while the Hong Kong company invested $150,000. The Hong Kong partner was to market 70 percent of this new joint venture's output to countries that did not impose trade quotas on such products. Thus, in addition to the original joint venture with four parties, the village operated another Sino-foreign enterprise. Furthermore, between 1991 and 1993, six enterprises were established in the form of joint operation between the village and other domestic collective enterprises. Three Sino-foreign joint ventures were also established. The influx of outside resources in the Yangtze Delta region in the early to mid-1990s indicates that this area's location had been recognized as an advantageous front line for export-oriented industry as well as domestic marketing.

Conclusion

This chapter has provided an analytic description of how local institutions have promoted and affected collective-oriented property rights arrangements in the Yangtze Delta region between the 1980s and the mid-1990s. The region is rich in resources, and local governments have long controlled collective resources. Also, in order to establish themselves as the core nodes in the local networks of economic activities, local officials suppressed the private sector. As a result, economic institutions, such as property rights relations and enterprise organizations, were embedded in local bureaucratic coordination characterized by patron–client ties and vertical social relations in local and external bureaucratic system. TVE development in this region shows how economic institutions arose from the initiatives of local leaders, and the collusion between these leaders, local residents, and a social network extending into state organs, state firms, and governments outside the locality. The key driving force of rural development in this period of reform era lies not with the 1978 central government's policy shift, but with local initiatives. In fact, the establishment of TVEs in the Yangtze Delta, particularly in southern Jiangsu, predated the reform period (also see Jacobs 1999). Such local initiatives became possible because of the local employment pressure and shortage of start-up capital, and external opportunities brought about by the havoc generated by the Cultural Revolution. For example, sent-down youths and urban technical workers served as important bridges linking previously isolated villages with human resources and productive factors in the cities.

Up until the mid-1990s, a collective unified management system prevailed over other property rights arrangements, then shifted into shareholding and even outright privatization in the years following. Under the collective unified management, village officials directed economic affairs by merging village enterprises with the village government. The arrangement of manager responsibility and shareholding did not lead to the separation of the party, the government, and the economy as anticipated. Rather, evidence suggests that local cadres, led by the party secretary, not only took charge of political affairs but managed economic affairs as well. To a certain degree, the shareholding system became an indispensable and legitimate means for the village cadres to wrest the control of collective assets from the public sector.

As reforms proceeded over the course of two decades, local institutions in the Yangtze Delta underwent a shift from hierarchies toward networks. The driving force of this region's institutional transformation shifted from the political leadership in the bureaucratic system to local elites whose power and authority were rooted in their local origins and local networks. The case studies in this chapter have shown the trend of convergence of corporate elites and local cadre networks, particularly their family networks. The early transfer of village enterprises' property rights through shareholding signals the rising power of local elites who exploited social and economic capital, drawn from their local networks, in order to increase their power and wealth.

This is the picture of transformation up to the mid-1990s in the Yangtze Delta region. TVEs continued to evolve through the late 1990s and early 2000s, with local institutions playing a pivotal role, as the next chapter will show.

3 The Yangtze Delta in the post-reform era

This chapter aims to illuminate the past, present, and future development of rural TVEs through a case study conducted in the heartland of rural China. This study shows that throughout the take-off period of the reforms, from the late 1970s to mid-1990s, rural industry in traditionally pro-collective southern Jiangsu operated as collectives and cadre-directed corporations. Throughout certain periods of the rural reforms, collective-oriented ownership existed together with fast industrialization and economic growth. Only in the mid-1990s has the pro-collective heartland begun to feel the privatization thrust.

A key issue addressed in this chapter is the level of benefit and domination in publicly owned enterprises by local cadres and corporate leaders. The case study presented here suggests that a symbiotic relationship has long existed between corporate entrepreneurs and village cadres, blurring the boundaries between village ownership and elite family ownership. Recent privatization in the early 2000s actually changed little of the resource allocation and power structure, but it did legitimize undervalued transfer of legal ownership to elites.

The financial distributional consequences of privatization are far reaching. The village under study in this chapter shows that those in the village government and enterprises have been a group of specific families and individuals. Before and after the privatization, their power and vested interest remained stable, if not strengthened. Thus, the questions are: who precisely were the village administrators and enterprise managers of the economic reform? How were property rights transfers processed? And who are the winners and losers in the transition process?

To answer these questions and illustrate property rights transformations, the following two chapters will be devoted to a case study of one village in southern Jiangsu, which once had a predominant collective sector in the rural economy. The first section of this chapter provides a brief description of the regional development trend in southern Jiangsu. It suggests that a downturn in the region's rural economy in the mid-1990s pushed government administrators to adopt privatization measures in the TVE sector. The central government's decision to sell and merge state-owned enterprises further encouraged local governments to give away money-losing TVEs. The next section reports the development and property rights transformation (particularly the privatization process after the mid-1990s) of village enterprises in a village in southern Jiangsu. It highlights the distributional consequences and power structure of the village, signaling a pattern of power persistence among a small clique of village elites, both in the past and foreseeable future.

Sunan model in transition

In the two decades of economic reforms, southern Jiangsu – known as Sunan, and referring to Suzhou, Wuxi, and Changzhou – spearheaded economic change in rural China to become famous as the heartland of rural public enterprises. The region had, at one time, received national acclaim for its efforts at collective ownership, and for following the path of socialist transformation with indigenous Chinese characteristics. The proliferation of its TVEs stood as a pillar of the region's economy, bringing in substantial incomes for rural inhabitants and generating fiscal revenues for township and village governments. Such developments created far-reaching implications in the local economies and in social transformation.

Yet there have been concerns. Since the mid-1990s, the Sunan model clearly faced a precarious future. The health of TVEs in southern Jiangsu has raised questions of long-term sustainability and economic viability. From 1990 to 1994, for example, the total industrial output value of TVEs in Suzhou jumped from 36 billion yuan to 179 billion yuan, with an average annual growth rate of 49 percent. But in 1994–1995, the industrial output value of Suzhou's TVEs fell from 179 billion yuan to 123 billion yuan, a decline of 31 percent.[1] Although output did recover in the next year, profits continued to shrink. In October 1996, the number of Suzhou's money losing TVEs increased by 31 percent over the previous year (Dong 2002).

The tumble of economic growth in 1994–1995 occurred without any warning symptoms. In the early 1990s, the rural collective sector in southern Jiangsu was still developing with full momentum. In 1992, public ownership accounted for 81 percent of total industrial output; township and village governments owned 92 percent of productive fixed assets. To be sure, by 1994 the government still proudly claimed that collective ownership is fully "adapted to the requirement of modern productivity" (Su 1994). Although the shareholding cooperative system (*gufen hezuozhi*) was advocated, and various forms emerged in other regions, municipal authorities in southern Jiangsu still adhered to collective ownership in the TVE sector. This created a problem when faltering TVEs in some townships and villages started to push local cadres to pioneer ownership reforms. As a rule of thumb, localities with smaller TVE sectors and weaker economic bases were more likely to be front runners in adopting "aggressive" or straightforward privatization measures.

For example, Yixing in Wuxi saw its small-scale and backward TVEs lag behind their highly industrialized counterparts in Sunan. To counter the downward trend, Yixing City authorities experimented with a shareholding cooperative system over a small number of its faltering collective TVEs in 1992. The experimental measures changed some 30 TVEs' collective ownership into shareholding cooperatives, allowing private parties to invest and share profits. Such experimental measures were conducted with a low profile, but it still displeased authorities in Wuxi's municipal administration and Nanjing's provincial government, who dispatched inspectors to check "whether the collective economy had been undermined to any degree" (*Caijing* 2001).

The resistance to privatization changed with the national economic downturn in 1994–1995. Local TVE performance tumbled, forcing provincial and municipal authorities to take more flexible measures to save money-losing enterprises. Therefore, loosening restrictions on TVEs' property rights arrangements was a necessary experiment.

In 1995–1996, property rights reforms in Sunan picked up speed and expanded rapidly throughout the region. During this period, about 70 percent of TVEs in Sunan practiced some kind of property rights reforms. Yixing, for example, one of the pioneering localities in ownership transformation, put 94 percent of its TVEs under ownership transformation, which included 74 percent of collective net assets (Li 1998). Whiting's study reports that, by 1996, local officials in Wuxi and Songjiang County of Shanghai suburbs started for the first time to push collectively owned enterprises toward outright privatization. The policy adopted was to maintain property rights over large enterprises but sell small enterprises to private individuals (Whiting 2001: 289).

The 15th Party Congress in September 1997 ushered in a sweeping privatization agenda, in which Beijing called for the sale, merger or closing of the vast majority of China's state-owned enterprises.[2] This gave momentum to TVE privatization in Sunan. Since then, local bureaucrats from provincial and township levels have had the confidence to further ownership transformation. They hung the slogan "changing the system" or "changing the institutions" (*gaizhi*). That winter, the Jiangsu government employed oblique language to lay out a blueprint for the future of TVEs:

> Collective ownership could and should take multiple forms in its realization. The principal aim of reforming ownership institutions is to change the single form of collective ownership, to develop multiple forms of investments and ownerships, to extensively build up shareholding and joint-stock cooperative system, and to accelerate the development of the non-public economy.
>
> (Jiangsu CCP Committee and Provincial Government 1997)

Following this policy statement, TVEs in Sunan underwent two waves of "institutional change." The first wave, in 1997–1998, focused on privatizing money-losing medium and small TVEs and promoting individual businesses and private enterprises. Because large money-losing TVEs could find no buyers, they were left for the second wave, which began in late 1998 and reached its peak in 2000, and pressed the directors of the large TVEs to either buy the company or take a share in the company if they were unable to buy it out. It was not planned as such, to be sure, but rather evolved in a two-step program. Faced with inadequate supplies of private capital to complete ownership shifts of the big TVEs in the late 1990s, authorities had to adopt shareholding to complete the process.

Pressed by the weakening economy and the escalating privatization fever, in 1999 the Jiangsu provincial government delegated a group of officials to inspect rural development in nearby Zhejiang. The inspection trip strengthened Jiangsu officials' determination, and it built a consensus on TVEs' privatization within different levels of the Jiangsu government. To transform the TVEs a provincial official motto prioritized policy priority: selling over shareholding; shareholding over renting; renting over contracting; withdrawing over maintaining; closing over protecting.[3]

An official document was circulated from the Jiangsu provincial government to local governments, which highlighted "learning from Zhejiang and outrunning Zhejiang." It further pushed reforms in big money-making TVEs. The document required local governments to withdraw their collective shares from TVEs with net assets totaling less than 5 million yuan. Also, collective shares were not allowed to occupy more than 30 percent of a firm's total shares; the extra shares had to be turned into debts owed by the private manager-owners. To achieve this goal, private manager-owners were allowed to be granted as much as 20 percent of a firm's net assets as discount value when buying ownership of a collective enterprise (He *et al.* 2000).

By 2000, it was reported that more than 95 percent of TVEs in southern Jiangsu had adopted some kind of property rights reforms. As local governments' financial contribution to TVEs gradually shrank, resources drawing from non-collective sources soared. Between 1995 and 2000, Sunan TVEs' financial capital drawing from private individuals, foreign ventures, and legal bodies had increased by 30 percent, 7 percent, and 5 percent, respectively (*Jingji ribao* 11 May 2001). During this time, shareholding had become a "politically correct" campaign. In practice, private manager-owners asked for more stakes of lucrative shares in moneymaking TVEs, while governments desperately wanted to shift collective shares of money-losing firms. A survey of 168 township enterprises in Jiangsu and Zhejiang also showed the privatization trend, finding that 82 percent of township enterprises in this region in 1994 were still fully or partially township owned, while 18 percent were fully private. In the following five years rural firms experienced a dramatic move away from the traditional collectively owned type. As a result, between 1994 and 1997, the number of fully private firms more than tripled (Li and Rozelle 2000).

In the second half of 2000, the second wave of ownership reform reached its peak, emphasizing a mission of the TVEs "taking off the collective caps" and selling out collective shares of large TVEs. Local governments in Sunan required TVEs under their jurisdictions to transform into either limited liability companies, joint-stock limited companies, or private enterprises. For those big-scaled TVEs beyond the purchasing power of private individuals, the governments required incumbent directors to hold a significant amount of shares – no less than 25 percent of total shares – and collective shares to be withdrawn step by step in the near future.

By 2003, the process of privatization was complete. The companies that were not sold off in the first wave were gradually transferred by shares to their directors (who often had direct relations with village authorities), and often at steep discounts.

Shuang village in perspective

The case study of Shuang village in Wujiang illustrates a profound change in management and ownership evolution in Sunan. The data from Shuang village draws from extensive fieldwork conducted between 1996 and 2002, where I visited the community at least once a year since 1996, and most recently in the fall of 2002. During these trips, I stayed for one to two weeks and conducted interviews with local cadres (including township and village cadres ranging from the party secretary to chief accountant), enterprise executives (including all enterprise directors and some engineers), workers and ordinary villagers.

Located in the center of Wujiang City, and 30 minutes drive south of Suzhou in the Yangtze Delta region, Shuang sits on a plain of fertile farmland and fishponds. It is also positioned across a newly developed town-run industrial park, and along the No. 318 highway between Shanghai and Nanjing. In 2000, Shuang village had 1,343 residents in 350 households, occupying a total area of 2.1 square kilometers. During the mid-1980s, Shuang was among the very first villages to witness an explosion of township and village enterprises in Sunan.

Like other villages in the region, Shuang owes its achievements to the one-time village-owned factories that dot its verdant fields. Between 1984 and 2001, the number of village enterprises increased from one to seven, while their industrial output raced ahead at an average annual growth rate of 60 percent, from 250,000 yuan in 1984 to 789.62 million yuan in 2001. Shuang's collective economy shifted onto a privatization track in the mid-1990s, and was fully completed in the spring of 2002 after the village government gave away its last share of a loss-making company.

The Yangtze Delta in the post-reform era 75

Over the past two decades, a small circle of village elites has come to dominate the village's economy and politics, receiving the lion's share of wealth generated from village enterprises. They started as entrepreneurial bureaucrats, then became bureaucratic entrepreneurs and cadre-corporate leaders, and now serve as government officials or private businesspeople, enjoying the fruits of the reforms.

The development of village enterprises in the reform era

The very first village-owned enterprise in Shuang was launched in 1974 as a chemical products factory, among the first in southern Jiangsu. After a decade, a metal foundry and a paper cartons plant joined the village's non-farm activities, followed by a chemical fibers factory established in 1987. By 1993, with the metal foundry taking the lead, these four village enterprises greatly contributed to the village's industrial output and money generating, and employed a native labor force of more than 600. However, in 1992–1994 these four enterprises suffered setbacks as their net profits dropped sharply. This slowdown coincided with the founding of the village's flagship enterprise: a differential polyester chip factory. It immediately overshadowed all other village enterprises by accounting for 38 percent and 54 percent of the village's total industrial output in 1994 and 1995, and led all the others in profit generating, earning 5.3 million yuan or 57 percent of the village's total and 13.4 million yuan or 71 percent of the village's total in 1994 and 1995 respectively (Table 3.1). In 1997, based on the chemical products factory and chemical fibers factory, the village set up its sixth enterprise specializing in manufacturing acrylic fiber chips. The next year, the village established a color master batch factory that produced dying materials for polyester chips. This step into the petrochemical industry offered the village new opportunities and resources by expanding and diversifying its products line from low-end chemical products to capital-intensive fibers, polyester chips, acrylic fiber chips, and color master batches. The other two village enterprises – the metal foundry and paper cartons factory – had been involved in different industries and actually maintained a relatively independent position in management and property rights relations.

Shuang's industrialization started in 1974 when the Cultural Revolution wound down. In that year, driven by the villagers' urge for development, Huang Wen, then the village's Communist Youth League secretary, was asked to search for any possible connections to help the village launch its industry. Through a relative who worked in a state-owned chemical firm in Shanghai, Huang Wen set up a chemical products factory, processing wood oil and paint materials. Of the start-up capital of 20,000 yuan, half came from a bank loan, and the rest collected from the village coffers and its nine production teams. In the first decade of the village's development, this chemical products factory provided the major non-farm income for

Table 3.1 Performance of TVEs in Shuang village, 1984–2001

	Total	Chemical products		Metal foundry		Paper cartons		Chemical fibers		Differential polyester chip		Acrylic fiber chips	
	Amount	Amount	% of total	Amount	% of total	Amount	% of total	Amount	% of total	Amount	% of total	Amount	% of total

Gross value of industrial output (10,000 yuan)

1984	25	25	100	–	–	–	–	–	–	–	–	–	–
1985	74	39	52	30	41	5	7	–	–	–	–	–	–
1986	145	65	45	58	40	22	15	–	–	–	–	–	–
1987	275	107	39	112	41	55	20	–	–	–	–	–	–
1988	635	159	25	183	29	171	27	122	19	–	–	–	–
1989	1,002	174	17	264	26	258	26	306	31	–	–	–	–
1990	1,344	297	22	355	26	269	20	424	32	–	–	–	–
1991	3,051	728	24	692	23	459	15	1,172	38	–	–	–	–
1992	5,153	1,288	25	1,507	29	711	14	1,648	32	–	–	–	–
1993	9,607	1,947	20	3,677	38	1,310	14	2,673	28	–	–	–	–
1994	15,009	1,809	12	4,008	27	1,603	11	1,912	13	5,678	38	–	–
1995	28,075	1,378	5	5,386	19	3,010	11	3,201	11	15,100	54	–	–
1996	31,256	2,645	8	6,687	21	4,055	13	3,028	10	14,841	47	–	–
1997	31,593	2,623	8	4,146	13	3,311	10	2,215	7	18,095	57	1,203	4
1998	28,745	1,196	4	2,380	8	2,829	10	386	1	19,876	69	2,079	7
1999	41,922	1,316	3	2,608	6	2,163	5	–	–	32,410	77	3,425	8
2000	67,874	1,417	2	2,140	3	1,501	2	–	–	59,540	88	3,276	5
2001	78,962	1,231	2	1,614	2	1,667	2	–	–	70,808	90	3,642	5

	Total	Chemical products		Metal foundry		Paper cartons		Chemical fibers		Differential polyester chip		Acrylic fiber chips	
	Amount	Amount	% of total	Amount	% of total	Amount	% of total	Amount	% of total	Amount	% of total	Amount	% of total

Net profit (10,000 yuan)

1984	4	4	100	–	–	–	–	–	–	–	–	–	–
1985	13	10	73	3	25	0	2	–	–	–	–	–	–
1986	25	12	45	13	50	1	5	–	–	–	–	–	–
1987	74	27	37	35	48	11	16	–	–	–	–	–	–
1988	144	39	27	46	32	29	20	29	20	–	–	–	–
1989	238	52	22	78	33	43	18	64	27	–	–	–	–
1990	250	53	21	82	33	50	20	64	26	–	–	–	–
1991	381	104	27	109	29	59	16	109	29	–	–	–	–
1992	649	105	16	259	40	68	10	217	33	–	–	–	–
1993	755	88	12	420	56	56	7	191	25	–	–	–	–
1994	940	33	4	294	31	11	1	69	7	533	57	–	–
1995	1,890	–5	0	301	16	51	3	201	11	1,341	71	–	–
1996	2,138	40	2	362	17	140	7	86	4	1,510	71	–	–
1997	2,421	363	15	214	9	111	5	422	17	1,218	50	93	4
1998	1,330	52	4	169	13	129	10	–2	0	717	54	266	20
1999	3,022	74	2	354	12	97	3	–	–	1,966	65	532	18
2000	4,565	71	2	655	14	73	2	–	–	3,029	66	737	16
2001	551	34	6	122	22	4	1	–	–	125	23	267	48

continued

Table 3.1 continued

	Total	Chemical products Amount	% of total	Metal foundry Amount	% of total	Paper cartons Amount	% of total	Chemical fibers Amount	% of total	Differential polyester chip Amount	% of total	Acrylic fiber chips Amount	% of total
Remittances submitted to the village (10,000 yuan)
1984	–	–	–	–	–	–	–	–	–	–	–	–	–
1985	0	0	100	–	–	–	–	–	–	–	–	–	–
1986	2	2	68	1	32	–	–	–	–	–	–	–	–
1987	23	9	38	11	46	4	16	–	–	–	–	–	–
1988	33	12	37	13	40	8	23	–	–	–	–	–	–
1989	68	16	23	22	32	12	18	18	27	–	–	–	–
1990	64	13	21	22	35	13	20	15	24	–	–	–	–
1991	93	24	25	29	31	15	16	26	28	–	–	–	–
1992	140	28	20	59	42	16	11	37	27	–	–	–	–
1993	137	28	21	59	43	16	12	34	25	–	–	–	–
1994	148	18	12	58	39	5	3	21	14	46	31	–	–
1995	295	7	2	68	23	20	7	40	14	160	54	–	–
1996	376	20	5	88	23	42	11	26	7	200	53	–	–
1997	361	73	20	48	13	32	9	80	22	127	35	–	–
1998	278	11	4	45	16	21	8	11	4	110	40	80	29
1999	754	11	1	90	12	21	3	–	0	534	71	98	13

Source: Author's fieldwork, October 2002.

Shuang. For example, in 1984 and 1985, it contributed 40,000 yuan and 100,000 yuan in net benefit, respectively.

After a decade, in 1984, Shuang set up its second and third enterprises, which coincided with the nationwide enthusiasm for township and village enterprises. The metal foundry was originally set up jointly by the village and the township government. However, within months it went into a deep loss and the township government soon withdrew from the partnership. Shuang's village authorities decided to take it over and Huang Wen also successfully seized a chance to link up with the state-owned Shanghai Electric Plant, which then subcontracted the melting of fan parts to the village's metal foundry. With an initial investment of 70,000 yuan and a steady subcontract relationship with the Shanghai state firm, the foundry has since gained stable earnings and played a significant role in village's income. The subcontract relationship was further formalized in 1988; the foundry became an extended manufacturing line for its Shanghai contractor and was renamed as the Second Workshop of Shanghai Electric Plant. Between 1985 and 1995, its contribution in net profits roughly accounted for 30 percent to 50 percent of total profits earned by all village enterprises (Table 3.1).

In 1995, the Shanghai partner moved one of its workshops to the village and further expanded the factory's scale and productivity. Then, in the same year, the village and the Shanghai state firm signed a joint-venture contract to turn the foundry into a limited responsibility company. Shuang village owned 48 percent of the company's stocks, including a cash investment of 1.34 million yuan and fixed assets of land, workshop, and equipment, amounting to 2.63 million yuan. The Shanghai state-owned partner owned another 52 percent of the company's stocks, including a technology investment of 100,000 yuan, equipment and machinery investment of 2.76 million yuan, and a cash input of 1.46 million yuan.

Also in 1985, a paper cartons factory was established by three villagers, who joined together to provide initial capital of 5,000 yuan for the new venture. In the start-up period, the partnership firm operated with backward equipment and labor-intensive production processes in a rental cottage, and earned a slim profit. Despite a newly issued national policy at the time granting privately-owned individual businesses permission to operate, this paper factory soon suffered hardships in a hostile climate and discrimination in the locality. Due to its private ownership, the factory was refused bank loans and even a plant site in the village; raw materials bought from state firms were more expensive. Even worse, when power was in short supply, which was common during the early years of rural reforms, the factory was among the first to get power cuts.

Village cadres kept "educating" the three founders to convert the factory's private ownership into a collective one, which was qualified to receive bureaucratic endorsement and resource allocations. In 1986, one year after the firm's establishment, the three owner-managers in partnership decided to make their firm politically safer and economically resourceful by converting it into a village-owned enterprise. Wang Jin and Zhou Min, the original co-founders, served as the factory's director and deputy director respectively. The factory's original assets, valued at 100,000 yuan, were entitled to the village, and the village government further invested 10,000 yuan for purchasing new machinery. As the operating climate improved, the factory started to make profits, climbing from 110,000 yuan in 1987 to a record high of 680,000 yuan in 1992, before slowing down to 510,000 yuan in 1995 (Table 3.1). In 1995, the factory added a new production line with a low-interest loan of 9 million yuan from the nation's "Spark Program" designed for promising TVEs.

In 1987, based on the village's chemical products factory, the village founded its fourth enterprise, a chemical fiber factory. Thanks to the state's supportive policy toward rural industry during the time, the factory's start-up capital of 500,000 yuan was drawn wholly from a bank loan, reflecting an abundant capital supply in the region.

The factory's establishment and its later success was the result of two outside engineers from Tianjin. Mr. Li Dong and Ms. Wang Hua, who were then research associates in the Tianjin Institute of Chemical Engineering, a subsidiary organ of the state's Textile Ministry. Before moving south to the backward countryside, they had long been involved in polyester research but lacked any chance to develop their ideas into the manufacturing industry. In 1987, through a connection of Huang Wen's relative, they were invited to contribute their expertise to help Shuang develop state-of-the-art polyester products. Before long, Li Dong and Wang Hua successfully materialized their laboratory ideas into a series of polyester products, including "low-melting-point polyester," which later won the state's accreditation and soon generated a huge amount of profits. It took less than a year to recover the initial investment.

Seeing this lucrative business, the township government was eager to have a share, and it quickly pooled 5 million yuan to expand the factory's manufacturing capacity. In the four years between 1988 and 1992, this chemical fiber factory contributed roughly one-third of the village's total net profits, jumping more than sevenfold from a mere amount of 290,000 yuan in 1988 to a remarkable 2.17 million yuan in 1992 (Table 3.1).

Shuang's well-known fame as the site of booming rural industrialization actually came from its largest "backbone" enterprise, a differential polyester chip factory. In 1993, based on two already well run and money-making factories in chemical products and fibers, Shuang's cadres launched an ambitious project involving a total investment of 32 million yuan. Huang Song, then the village's party secretary, was in charge of the task and afterwards served as the new factory's director.

In the initial stage, the factory was accepted into the state-level "Suzhou-Wuxi-Changzhou Spark Program" which aimed to promote the transfer of advanced technology from research institutes and state firms to rural enterprises. Thanks to the Spark Program, the differential polyester chip factory was entitled to a low-interest loan of 10 million yuan from the Agriculture Bank and the State's Science and Technology Commission. In addition, the village received another loan of 7 million yuan from the Agriculture Bank, and formed a collaborating relationship with the Nanjing-based Yangzi Petrochemical Corporation, a state-owned petrochemical giant, which provided raw materials and had a one-fifth stake in the factory.

The entry timing for the polyester chip factory was exactly when such material was in short supply but high demand. Thus the profits it created in its establishing years were more than striking. In 1993, after a three-phase construction period, the chip factory was completed with a total investment of 32 million yuan. In 1994 and 1995, it earned 5.33 million yuan and 13.41 million yuan in profit, accounting for 57 percent and 71 percent of total profits earned by all village enterprises, respectively (Table 3.1).

Within two years, by 1995 it had paid back the start-up loan of 17 million yuan, and by the late 1990s, the differential polyester chip factory had brought fortune and fame for Shuang and, more importantly, for its small circle of village elites.

The property rights transformation and privatization of Shuang's enterprises

Throughout China's countryside, different property rights arrangements have emerged to dominate the enterprise landscape at different times and locations. Walder and Oi outline five types of ownership arrangement that can be arranged along a continuum, ranging from traditional collective to the recognizably private, with three intermediate types, including reformed collectives with management incentive contracts, contracted public firms with government–management partnerships, and leased public assets (Walder and Oi 1999). In practice, the intermediate types bear different contract management systems. Under the collective contract systems which were widely adopted in pro-collective regions in the 1980s, management and workers presumably shouldered risks together and hence had common interests. But under the individual contract system, individual contractors who rented the public assets and took responsibility for any gains or losses shouldered risks. In addition, the shareholding system had been adopted and advocated across regions with various indigenous forms. However, it is important to note that property rights transformation did not necessarily proceed along a linear line from collective to private ownership, passing through collective and then individual contract systems. Actually few localities have really experienced all those theoretically continuous property rights transformations.

Shuang illustrates a typical evolutionary pattern in property rights transformation in southern Jiangsu. It maintained conventional public ownership in the 1980s but shifted to private ownership in the late 1990s and early 2000s, with collective contract systems and shareholding systems inbetween. In the years between 1998 and 2002, all of Shuang's village-owned firms were finally sold off to individual owner-managers. The once widely reported official-led collective ownership no longer exists.

The development from collective to private ownership can be traced back to the 1970s and 1980s, when Shuang's enterprises were run under traditional collective ownership, called "collective unified management," (*jiti tongyi jingying*). Under the system, the village government took on a twofold role – as community administrator and as enterprise owner; key property rights for the use, transfer, and residual income of collective enterprises belonged to the village government commanded by the village party secretary. Like nearby Shanghai villages and other pro-collective regions, Shuang incorporated itself as an industrial corporation that appointed factory directors and managers who mostly also occupied cadre posts in the village administration. As the village political apparatus and corporate organs mingled with each other, key decisions were made in the village party-government office. That is, from the collective era of the mid-1970s to the market-oriented 1980s, the village government retained complete control of property rights, including personnel appointment and managerial decisions as well as profit allocations among the collective, firms, corporate managers, and workers.

In 1987, a contract responsibility system began to change the income rights of village enterprises in Shuang. The contract responsibility system was implemented to set production and profit targets, and more importantly, to decide the distribution of residual income. A contract was signed between the factory's director and the village administration, which received an annual economic target from the township government. According to the contract, the enterprise director's annual pay was determined by a formula based on the profits achieved by the enterprise above the set quota. In this respect, enterprise directors should have had incentive to perform well because they were guaranteed the rights to share surplus income. However, it turned out that the implementation of the contract had been flexible and the targets and promises often became "soft." For example, in 1994, the contract for all village enterprises stated that 30 percent of the above-quota profit would be handed over to the village government, 30 percent to the enterprise bonus fund, and 40 percent to the enterprise development fund.

The village records showed, however, that the remittances handed over to the village's coffers from each enterprise were much lower than the amount stated in the contract. According to a cadre-manager, "it made no difference to save the money in the enterprises or in the village's coffers, because the enterprises and the village belong to one family (*yijiaren*) who always helped each other." It was common that management contracts were not enforced and were outweighed by bureaucratic command. For example, In 1995, according to the distribution scheme for above-quota profit, the director of the differential polyester chip factory was entitled to a bonus of 140,000 yuan. However, considering the struggling businesses and declining income of nearby villages, the township government intervened and adjusted the director's final bonus to 40,000 yuan.

In the late 1990s, the collective contracting system was gradually replaced by a profit-sharing system in Shuang and its nearby villages. It reflected the decline and withdraws of the village and township governments in coordinating property rights of collective assets. In 1996, an experimental program of distributing above-quota profits was implemented, by which 50 percent of the above-quota profit earned by each enterprise would be rewarded in cash to key managers and cadres, including the enterprise director and deputy director, the village party secretary and deputy party secretary, the villagers' committee chairman, and the village accountant; the other 50 percent would be converted into an enterprise development fund.

In 1997–1998, together with a mass privatization of small- and medium-sized state-owned companies across urban China, Shuang started to arrange the selling of its village-owned enterprises. At the forefront of the privatization movement were smaller-scale but debt-ridden enterprises; namely the chemical products factory, the chemical fibers factory and the paper cartons factory. As the big differential polyester chip factory joined the village's industrial production in 1994, and later the acrylic fibers chip factory in 1997, these three one-time moneymakers became unimportant and marginal in generating profits for the village coffers.

Since their establishment in the 1980s till 1993/1994, each of these three enterprises had generated a significant portion to the village's industrial production and net income, as well as remittances submitted to village coffers. For example, in 1993 the net profits contributed by these three enterprises totaled 3.35 million yuan and accounted for 44 percent of all profits earned, including a profit of 1.91 million yuan by the chemical fibers factory, 880,000 yuan by the chemical products factory, and 560,000 yuan by the paper cartons factory. In the same year, their remittances submitted to the village totaled 780,000 yuan, which was 56 percent of all submitted remittances. However, since the mid-1990s, they suffered market slowdown and barely eked out a profit.

These enterprises' contributions to village coffers shrank as further risks emerged. For example, after 1994, despite an exceptional single-year boost in 1997, the share of net profits contributed by the chemical products factory dropped to single digits, compared with an extraordinary 71 percent contributed by the differential polyester chip factory in 1995 and 1996. Also, the share of net profits contributed by the chemical fibers factory plunged from 25 percent in 1993 to 7 percent in 1994. Likewise the paper cartons factory's contribution began to drop after 1993, accounting for 10 percent of all village enterprises remittances in 1992 and 5 percent in 1997 (Table 3.1).

As these enterprises' profits declined, their bad loans, "dead" receivables, and unsold stocks in the warehouses climbed. By 1998, the bank debts owed by these three enterprises totaled 14 million yuan, of which 8.53 million yuan by the paper cartons factory, 3.38 million yuan by the chemical fibers factory, and 2.21 million yuan by the chemical products factory. These heavy burden of non-performance loans worried village authorities who decided to take steps to prevent further loss. On the other hand, compared with the backbone differential polyester chip factory that alone carried a loan of 35 million yuan, these cases were more manageable and feasible in property rights transformation.

Negotiating the sale terms began in 1997 and took more than a year to complete. In February 1998, an audit determined the assets and liabilities of these three factories, figuring each item of their assets and liabilities. The chemical products factory's assets totaled 10.27 million yuan, against 9.22 million yuan in liabilities. Its assets were mainly composed of receivables (39 percent), stocks (15 percent), and fixed assets (41 percent); the liabilities included bank loans (24 percent), payables (53 percent), and wages to be paid (10 percent). In total, the chemical products factory still had a net asset of 1.05 million yuan, which the village government claimed was reimbursed for its ownership transfer. In the same way the audit concluded the chemical fibers factory had a net asset of 600,000 yuan (8.81 million yuan in assets and 8.21 million yuan in liabilities) and the paper cartons factory 300,000 yuan (18.14 million yuan in assets and 17.84 million yuan in liabilities) (Table 3.2).

The village government set the game rule simple: the amount of the firm's net asset was its price for sale. Actually, and not surprisingly, the books were cooked throughout the auditing and negotiating process to satisfy both sides and make deals feasible.

The ownership transfer was discussed and negotiated between the manager-owners and village authorities; there was no public bid, nor any competition from other interested individuals. The deals and transfers of these three enterprises occurred in February 1998. Buyers, all incumbent factory directors, signed ownership transfer contracts with the village administration represented by the village party secretary. According to the transfer contracts, the enterprise owners paid the village the amounts of the enterprises' net assets, shouldered the enterprises' outstanding debts, and from then on took full responsibilities for any wins and losses. The chemical products factory was sold to Zhou Min, who co-founded the one-time privately owned paper cartons factory with Wang Jin in 1985. After a six-year appointment as the deputy general manager in a township-owned foreign trade company, Zhou then took over the village-owned chemical products factory in 1995. Huang Wen, one of the village's elite cadres and

Table 3.2 Financial indicators for village enterprises in Shuang village, February 1998 (Yuan and % of total)

Village factory	Net assets[a]	Total assets								Total liabilities						
		Total	Receivables		Stocks		Fixed assets			Total	Bank loans		Payables		Wages to be paid	
			Amount	%	Amount	%	Amount	%			Amount	%	Amount	%	Amount	%
Chemical products	1,050,000	10,270,900	3,961,020	39	1,508,859	15	4,255,868	41		9,220,900	2,209,800	24	4,856,157	53	955,968	10
Chemical fibers	600,000	8,805,538	4,856,000	55	1,055,196	12	2,562,787	29		8,205,538	3,380,000	41	3,612,885	44	655,743	8
Paper cartons	300,000	18,138,339	4,817,577	27	3,303,603	18	7,755,375	43		17,838,339	8,525,414	48	7,345,696	41	1,037,602	6

Source: Author's fieldwork, October 2002.

Note

a Net assets = Total assets − Total liabilities.

the founding director of the chemical fibers factory, finally acquired the firm's ownership. The paper cartons factory went back to Wang Jin, its co-founder and director since 1990. Thus, these once-collective village enterprises shifted into fully-fledged private firms owned by their long-time directors.

Compared with the privatization practice in 1998, the ownership transfer of other larger-scale enterprises in Shuang were much more complex. The values of these enterprises were simply too high for any individual owner-manager to take over in a one-time shot deal. As a result, shareholding was adopted for ownership transfer.

For the metal foundry, in 1995, the village owned 48 percent of its shares and a Shanghai state firm had the other 52 percent. Over the following years the Shanghai state firm's shares originally obtained from machinery investment shrank due to machinery depreciation. In 1999, the village government began to negotiate with the incumbent director, Jin Hairong, who just inherited the metal foundry from his uncle Fu Ya who remained single and served as its director in 1985–1996. In 1999, an audit figured the foundry's assets of over 24 million yuan, of which 36 percent was receivables and 29 percent fix assets. The liabilities totaled nearly 13 million yuan, mainly including payables (62 percent) and bank loans (19 percent) (Table 3.3). Its net assets equaled 11.04 million yuan, of which 7.5 million yuan (68 percent) belonged to the village government, and 3.54 million yuan (32 percent) owned by the Shanghai state firm. Following the audit, the village authorities wanted the foundry's incumbent director to join the shareholding company by buying the village's 5.5 million yuan-worth of shares and putting down another 2 million yuan to buy a 27 percent stake. The incumbent director accepted the terms and first paid the village government 2 million yuan in cash, while the remaining 3.5 million yuan put in debt to be returned within five years.

As a result, the foundry transformed from a two-party to three-party shareholding company involving the village government (holding 27 percent of shares), the Shanghai state-owned Electric Plant (holding 47 percent of shares), and the incumbent director Jin Hairong (27 percent of shares). By the end of 2002, the village sold out its last part of 2 million yuan-worth shares to the director; the metal foundry became a two-party shareholding enterprise in which the director's share increased to 54 percent (Table 3.4).

Following the deal of the metal foundry, the next task to tackle in the spring of 1999 was the newly founded color master batch factory. In 1998 Huang Wen persuaded the village and township government to step into manufacturing color master batches – a kind of raw materials mixed in polyester production to produce colored chips. The village government invested 1.1 million yuan and the township government 550,000 yuan. The firm then acquired bank loans totaling 4.8 million yuan. However, this newly founded village-owned firm could not resist the privatization

Table 3.3 Financial indicators for TVEs in Shuang village, 1998–2001

	Net assets	Total assets					Total liabilities				
	Total	Total	Receivables		Fixed assets		Total	Bank loans		Payables	
			Amount	%	Amount	%		Amount	%	Amount	%
Metal foundry, 1999	11,041,005	24,003,257	8,639,219	36	6,869,519	29	12,962,252	2,400,000	19	8,063,092	62
Color master batch, 1998	3,150,000	12,853,234	2,074,941	16	5,493,271	43	9,703,234	3,180,000	33	3,887,233	40
Acrylic fiber chip, 1999	7,000,000	18,014,500	228,000	1	16,248,500	90	11,016,500	1,500,000	14	253,000	2
Acrylic fiber chip, 2001	6,300,000	21,578,000	5,720,100	27	10,596,100	49	15,278,000	2,500,000	16	2,941,500	19
Differential polyester chip, 1999	39,247,006	85,198,854	7,913,297	9	52,343,229	61	45,951,848	35,035,000	76	4,122,370	9

Source: Author's fieldwork, October 2002.

Table 3.4 Changes of share divisions for TVEs in Shuang village, 1998–2002

	Total	Net Assets and Share Divisions, 1999							
		Township shares		Village shares		Corporation shares		Individual shares	
		Amount	%	Amount	%	Amount	%	Amount	%
Metal foundry									
1999	11,041,005	0	0	7,500,000	68	3,541,005	32	0	0
1999, after shareholding	7,541,000	0	0	2,000,000	27	3,541,000	47	2,000,000	27
2002, after privatization	7,541,000	0	0	0	0	3,541,000	47	4,000,000	54
Color master batch									
1998	3,150,000	550,000	17	1,100,000	35	0	0	1,500,000	48
2002, after privatization	2,100,000	0	0	0	0	0	0	2,100,000	100
Acrylic fiber chip									
1999	7,000,000	1,650,000	24	2,200,000	31	1,650,000	24	1,500,000	21
2001 after shareholding	6,300,000	509,000	8	2,200,000	35	1,161,000	18	2,430,000	39
2002, after privatization	6,300,000	0	0	0	0	0	0	6,300,000	100
Differential polyester chip									
1999	39,247,006	4,553,000	12	21,034,006	54	13,660,000	35	0	0
1999 after shareholding	22,000,000	2,111,500	10	9,754,900	44	6,333,600	29	3,800,000	17
2002 after shareholding	22,000,000	1,300,400	6	6,096,700	28	6,333,600	29	8,269,300	38
2002, after privatization	18,890,778	0	0	0	0	6,333,600	34	12,557,178	66

Source: Author's fieldwork, October 2002.

command of the county government. This was in 1998, when the firm's net assets equaled 3.15 million yuan with 12.85 million yuan in assets and 9.70 million yuan in liabilities (Table 3.3). Huang Wen put down his personal 1.5 million yuan to buy shares from the township and village government and thus became an individual shareholder.

As a result, the reorganized firm became a shareholding company with three shareholders: the township government holding shares of 550,000 yuan or 17 percent, the village government holding shares of 1.1 million yuan or 35 percent, and Huang Wen with individual shares of 1.5 million yuan accounting for 48 percent.

After three years, in 2002, as privatization zeal filled the area, the township and village authorities were eager to get rid of the firm's ownership, even at the expense of big losses. Thus the color master batch factory's assets were stripped of 1.05 million (Table 3.4). The ownership transfer contract reveals that Huang Wen paid the township government a lump sum of 200,000 yuan and the village government 400,000 yuan respectively, in exchange of the firm's full ownership. Then, Huang Wen became the sole owner of the color master batch factory and was obliged to take over loan repayment (Table 3.4).

For the acrylic fibers chip factory, the ownership switch also occurred in 1999–2001. The factory's founding capital came from three parties: the township government, the village government, and the differential polyester chip factory. In 1999, the factory's net assets amounted to 7 million yuan, with 18 million yuan in assets and 11 million yuan in liabilities.

At first, the incumbent director Xu Kun was asked to buy 1.5 million yuan-worth of shares from the township and village government. As a result, the firm had four shareholders: the township government (1.65 million yuan or 24 percent), the village government (2.2 million yuan or 31 percent), the differential polyester chip factory (1.65 million yuan or 24 percent), and the incumbent director Xu Kun (1.5 million yuan, or 21 percent). In the following two years, by December 2001, Xu Kun had put down another 930,000 yuan buying shares from the township government. His individual share worth rose to 2.43 million yuan, or 39 percent of the enterprise's total shares. Then in 2002 Xu Kun signed a five-year loan document with the factory's three collective shareholders, turning their remaining shares into private debts owed by Xu Kun. Consequently Xu Kun became the sole owner of the acrylic fibers chip factory, despite carrying a heavy-loaded debt (Table 3.4).

Among Shuang's privatization tasks, the differential polyester chip factory was the biggest headache for village authorities, mainly because of its heavy-loaded debts, which had mounted over the years. Selling the burden was deemed impossible without any extraordinary discounts. In 1999, the firm's liabilities totaled almost 46 million yuan, of which bank loans totaled over 35 million yuan and unpaid trade credit over 4 million yuan. Its fixed assets were calculated at over 52 million yuan, actually highly overestimated, and the firm's net assets were set at over 39 million yuan (Table 3.3). Shares of this firm were initially divided among three parties: the township government (12 percent), the village government (54 percent), and the state-owned Yangzi Petrochemical Corporation (35 percent).

To find a slot for the incumbent director's investment, the three shareholders agreed to strip 17 million yuan from the firm's book, forming a shareholding corporation with net assets valued at 22 million yuan, including shares of 2.11 million yuan or 10 percent owned by the township government, 9.75 million yuan or 44 percent by the village government, 6.33 million yuan or 29 percent by the Yanzi Corporation, and finally 3.8 million yuan newly injected by the incumbent director Sun Xue, whose shares accounted for 17 percent.

The next year, 2000, saw a tremendous market boom for polyester chips, which gave the restructured shareholding enterprise its most profitable year, earning a net profit of 30 million yuan. However, high demand in such products attracted far more producers than the market could sustain. Price wars erupted among the large state firms, which suppressed profitability and destroyed smaller manufacturers. The result made the next year the least profitable year ever for Shuang's differential polyester chip factory, which had just seized a new loan of 10 million yuan to expand its production capacity.

The firm faced a dilemma: the more it produced, the more it lost; the longer it hung on, the worse the crisis. But on the other hand the factory director believed that those who hang on longest survive eventually and would benefit more in the long run. Seeing day-by-day losses and feeling continuous pressure from the county government to privatize collective-owned firms, the village authorities became increasingly anxious about the ownership transfer for this suffering giant firm.

Between 1999 and 2002, Sun Xue borrowed money from fellow managers and local banks to buy township and village's shares valued at 4.47 million yuan. As of February 2002, the ratio among the stocks owned by township government, village government, Yangzi Corporation, and the director Sun Xue was 6:28:29:38. By 2002, Sun Xue owned 38 percent of the firm's shares valued at 8.27 million yuan. The recession in 2001 put great pressure on Sun Xue but also offered him an advantageous position to buy out the firm at a good price. Negotiating the sale terms took months before the village government made substantial concessions.

Both sides agreed on a deal of which the village government sold Sun Xue its stock with a 6-million-yuan book value at a price of 3.79 million yuan, approximately 38 percent off. Likewise, the township government sold Sun Xue its stock with a book value of 1.30 million yuan at a discounted price of 500,000 yuan. In total, according to the contract signed in February 2002, the ownership transfer cost and previous debts Sun owed to the village government amounted to 6.17 million yuan, which had to be returned on hire-purchase and completed in two years. This watershed ownership transfer in 2002 signaled the end of Shuang's collectivism in village enterprises and a new beginning of private ownership in its non-farm economy.

The distributional consequences of reforms

Like elsewhere in rural China, Shuang's village administration merged with its enterprises, which made the directors board members of the villagers' committee. However, unlike the centralized one-man command structure widely reported in other glorious villages,[4] Shuang's leadership was cliquish. A small group of elites occupied the posts with few turnovers.

The village's collective non-farm sector was a "talent-type" economy where the success of a firm depends heavily on its director. Before the privatization transition in the late 1990s, the appointment of directorship was controlled by the village authorities headed by its party secretary. Table 3.5 documents Shuang's leadership structure specifying those who occupied cadre and director posts over the past two decades. On the top echelon are Huang Wen and Huang Song, who held the party secretary post in 1984–1994 and 1994–1997 respectively. Despite carrying the same surname, they are not related, though they have dominated the village's administration and collective enterprises since the early reform era.

Huang Wen, born in 1945, worked as a technician in one of the village's production teams after his junior high school education. During 1974 and 1984, he acted as the director of the village's sole enterprise, the chemical products factory. He then founded the metal foundry in 1985, and the chemical fibers factory in 1987, serving as the director of the latter until 1998 when the factory's legal ownership was sold to his son-in-law. Huang Wen also launched the color master batch factory in 1997 and served as its director. In village administration, Huang Wen was the village's industry head (*gongye shezhang*) in 1975–1986, then the village head (later villagers' committee chairman) in 1987–1990, the village's deputy party sectary in 1990–1995, and finally the party sectary in 1995–1997.

Huang Song served as the village militia head in 1981–1982, the village head in 1982–1983, and then the village party sectary in 1984–1994. In 1993, He founded the village's biggest moneymaker, the differential polyester chip factory, and served as its director till 1994, when he was promoted to be the township party secretary. Other local elites in the village's upper echelons mainly served as the village's enterprise directors. For example, Zhou Min was the co-founder and director of the paper cartons factory in 1985–1989. In 1989, his entrepreneurship and talent earned him an appointment from the township government to set up and supervise a township funded Sino-foreign joint venture. In 1991–1995, Zhou served as the deputy general manager of the township's foreign trade

Table 3.5 Cadre and director posts in Shuang village, 1970s to 2002

	74	75–81	82	83	84	85	86	87	88	89	90	91	92	93	94	95	96	97	98	99	01	02
Township government																						
Party secretary	–	–	–	–	–	–	–	–	–	–	–	–	–	–	B	B	B	B	B	B	B	B
Township-run company	–	–	–	–	–	–	–	–	–	–	C	C	C	C	C	C	–	–	–	–	–	–
Village cadres																						
Party secretary	–	–	–	–	B	B	B	B	B	B	B	B	B	B	B	B	A	A	J	J	J	J
Vice party secretary	–	–	–	–	–	–	–	–	–	–	–	–	–	–	–	–	J	J	–	–	–	–
Villagers' committee chairman	–	–	B	B	L	L	L	A	A	A	A	K	K	K	K	J	I	I	I	I	I	I
Village enterprise directors																						
Chemical products	A	A	A	A	AE	E	E	E	E	E	E	E	E	E	E	C	C	C	C	C	C	C
Metal foundry	–	–	–	–	–	A	AG	H	H	H	H	H	H	H	H	H	H	Hx	Hx	Hx	Hx	Hx
Paper cartons	–	–	–	–	–	CD	C	C	C	C	D	D	D	D	D	D	D	D	D	D	D	D
Chemical fibers	–	–	–	–	–	–	–	A	A	A	A	A	A	A	A	A	A	A	Ax	A	A	A
Differential polyester chip	–	–	–	–	–	–	–	–	–	–	–	–	–	B	B	F	F	F	F	F	F	F
Acrylic fiber chips	–	–	–	–	–	–	–	–	–	–	–	–	–	–	–	–	–	–	M	M	M	M
Color master batch	–	–	–	–	–	–	–	–	–	–	–	–	–	–	–	–	–	–	A	A	A	A

Source: Author's fieldwork, 1995 and 2002.

Notes
(A) Huang Wen; (Ax) Wang Yuzhong (Huang Wen's son-in-law); (B) Huang Song; (C) Zhou Min; (D) Wang Jin; (E) Wu Shi; (F) Sun Xue; (G) Huang Ya; (H) Fu Ya; (Hx) Jing Hairong (Fu Ya's nephew); (I) Xu Gen; (J) Meng Jiang; (K) Xu Xingsheng; (L) Zhou Maoling; (M) Xu Kun.

company, before returning to the village taking charge of the chemical products factory in 1995. Finally Zhou bought the ownership of the chemical products factory in 1998. Sun Xue is also a village native who had been the accountant for the chemical products factory and then the differential polyester chip factory before becoming its director in 1995. Sun Xue became one of the village tycoons after serving as the director of the once lucrative differential polyester chip factory. Between 1998 and 2002, Sun Xue increasingly purchased shares of the differential polyester chip factory, ballooning his assets to 8 million yuan as of the spring of 2002.

Before the privatization in the late 1990s, Shuang's village administration, headed by the village party secretary, had delegated management rights to the enterprise directors. The village administration was not divorced from managing the enterprises, especially with respect to procuring bank loans and distributing profits earned. As time passed, some of the delegated directors accumulated knowledge pertaining to their firms from the idiosyncratic association with their work environments, physical equipment, and outside connections. On the other hand, the village administration and township government were unable to effectively monitor the day-to-day management and resolve problems. As a result, effective control and monitoring of the village party secretary on enterprise directors mostly relied on personal ties and informal restraints.

It turned out that two kinds of managerial elite emerged in Shuang. The first group of directors, like those of the metal foundry and the paper cartons factory, had gradually transformed their roles as managerial cadres of the village administration to private businesspeople able to dance out of the village's monitor and control. The other group of managerial elite, like the directors of the differential polyester chip factory, the acrylic fiber chips factory, and the color master batch factory, all belong to the inner circle of Huang Song, who wields authority and power as the locality's strongman. In any case, all of these directors have made themselves indispensable to the enterprises delegated to their management after a significant period of time. The enterprises' operation and profit generation, which supplies the village's revenue, hinges on these managerial elites. Therefore, when privatization occurred in the late 1990s, Shuang's enterprises were invariably sold to the incumbent directors whose power and resources were further consolidated and even strengthened.

In the village government, although Huang Song was promoted to the township government in 1994, he has no intention of fading away and still weighs in on major decisions of village affairs. Huang Song has skillfully made sure he exerts major influence over the village's decision makings and income distribution. His wife has served as the chief accountant of the lucrative differential polyester chip factory since its establishment. Huang Wen, Xu Gen, and Meng Jiang, all his protégés, have worked closely with

94 *The Yangtze Delta property rights transformations*

Huang Song. Xu and Meng, the incumbent villagers' committee chair and party secretary, were handpicked by Huang Song to be the village's next-generation leaders. However, until the early 2000s, Huang Song has continued to openly pull the strings of power and overshadowed top leaders in the village administration.

To highlight the distributional consequences of Shuang's transformation, Table 3.6 presents average annual pays of the village party secretary, enterprise directors, and workers. It shows that Shuang has been getting richer, but more unequal as well. The earnings of the elite group, the village party secretary and enterprise directors, have been consistently parallel, particularly compared with workers' wages. Up to the late 1990s after a long time of market expansion, there had not been any decline of cadre privilege in this region. Nevertheless, the income gap between elites (cadres and directors) and ordinary workers has been growing. From 1987 to 1999, for example, average annual wages for village party secretary and directors increased from 4,500 yuan to 49,000 yuan, climbing at an average annual growth rate of 22 percent, whereas average annual wages for workers improved from 1,707 yuan to 6,540 yuan, with a smaller growth rate of 12 percent.

The income spread between elites and workers has undergone three phases. The first phase, from 1987 to 1992, saw income gap narrow, with elites earning two to three times workers. The gap widened from 1993 to 1998, with the elite group earning roughly five to six times more than that of workers. Since 1999, the income gap continued to enlarge; the ratio of elite-to-worker income stood at over 7:1 (Table 3.6).[5]

The increasing income divergence between the haves and the have-nots in Shuang echoes the national trends of rising inequality, but it is noteworthy to see such a quickly increasing income disparity occurring in once pro-collective southern Jiangsu, which used to impose a ceiling on income differences between directors and workers within a community.[6] Ideological constraints against high personal income in this region have been rapidly eroding, even though an ethos of socialism and community obligation remains, which gives villagers the first chance at available employment in village enterprises. Despite remarkably increasing annual pays for the directors, the massive assets accumulated by TVEs in the reforms that were later transferred to private owners may further increase their relative returns (see also Walder 2002). All in all, growth in personal incomes has been associated with substantial increases in inequality between local elites and ordinary villagers, particularly after recent privatization transition.

One important question is to what extent the privatization of village-owned enterprises has restructured the resource base of village administration (Oi 1999). Does the village government still have access to the associated enterprise profits and non-tax revenues? If not, where will the village's alternative financial resources, if any, come from?

Further inquiry in Shuang reveals that the shift from collective to

Table 3.6 Average annual earnings in Shuang village, 1987–1999

	1987	1988	1989	1990	1991	1992	1993	1994	1995	1996	1997	1998	1999
(1) Village party secretary	4,478	6,928	7,149	7,914	8,808	10,844	20,030	23,676	30,000	38,000	45,600	41,500	48,000
(2) Directors of village enterprises	4,506	7,234	6,923	7,129	8,190	11,025	13,950	18,420	28,346	35,920	52,393	45,435	49,626
(3) Workers in village enterprises	1,707	2,607	2,550	2,600	2,753	3,041	3,588	4,402	5,170	5,840	8,201	7,843	6,540
(1)/(3)	2.6	2.7	2.8	3.0	3.2	3.6	5.6	5.4	5.8	6.5	5.6	5.3	7.3
(2)/(3)	2.6	2.8	2.7	2.7	3.0	3.6	3.9	4.2	5.5	6.2	6.4	5.8	7.6
(1)/(2)	1.0	1.0	1.0	1.1	1.1	1.0	1.4	1.3	1.1	1.1	0.9	0.9	1.0

Source: Author's fieldwork, 2001.

private ownership did not necessarily undermine the resource base and power of village administration. Privatization should strip village authorities property rights pertaining to village enterprises. Yet the Shuang village administration still holds administrative power over private enterprises in its jurisdiction and is entitled to charge them for various kinds of service fees. Following Shuang's privatization there were still a bundle of fees imposed on private enterprises to support village coffers and discretionary funds. The privatization contracts signed between village authorities and private entrepreneurs in 1998 spelled out amounts of various fees that privatized enterprises had to pay as an annual base. These fees included management fees, support of agriculture, social services, union fees, and pension funds (Table 3.7). In addition, rental contracts formalized the rents to be paid by enterprises for factory sites, buildings, and utility facilities such as transformers and waste-pipes. For example, in 1998, the annual rent for land and electricity transformers was 116,000 yuan for the privatized paper cartons factory, and 40,000 yuan for the chemical products factory. As a result, the total fees of 555,294 yuan plus rental payments collected by the village administration from the three privatized enterprises in and after 1998, actually were no less than those submitted in the collective period.

Privatization offered private business people complete rights pertaining to their property, but did not change their subordinate positions to village administration and obligation to the community. In an earlier work, Oi pointed out that the reforms up to the mid-1980s have transformed the primary function of village government from implementing government policies and managing agricultural production, to being the general contractor of collective property (Oi 1986).

After two decades, the village administration's role as a business corporation is fading, but its role as land manager and infrastructure provider is further reinforced. Since the early 2000s, Shuang village started to reallocate and develop its land for industrial use, launching a so-called industrial park in which the village constructs factory buildings, warehouse, and other facilities for a more profitable use in industry.[7] Parallel to the "park fever" in Jiangsu and similar development experiences in other economically developed coastal regions, the village administration now acts as a real estate and land-contracting company, appropriating land ownership rights to facilitate land planning and industrial development.[8]

Concluding remarks

The transformation from plan to market in Shuang village has gone through two distinctive stages: first when enterprises were cadre dominated, and second when enterprises were turned over completely to private ownership. Outright privatization in 1998 marks the point between them.

Table 3.7 The annual fees paid by the enterprises after privatization in Shuang village, 1998–2000

	Total	Management fees	Education surcharge	Support of agriculture	Pension fund for workers	Pension fund for one-child parents	Subsidies for military dependents	Sanitation	Public safety	Greening the environment	Union fees	Fund for flood control
Chemical products	185,840	33,000	35,000	7,700	39,600	39,600	2,200	7,920	880	440	10,000	9,500
Paper cartons	264,956	65,700	40,000	10,430	53,640	53,640	2,980	10,728	1,192	596	14,300	11,750
Chemical fiber	104,498	10,000	22,000	4,690	24,120	24,120	1,340	4,824	536	268	6,400	6,200
Total	555,294	108,700	97,000	22,820	117,360	117,360	6,520	23,472	2,608	1,304	30,700	27,450

Source: Author's fieldwork, October 2002.

Between the 1980s and mid-1990s, Shuang's village industrial enterprises in the traditionally pro-collective southern Jiangsu were owned and operated by a village administration whose entrepreneurial cadres were deeply involved in all major decision makings. In southern Jiangsu where the bureaucratic coordination played a vital role in promoting local economy, the talent and commitment of local cadres in obtaining support and resources for village enterprises were crucial for their successes. In this regard, privatization was indeed not the only way to stimulate economic growth in reforming communist systems. The success of rural collective TVEs in Chinese reforms is thus seen as belying belief in the superiority of private property rights, and as a sign of the least temporary expediency of collective ownership (Weitzman and Xu 1994; Chang and Wang 1994).

Like state-owned enterprises, "progress without privatization" was possible for a certain period of time in Chinese reforms. However, this does not imply that property rights do not matter, but, as Walder points out, it emphasizes the distinction between property rights reform and privatization, in which the former refers to the clarification and reassignment of various ownership rights among economic actors and the latter denotes narrowly to the reassignment of rights from government to private firms (Walder 1995a). This case study shows that there had been a rule of game, mainly in the form of social norms and group consensus, as to property rights relations among village government, enterprises, and cadres and executives involved. Peng's study in Jianying in southern Jiangsu also confirms that village collective ownership, relative to township collective ownership, was feasible and productive as long as there existed an adequate incentive arrangement, which might be based on interpersonal relations and collective legacy rather than on private legal ownership rights (Peng 2002).

Shuang's experience indicates that grassroots cadres in traditionally pro-collective villages were entitled to gain control over lucrative collective assets. The larger the industrial enterprise, the greater cadre advantages and returns. Compared with other coastal regions like southern Fujian, southern Jiangsu had a larger industrial base producing higher value of industrial products such as machinery and chemicals, which also require higher entry barriers in terms of start-up capital and technology.[9] The high entry barriers for TVEs also provided cadres with greater advantages in initiating enterprises and controlling profits earned. The institutional foundations in once pro-collective southern Jiangsu actually reflect characteristics of the "local state corporatism" proposed by Oi (1992, 1999). The dual role of village government as both community government and business corporations leads to a symbiotic relationship between village cadres and corporate entrepreneurs, causing the blurring of boundaries between village ownership and elite family ownership.

As reforms began to bear fruit, local elites, cadres and corporate elites, appeared less willing to share the fruits of their enterprises with the community administrations and villagers. They took steps to claim ownership from the local governments, the original legal owners, while at the same time keeping it away from the workers and villagers. Even worker-stockholders played a marginal role, with little say in how shareholding was carried out. The privatization in the late 1990s and early 2000s saw the collective ownership undervalued and diluted. Deliberate undercapitalization had been used to reduce the proportion of collective shares so that the process of conversion could be achieved.[10] Liu's study in Wujiang also confirms such a trend in which large-scale privatization was finally embraced due to political pressure from above and the desire for individual returns (Liu 2001). Other studies on TVEs in the mid to late 1990s in Jiangsu and Shandong also reports the privatization process actually better served the interests of some agents, mostly township governments and enterprises managers, than ordinary workers and villagers (Ho et al. 2003). As a result, a legal separation of village administration and enterprises emerged. There is a divergent trend between corporate leadership and political leadership. However, those who position themselves in the village administration and enterprises have been the same group of specific families and individuals. Economic expansion and privatization created ample returns and autonomy for private entrepreneurs, but did not lead to reductions in cadres' income advantage and administrative power. Being stripped of property rights on village enterprises following privatization, village administration became much more anxious to secure adequate revenues from other sources. It pushed local authorities to formalize a legal rent-generating structure.

At the same time, the transfer of undervalued corporation property rights signals the rising power of local elites whose power derives from political positions and clique networks centered on particular local leaders. One visible consequence of the transformation is the shift from bureaucratic coordination in the government hierarchy toward networks in a locality.

Two distributional consequences are emerging and noteworthy. One is that workers have largely been disfranchised in property rights transformation. As the local economy thrives, elites retain the lion's share of the benefits. If and when the economy slows, workers may be laid off or fired. If so, it would add a much more volatile dimension to the locality because farming land is no longer available to villagers as it has been shifted to industrial use. However, villages in southern Jiangsu have not experienced such a crisis as of yet. The village administration actually uses its land ownership to collect substantial amounts of revenue to support the village's infrastructure and social services, and certainly for the cadres' benefits.

4 Shuang village
The case study

In October 2002, on a gray Wednesday morning in Taipei, a curious fax spooled into the offices of one academic and a dozen small- to medium-sized Taiwan enterprises. "This Friday at the Grand Hotel we will treat our Taiwanese compatriots. Your business friends and clients are welcome to join us," the fax read. It was signed Huang Song, the party secretary of Mei township, one of the 23 townships of Wujiang City in Suzhou municipality. On the trip to Taiwan he was acting as the head of a seven-person delegation of mainland Chinese officials.

The invitation was, for all intents and purposes, extremely sensitive. Just two weeks prior, a Jiangsu delegation had strung up a red banner in front of the Taipei Grand Hyatt Hotel welcoming Taiwanese investors. "Conference to Welcome Taiwanese Investors in Jiangsu" it read. Taiwan's government promptly deported the party for illegal activities. Under Taiwan government regulations, mainland Chinese are only allowed onto the island in tour groups coming from a third country. Three months before their arrival they must submit an itinerary with their application for a travel permit. The Chinese visitors must strictly follow this itinerary, in which soliciting investments and business dealings are strictly prohibited. The gray areas are, of course, many in a democracy. Taiwan's investigators and officials would have a hard time prosecuting Chinese visitors for meeting with local "friends" as long as everything remained low key and non-commercialized.

The red banner advertisement and a high profile and publicized event had gone a bit too far. Three weeks later, Huang Song knew as much, and knew the government was watching them. Just days earlier one local newspaper had reported their arrival. A short two-inch column buried on the inside pages noting that the Mei township delegation had arrived and was traveling around the island. Although the placement of the article would not call much attention, it was publicity all the same, and one morning Huang Song awoke to find that single page under his door, the article circled in bright yellow.

This is all to say, that Huang Song and his delegation were not just tourists curious over the Taiwan scenery. They had come to woo

Taiwanese investment. Their small township with an area of 53 square kilometers and exercising administration over 21 villages and 31,000 residents in the southern Jiangsu countryside was partaking in the Wujiang City government's game of attracting foreign investors.

Beginning in 2002, the order went out to all the 21 townships in the vicinity: the township party secretary who brought in the least amount of foreign investment for the year would be replaced. It created a nervous tremor among the township officials whose political careers were now placed on the line, threatened to get cut altogether and possibly even deprive them of a livelihood. "Now all of our efforts are concentrated on seeking foreign investment; we are doing OK, not falling behind, but we are still under a lot of pressure and are becoming nervous," noted one Mei cadre. With Taiwanese large-scale listed companies moving into several state-level development zones of Suzhou and Shanghai, townships like Mei township hoped to attract small- to medium-sized manufacturers. This journey to Taiwan was their first, and one of the first by these Chinese local governments now thrown into competition with each other.

This newly developing trend took root in the need to continue to raise capital inflow and boost industrial output. Bringing in foreign investment creates a larger industrial base that will raise the overall industrial output. This translates directly into sustained long-term growth and development, which the local governments are desperate for.

Furthermore, the local governments now face large-scale underemployment problems. When rural collective enterprises began to privatize in the mid-1990s, labor surplus quickly followed, creating a dire need to re-employ the swelling ranks of a potentially dangerous social class of jobless.

Of course, by definition, there is no unemployment problem for Chinese peasants because each household has its farmland allocated by the village. However, the high ratio of peasants to land has long rendered farming inadequate for the peasants to make a living, not to mention a profit. Since the 1980s most peasants in the area have worked away from the farms in order to have cash income. It goes without saying that they enjoyed a much higher standard of living compared to their counterparts in the inland provinces.

Privatizing collective enterprises and concurrently selling off farmland began to cast doubts about the peasants' work and life. Local governments no longer owned their community enterprises, which were obligated to help employ community peasants. To make matters worse, local governments in the area joined the "zone fever" in coastal provinces to earmark farmland for newly developed industrial parks. Peasants who lost their farmland were happy to receive a lump sum of indemnity and work in village enterprises, before encountering any employment problems in the enterprises.

This happiness may change if the peasants later find no off-farm jobs and must return home to no farmland. Foreign investment is one solution to this problem. "Even if foreign investors do not create any real economic incentives, they do help with employment," said Huang Song. As a township party secretary in Suzhou municipality, he for one is extremely concerned about such developments, for the local government is directly responsible for peasants' employment (or lack there of) in this traditionally pro-collective region.

Such pressures have created drastic changes in the practices and attitudes of the local officials. Foreign visitors who were greeted cordially, but largely ignored in 1996, are now treated with honor. A chauffeured sedan ride from the Shanghai airport and large banquets now greet the village's foreign guests. Between friendly chats and rice wine toasts they offer commission in the amount of 3 percent of any foreign investment brought in. "Professor, we know you're a scholar. You don't do business. But you have friends and relatives in Taiwan who are interested in exploring investment projects here. You have my word. For each case you bring in you get a 3 percent commission," Huang Song said offering a toast.

"Yes, professor, he means it. This is a common practice here. Don't feel shy. Keep it in mind," whispered an engineer in echo of Huang's words.

The most startling developments, however, are the trips to Taiwan to seek and convince Taiwanese small- and medium-sized enterprises that

Plate 4.1 Overlooking Shuang village industry.

Shuang village

their township and villages are among the best investment choices. On his trip in October 2002, Huang Song handed out glossy information packets detailing his township and home village. "Half an hour to Hangzhou and thirty minutes to Shanghai," Huang said between mouthfuls of shark fin soup. He stretches the truth by about twenty minutes, but the village is on the freeway just inland of these major trading ports. Huang also offers deep discounts on land, making it a minimal overhead cost, or "basically free," as one of the businessmen put it. Further perks include as much as 10 percent lower taxes than those in Suzhou.

The incentives are all very appealing to the Taiwanese manufacturers gathered around the round table in Taipei's Grand Hotel. Land and labor costs in Taiwan have risen tremendously since the mid-1980s, pushing traditional industries that rely on cheap unskilled labor to areas that can supply it. The machinery, garment, umbrella and shoe factories that Taiwan raised in the 1970s and 1980s made the move across the strait early on, followed by tech companies in the mid- to late 1990s. Serving mainly export markets, these companies mushroomed around the ports – Guangdong, Fujian, and Shanghai. As larger listed companies such as Acer and Giant began to become attracted by the incentives in places like Suzhou, the Taiwanese manufacturers in electronics and precision machinery soon followed. Now they are not exporting though, they are exploiting the vast potential of the Chinese market.

Mr. Chen, one of the first Taiwanese investors in Mei, for example, has already set up a textile factory in Shuang village. His small factory employs twenty workers which produce yarns that are sold to local cloth factories. The five-year investment in Shuang has not, however, brought him much fortune. He spends whatever profits he makes on KTV drinking, and feels little ambition to further improve and expand his manufacturing. Yet, he looks proud of his decision to invest in China. "Five years ago my Taiwan factory closed. If I didn't go out, who knows where I'd be lying half dead," he said with a cheek swollen full of blood-red betelnut.

"What's wrong with China? You can get a maid for 500 yuan a month to cook for you and wash your clothes," he informed his Taiwanese compatriots. "In China I feel good."

"There is a common saying: 'You need to share good things with everyone.' I am speaking to you with this kind of sincerity."

His compatriots gathered around the table, letting Huang entertain them with $120 bottles of wine, have also made the decision to invest across the strait, only not yet sure where. For 45-year-old Lin Songfei, owner of a factory in Taoyuan that makes textile machinery, the Suzhou suburban area is now his major market. He currently works out of Taiwan shipping orders to Suzhou. "It doesn't make much sense with higher overheads, and then transportation costs on top of that," he said. "I want to set up a factory in southern Jiangsu. At present I am just debating whether I need to also move my R&D personnel to China, or leave it in Taiwan."

The other bosses of freezer equipment, of packaging printing and design, of frozen foods also want to relocate their factories to China.

The collective years

It would appear to be an unusual development in a region that once downplayed foreign investment; for a local government that has long been suspicious and uncertain about outsiders. In fact, less than a decade ago Huang Song had little to say to foreign visitors touring his village, wishing instead they were elsewhere other than poking around the Sunnan countryside and chatting up Shuang residents on village affairs. So why the complete turnabout in policy and attitude, allowing government officials to not only welcome outsiders with money, but even go overseas and recruit them to come? It's a brief history of Chinese reforms and its transformation of property rights. For unlike southern Fujian which has built its economic transformation on family, kinship, and small businesses, southern Jiangsu is an economic story of mammoth industry controlled by a small few; they run the factories as well as the government; they make the decisions and enjoy the profits. It is a tale of the rise and sell of China's rural collective industries. And in Shuang village it begins in the 1970s with Huang Wen.

A short wiry man standing under 160 centimeters, Huang Wen was born in Shuang village and grew up in Shuang village. Although his dark leathery skin and rotten teeth do not set him apart from his fellow peasants, he is considered educated with a junior high school degree, which he obtained from a neighboring village. When he returned to Shuang from school in the early 1970s he joined one of the village's production teams as a technician, fixing tractors and other farm machineries. During the Cultural Revolution he became the secretary of the village Communist Youth League in charge of propaganda and education. He was sent to the township for two years to partake in educating offenders. When he returned to Shuang in 1974 he was made chief of the village's industrial association (*gongye she*).

This politically correct background, as well as his education, made Huang Wen the ideal candidate for village cadres looking to expand village production output. Furthermore Huang's passive yet hard working personality meant that one could give him a task and he would set about accomplishing it. He did not give orders nor think much beyond completing the orders given to him. So when the village party secretary told Huang to go out into the world and find an opportunity for the village; to find something other than rice to invest in and begin producing, Huang went, just like he always did, and succeeded.

The problem the villages in the southern Jiangsu countryside faced in the early 1970s was, as local government officials put it, "too many people and too little land." Traditionally, agricultural areas relied on farm output to sustain economic growth and support their local populations. But when the villages faced increases in population for which the agricultural industry could not support, labor surplus followed.

The solution to such problems was to diversify into the manufacturing industry. The question, however, was how to do it? In 1974, the village had 20,000 yuan ready to invest, but knew no industry, had no markets, no connections, no base and no expertise in anything except hoeing fields. Huang Wen's job, the village party secretary told him, was to make connections and find a manufacturing industry to invest in.

Huang Wen had a relative in Shanghai who had a neighbor who worked at a Shanghai state firm mixing chemicals to make paints and other construction supplies. Could Huang, perhaps, meet the factory manager? He could, and when the four sat down over cigarettes and heavy green tea, Huang explained the village predicament. The manager said that with the end of the Cultural Revolution China was in a building phase, reconstruction of broken architecture now boomed and the country needed lacquer. For a fee, the manager said, his Shanghai state firm could help Shuang set up a production line to manufacture lacquer; he could provide the necessary technology and know-how, as well as the raw materials. The Shanghai firm also sold Shuang village equipment and training. But more importantly, the firm provided a long-term partnership for procuring resources.

Such agreements were common for the day. Technologically backward villages turned to state firms in the cities for support in starting up their own factories. Not only did the provider receive financial compensation for their services, but the manager in the state firm could also start a small but lucrative business on the side by funneling off small amounts of state resources to sell. In the 1970s, industrial raw materials or semi-products were produced and distributed within the bureaucratic system according to the state plan; there was no market, let alone price mechanism. Therefore, building connections with someone in the bureaucratic system in charge of production mechanisms and know-how was the key for a village enterprise outside the planned economy.

That same year, in 1974, Shuang's chemical products factory was established. Sixteen workers produced lacquer for the local market. No packaging and no advertising. Only by word of mouth those that needed it would come to the factory with their own containers and ladle out what they needed.

The chemical products factory was a village collective in name, and initially in form. Of the initial investment of 20,000 yuan, half came from a bank loan, while the village invested 1,000 yuan and the rest of the 9,000 yuan came from the nine production teams, each contributing 1,000 yuan. These production teams were organized village peasants, and formed a brigade before the reforms during the commune period. They recorded workloads, hours worked, even the wind direction and slope inclination, determining the amount of effort expended. In the first decade of the village's development, this chemical products factory provided the major non-farm income for Shuang. For example, in 1984 and 1985, it hired some 90 workers and earned 40,000 yuan and 100,000 yuan in net benefit, respectively.

With each production team investing in the village's new experiment of industrial production, villagers where theoretically all joint owners who would all share profits from the venture. The reality, however, left only township and village cadres in charge, making decisions and dividing the profits. Local cadres, headed by the party secretary, thought they were serving their people's best interests on behalf of the party by running collective enterprises, employing more villagers, and generating more cash income. The issue of distribution and redistribution was rarely a concern in the village between the masses and the cadres.

The interesting thing was that even though such facts were open and obvious no one seemed to mind.

"Who owns this factory?" I asked the villagers.

"The collective," the villagers replied.

"What does a collective mean?" I asked the villagers again.

"A collective is just a collective!"

"Then who are entitled to receive the earnings of the factory?"

"The collective," the villagers replied.

"Excuse me? Who are the collective?"

"All of us; a collective belongs to all villagers; it's a collective." they replied.

Legally speaking, in the 1970s, Shuang's village-run chemical products factory fell under the central government's rural non-agricultural regulations that allowed non-farm activities in restricted industries in a bounded locality. During the Cultural Revolution era, when Shuang's chemical products factory was set up, non-agricultural activities not directly supporting farming were discouraged – if not directly prohibited – by state policy. Rural industries, if any, were permitted only in the "five small industries," i.e. locally operated small enterprises producing iron and steel, cement, energy (coal and hydroelectricity), chemical fertilizers, and agricultural machinery. State policy also required these enterprises to follow the principle of self-reliance and self-sufficiency, in which they were only allowed to use local resources and human capital, no matter what the cost or price.

The purpose and implications of state policy over TVEs were to make TVEs supplements to agricultural production rather than profit-oriented businesses in themselves. Until further economic reforms of the mid-1980s, rural trade, commerce and service businesses were not liberalized. That is, rural residents were not allowed to engage in the transport and sale of selected goods between town and countryside. Despite such policies, Shuang had established its chemical products factory in 1974 because local officials were at the head of the operation and able to pass it off as an entity "fully supporting agriculture."

Since 1978, economic reforms and the open-door policy paved the way for a favorable macro environment for TVEs' development. By the early 1980s, local governments in southern Jiangsu were no longer ideologically inhibited from establishing profit-oriented industrial activities. In the mid-1980s, the central state issued a series of documents to formalize the political and legal status of TVEs, allowing them to obtain bank loans as "legal persons," and offered particular funds to promote the technological advance of TVEs. Since then, townships and villages in southern Jiangsu enthusiastically began to establish collective enterprises in industrial manufacturing. Mei township in Wujiang City, for example, set up eighteen metal foundries serving the Shanghai market. The town came to be known as "the home of metal foundry."

By that time Shuang's chemical factory had slowed down and become only marginally profitable. Observing the success of Mei's metal foundries, Shuang's village cadres also wanted to go into the metal business, hoping to take on overflow from the surrounding villages. This was Huang Song's task when he came into office in 1984.

Appointed as the village party secretary in 1984, Huang Song knew that the village was too small, and home to too many people to maintain an agricultural base. He wanted to exploit the potentially vast reserves of its labor capital. "By setting up a manufacturing industry we could solve the surplus labor problem and put the village on its feet," he said reflecting on the time.

The metal foundry was his first brainchild and he plucked Huang Wen out of the chemical products factory, making use of his business talents by putting him in control of the metal foundry. He also convinced the township government to invest 20,000 yuan into the venture. Within two months, however, the factory was not turning profit; it was not even making revenue. They had no orders. The problem was the complete lack of expertise in casting metal, which made the whole thing a hack operation. They had no technology, no training and no skill. They were supposed to be making cast metal products like lamp bases or fan casings but the craftsmanship left much to be desired, and the miscalculations in casting and design led to disaster.

"For products in demand, we didn't have the know-how," Huang Song recalled. "It was just like in the Great Leap Forward, when no one knew what to do and a bunch of metal scrap was produced. For inferior products like nails, screws, and hammers, there was a market oversupply and no orders."

With no orders the township pulled out, but Huang Song refused to give up on the plant. He poured in another 30,000 yuan, increasing total investment to 70,000 yuan, purchasing new machinery and raw materials, and hiring a technician from Suzhou. Such efforts still did not help much until Huang Wen was sent off again with the mission to find a partner in the state sector.

Through a relative of a friend, Huang Wen made connections with a Shanghai electric machinery factory, which agreed to give the village subcontract orders to manufacture the base of a cooling fan. The subcontract relationship was further formalized in 1988, when the metal foundry became an extended manufacturing line for its Shanghai contractor. It was renamed as the Second Workshop of Shanghai Electric Plant. In the decade between 1985 and 1995, its contribution in net profits accounted for 30 to 50 percent of total profits earned by all village enterprises in Shuang.

By 1995, the Shanghai firm made Shuang's metal foundry a partner. It moved its workshop to Shuang village and gave all its metal casting needs to the village's metal foundry. The village had a 48 percent stake in the foundry, and the Shanghai state firm held the other 52 percent. The village invested 2.63 million yuan in land, equipment, and the building, plus another 1.34 million yuan. The Shanghai factory invested its skill, valued at 100,000 yuan, 2.79 million yuan in equipment and machinery, plus another 1.46 million yuan cash.

Huang Song's ambitions for building industry in Shuang did not stop there, however. In fact it accelerated. Just two years after the founding of the metal foundry he pulled Huang Wen out of the company's managerial position and made him the village committee chairman. This position worked closely with the villagers' secretary and brought with it a legitimacy to oversee all of the village's industry. Particularly in the 1980s, decision making in village-run enterprises – from bank loans to daily productions – was completely controlled by village cadres. Huang Wen's new task was to break into the chemical fiber's industry.

Sunan supported a booming silk industry. Traditionally, the town grew mulberry and was renowned for its family-based textile factories and silk fabric handicraft. With limited supply, and an insatiable demand for chemical fabrics increasing, many traditional silk factories and talents turned to manufacturing synthetic fibers. This increased the demand for chemical fiber processing and production. It was this market that Huang Song hoped to capitalize on.

Huang Wen again went forth to find connections and expertise to help in opening a chemical fibers factory. He asked around at a township firm and came up with someone who had a relative in Shanghai who had a neighbor who did chemical research for a state firm who knew someone in Tianjin who worked in the same bureaucracy.

So it was that Huang Wen took a 30-hour train to Tianjin and met Li Dong and Wang Hua, the two chemical engineers who would move to Shuang and remain there for the next 12 years as the chief engineers of Shuang's chemical fibers industry. They would develop new products, the most successful of which was a material that could be stretched thin and still maintain its strength. It also had its own color and did not need to be dyed. "The only other thing like it in the world are Dupont's products imported from abroad but with much higher prices," Huang Song boasted.

In the mid-1980s, Li Dong and . Wang Hua were research associates in the Tianjin Institute of Chemical Engineering, a subsidiary organ of the state's Textile Ministry. Li completed his college education before the Cultural Revolution and had committed himself to scientific research since his youth. The Communist government's political repression over intellectuals hindered his research but did not stop his passion. He led his students, among whom Wang Hua was the most brilliant and trusted, in building lab facilities. They conducted a series of research projects with limited resources. Before moving south to the backward countryside, they had long been involved in polyester research but lacked any chance to develop their ideas into manufacturing.

In 1987, after meeting Huang Wen, they were invited to contribute their expertise to help Shuang develop state-of-the-art polyester products. At that time, compared with metropolitan Tianjin, Shuang had nothing compatible except a place to realize their scientific dreams. It was a bold and unrealistic decision to quit their jobs in a state institute and to step into the rural field, yet it was from their genius that the village's chemical fiber plant was born.

Plate 4.2 Roof of differential polyester chip factory in Shuang.

They developed synthetic fiber which could be spun into thread and sold to the textile and silk manufacturers. In 1987, the village obtained a bank loan of 500,000 yuan for an initial investment for its establishment. So successful was the engineers' development that in its first year of establishment the company had earned back its initial investment, and every year thereafter profits grew steadily. The chemical fiber plant generated profits of 290,000 yuan in 1988, 640,000 yuan in 1989 and 1990, before jumping ahead to 1.09 million yuan and 2.17 million yuan in 1991 and 1992, respectively.

The chemical fiber factory's success lasted through the mid-1990s, but then, with an abundance of similar products dumping onto the market, closed its doors in 1998. While the village-run collective could still compete with other TVEs entering the market with simple machinery and limited financial support, they could not compete with the large state-owned enterprises.

When they decided to completely undercut the market and drive out all their competitors the state firms could sell at the lowest costs possible because they had less overhead and softer budgets. When these state firms carried heavy debts and encountered severe competition from multinationals, their only choice to stay alive was to dump their products onto domestic markets and collected as much cash as possible. Thus, they sold at any cost and used the revenue as income flow for workers' wages and other necessary expenses. The consequences were left to the central government.

Such is the story of the chemical fibers market in the late 1990s in China. And it led to the demise and bankruptcy of many chemical fibers enterprises in southern Jiangsu, including Shuang village's chemical fibers enterprises. By that time, however, Shuang's main industrial production had shifted to another company, a differential polyester chip factory, that also faced severe challenges on the market.

The differential polyester chip factory was established in 1993 with Wang and Li's development of a new lighter and stronger synthetic thread. This new material possessed its own color, eliminating the need for dyes that would fade and bleed.

When the company was launched, it claimed to be the only one on the free market that possessed such a technology. In fact, they claimed that the only other company in the world that could spin thread so thin while still maintaining its strength was Dupont. It is true that the state-owned companies did produce such a material, but it was expensive and was only distributed in the plan system in the early 1990s. Other TVEs or private companies did not have the ability to make such a thread. As for Dupont, it was yet not available or affordable for local companies.

In 1994, when the factory started its production line, it made a good quality product and found huge markets for it; clothes that could be made softer and stronger, and in colors that would not fade or bleed. Local textile companies rushed to order polyester chips to make blended fabrics with silk and cotton.

It became Huang Song's cash cow and his stairway to promotion and wealth. Shuang village invested 32 million yuan into the company through loans and joint investments, and made Huang Song director for its early years in operation. Those years saw tremendous growth. The first year in operation pulled in 5 million yuan in profits and then doubled the next year and continued to grow for the next three years. In 1995, Huang Song was recognized by higher authorities for his success and was appointed the township party secretary. Still, he left his wife watching the differential polyester chip factory, making her the chief accountant, which gave him control of the financials even if someone else sat in the director's chair.

In Sunan, village officials controlled the village-run collective enterprises, which were the backbone of the local industry. Before the mid-1990s, private enterprises that tried to rise up among the collectives were quickly strangled, just as Zhou Min and Wang Jin found out.

Zhou Min and Wang Jin are among the village's talents, but did not start their careers as village cadres. Zhou Min, born in 1953, completed his senior high school education in 1974 and started work as a technician in the village chemical products factory. Wang Jin also had a senior high school education, and had been serving as a teacher in the village's elementary school before joining Zhou to set up a paper cartons factory in 1985.

In the early 1980s, when reforms were just launched, their market sense told them that the Sunan silk industry needed paper carton packaging for market display. It was an easy enough industry to get into. The low entry level meant it required almost no skill and minimal technology to begin production. One just needed to collect old paper and cardboard, soak it and beat it into a thick paste then repress it into boxes.

Their entrepreneurship was short lived in private business, but ironically well developed in collective economy. In 1985, Zhou and Wang and another villager pooled together 5,000 yuan for establishing a private factory manufacturing paper cartons. The next year it had become a village-owned enterprise. The first problem they ran into was that as a private company, government policy restricted them from borrowing money. Thus they could not expand until they had accumulated enough working capital to self-fund one. But even if they did garner capital the village was not willing to give them land to build another factory or even enlarge the one they had. The village authorities intended to impede its development as long as it remained under private ownership.

Still, the worst of it all was the power outages. With regulated power supply to the villages, blackouts came often, though officials could control whose power went out first. As a private enterprise, Zhou and Wang topped the list. "We could not continue to do business. It strung us out very thin," said Zhou remembering that time. "Regularly we would have no power for two to three days. How can you continue to do business like that?"

One could not, was the rhetorical answer, and Huang Song made sure that they understood that. In September 1985, Huang Song, the village party secretary, called Zhou and Wang to come down to the office, where he proceeded to "educate" (*zuo gongzuo*) them on the need to turn their private-owned factory into village property. "There is no room for private business in our socialist territory," he said. "However, there is plenty of good stuff for collective entrepreneurs here." Huang Song lured them with the advantages of collective enterprises and the "opportunity income" a cadre-entrepreneur could enjoy.

The manager-owners agreed to serve the collective's interests. The deal was that the paper cartons factory would be valued at 100,000 yuan, and Wang and Zhou would continue at the factory as director and deputy director. The village would also put another 10,000 yuan into the factory to purchase new machinery. As the operating climate improved, the factory started to make profits, climbing from 110,000 yuan in 1987 to a record high of 680,000 yuan in 1992, before slowing down to 510,000 yuan in 1995. In 1995, the factory added a new production line with a low-interest loan of 9 million yuan from the nation's "Spark Program," a funding project designed for supporting TVEs. The factory upgraded its products to manufacture high-quality air filter papers, that won a number of state and provincial products awards.

The privatization years

By the late 1990s the collection of collectively owned enterprises in Shuang had brought wealth and prosperity to the village. Gravel roads had been paved, mud shacks had been replaced by concrete apartments, tap water and gas had been installed in the villagers' residences. Most spectacular was the 2,400-square-meter village hall completed in 2002, equipped with cadre offices, a clinical room, and a 40-seat theater. Residents of Shuang lived comfortably. Employment at the factories was steady, and salaries gave them enough buying power for home electronics, among which DVD players and cable televisions were the most recent items. Life was even better for the cadres who rode in the chauffeured Volkswagen and occasionally took foreign recreational "business trips." Huang Song, who had masterminded the village's rise throughout the reform years, now sat at the head of the township government, and his old village party secretary post first occupied by his partner at hand, Huang Wen and then his apprentice, Gao Xin. Both of them kept their fingers in the enterprise pie. Huang Wen remained director of the chemical fibers plant until 1997, after which he started the lucrative color master batch factory and still remains the director.

Huang Song, while he has personally given up directorship of all enter-

Plate 4.3 Shuang village government office building.

prise, has Huang Wen under his thumb, and has kept is wife as the chief accountant at the money-making polyester chip factory. Every Chinese New Year, it is said, the factory's director comes to Huang's home and lays out stacks of money on his desk. Only Huang himself knows the amount of his own riches, but their plethora is far reaching. His son, for instance, has been sent to high school in Australia, where Huang bought him a house to live in for his stay. The last time he took the cadres for a visit down under, they were held up at the airport for concealing cash in excess of customs regulations, which they had planned to bring back to China. On his trip to Taipei, where, after consuming six bottles of $100 French wine, he went out on a shopping spree in Taipei's most upmarket department store, plopping down $2,500 cash for a notebook computer.

Personal finances remained more than comfortable compared to the past, but village finances had already begun to deteriorate. On the surface heavy debt burdened village enterprises for which the village government guaranteed their bank loans. The village's book of net assets would turn to a painful loss if enterprises' unpaid bank loans were considered. Nevertheless, ignoring these loans meant the village still had much cash to spend. As a next generation village head put it, "In our village the richest people have more money than they can spend, and more debt than they can pay!"

This was the case throughout China. The highly leveraged TVEs had burdening debts, none of which were getting repaid. In government hands, they remained government responsibility, making the whole system look incestuous and corrupt. These loans were, after all, non-performing, jacking up the banks' national non-performance-loan ratio to over 50 percent, according to some.

The problem began in the mid-1990s, and in Sunan it dilated when foreign direct investment began to flood in. By mid-decade, revenue from FDI in Sunnan had surpassed that of profits from the TVEs. Some constitutions, such as Yixing, faced such a crisis that authorities took to extricate themselves from the predicament, and thus responsibility. The solution was to get rid of the enterprises by selling them to the factory directors, who would take on the debt themselves, and leave the village free from debt. As early as 1995, 94 percent of Yixing City's enterprises were privatized.

Yixing was two years ahead of the national impetus. In September 1997, the 15th Party Congress ushered in a sweeping privatization agenda, in which Beijing called for the sale, merger, or closing of the vast majority of China's state-owned enterprises. This gave momentum to TVE privatization, which instilled local bureaucrats from provincial and township levels with confidence to further ownership transformation. They hang the slogan "changing the system" or "changing the institutions" (*gaizhi*). That winter, the Jiangsu government laid out a blueprint for the future of TVEs, encouraging multiple and "creative" forms in collective ownership in order to accelerate the development of the non-public economy.

Such statements were followed by direct pressure from provincial and city governments on their subordinates. Wujiang City, for instance, came under fire from Jiangsu province for having such high debt on its books. In turn the city put pressure on Huang Song, as Shuang township party secretary, to rid the town of its debt. Huang told Shuang village to sell off the enterprises.

Shuang village was not as eager as neighboring Yixing to privatize its enterprises. Shuang's enterprises were profitable for the people who controlled them. And the people who controlled them controlled the village. Huang Song had been promoted to township party secretary in 1994 for his success with the differential polyester chip factory, and left his man in the factory's director chair. Huang Wen stepped into Huang Song's vacated village party secretary post while simultaneously maintaining the directorship of his profitable chemical fibers factory. Everyone else in the village government were placed there by Huang Song, young, inexperienced, and obsequious to Huang Song.

Even with an ideal set up for those in charge, there was no firm opposition to privatizing the village industry. The clique that led the local government and controlled the economy would design the privatization process so that it was not really free market privatization of industry, where competitive bidding is the rule and healthy competition is the norm. Rather, Huang Song and his men would make sure that their clique remained intact and their profits salient. The privatization of Shuang village, when complete, would find all of the very directors that Huang Song put in charge of the collectives now the full owners of the enterprises; burdened with debts, no doubt, but knowing full well that they would never have to repay them.

Such a property transformation was not just unique to Shuang. Throughout Sunan and Shanghai such developments were sweeping the countryside, phlegmatic ardor for privatization wrapped up in the benefits to be incurred through inveterate design of the process by a few in control of it.

Phase one

The process began in early 1998. With orders coming down from the city government for the townships and villages to get rid of their money losing and debt ridden enterprises, Huang Song had to act. He oversaw the entire process of turning the town and village enterprises from collective entities owned by the local governments, into privately held companies. Everything had to be converted, and here Huang Song faced a problem: four of the TVEs had net assets well over a billion yuan – one with assets over 39 billion yuan; cash that no single buyer had access to. In fact, it was a problem that plagued much of Sunan. The natural solution was a system of shareholding, in which two or more parties would purchase the entity. Yet that solution would have to wait a few years, until the townships and villages dealt with the enterprises that they could handle: those with assets under one billion yuan.

In two days in February, Shuang's three small- to medium-sized enterprises were privatized. Huang Song had evaluated the assets over the past few weeks. He had assessed the prices and the amount of debt of each. Likewise, the directors had much to consider in the bargaining: how much were they willing to pay for a debt ridden enterprise? How big was the risk of a bank seizure? How much profit could the firm make?

The two sides negotiated the price, and Huang Song laid down the terms and conditions. On February 9, 1998, Zhou Min, the previous owner and founder of the paper cartons factory, was sold the chemical products factory. He had been running the factory as a collective since 1995, placed in the director's chair by Huang Song. Now he had been given the entire company, debt and all, for the bargain price of 1.05 million yuan. Later that afternoon, the chemical fibers factory was signed over to Huang Wen's son in law for 600,000 yuan. The next day, the last deal of the first wave of the privatization of Shuang's TVEs was complete. The paper cartons factory was sold to Wang Jin, the factory's previous owner who was forced to sell it to the collective in 1985. At 300,000 yuan even, the price was not just prearranged, but also deflated considerably, as were all the deals reached. The price was determined by the company's total assets, less its total liabilities. In the case of the paper carton's factory, total liabilities, including bank loans, debts to suppliers, and back wages, equaled 17.84 million yuan. Total assets, including receivables, stocks, and fixed assets just happened to equal 18.14 million yuan, producing the nice round number of 300,000 yuan. In fact, this was arranged by deflating the company's fixed assets to a price agreeable to both parties.

By selling these companies to their directors, Huang Song ensured that everything remained in the family, so to say, even if it was now legally out of collective hands. This also ensured certain conditions of the sale, which were of the utmost benefit to the village. A typical contract looked something like this:

> In accordance with the opinion of the city government, we both agree to transfer to the buyer the assets and liabilities. The buyer takes full responsibility of the assets and liabilities from the village government.

The contract then lists all the assets and liabilities of the said firm, followed by the statement, "after the buyer takes over the assets and liabilities, he takes on full ownership of the company and is fully responsible for the firm's debts."

On the subsequent pages of the contract is a long list of annual fees that the new owner is obligated to pay to the village government. They include management fees, for managing the village; education fees in order to raise the standard of education in the village; agricultural fees to support the farmers whose land the factory occupied; village pension fund fee; village sanitary fee; public security fee; environmental fee; union fee; flood control fee. It was a lump sum that the factory paid, and the village did not necessarily spend the itemized amount on the service detailed. Thus, annual fees for the paper cartons factory totaled 264,956 yuan in its contract, much of which went to entertaining and supporting the cadres. Also, electricity fees over the next eight years were to be paid out in the sum of 116,000 yuan. These fees are all stipulated under "the opinion of further improving property rights reforms of the TVEs," of which "both parties sign on equal, voluntary, and pay as you use terms."

The last note on the contract is that a copy is to be sent to the city government as the overseer of the transaction.

And so the first wave of privatization was completed. Three enterprises and three directors made owners through arranged buyout terms. All parties involved were quite happy with the results. The village alleviated itself of its debts and of a money-losing business; it also got the added bonus of continuous revenues from the agreed assortment of fees. While the government did collect percentages of profits in the past, it constantly ran into the problem of the equivocate factory director who dissembled profits, informing the government that they just did not make money.

Likewise, the directors were happy because the contract spelled out very clearly the relationship between themselves as company directors and the village. They were, in essence, set free. The previous ambiguity of the relationship would find government authorities demanding more money from the company if it made money that year. Or it would involve itself in the hiring and firing of workers, telling them to hire more workers if unemployment was up, or disallowing them to fire workers. Government officials might bring guests by for lunch leaving the director with a large bill to pick up and his afternoon wasted. Under the new terms, as set forth in the contracts, fees were set, not to be arbitrarily adjusted according to profits.

As for the debts the new owners were now burdened with, well, they just would not pay them. With liabilities running into the tens of millions of yuan, the directors really had no intention to repay. When the bank collectors happened to come around to demand payments, they would be treated to a lavish lunch at the village restaurant reserved for village VIPs, perhaps slipped a red envelope and then sent on their way without so much as a word about debts owed, for they all understand by now that these companies are "not profitable." And who would know otherwise? The collectors perfunctorily make their rounds, returning to the office to inform superiors that the companies have no money to pay back loans. No

Plate 4.4 Entrepreneur and cadre residences in Shuang village.

legal system of collection exists, giving the banks only the option to take the company to court in a legal suit, possibly win the company's assets, which it will have limited means to unload.

While both parties of this privatization transaction come out ahead and happy, the state banks suffer. The state banks understand these unpaid debts are already dead, and have given up on reclaiming them. "The one-time 'robber economy' in the 1990s may pay the way for a legal-based market economy in the 2000s," one local bank official noted, adding that only by returning everything to ground zero can things progress.

Phase two

The second wave of privatization began in mid-1999 and took over three years to complete. Due to the size of the remaining four Shuang TVEs, they could not be sold and purchased outright, but instead had to undergo rounds of shareholding and devaluation of stock or assets or both before the director could claim complete control of the company – or the village be free from it, depending on one's perspective.

While the process appears straightforward enough, with two steps undertaken: first a divesture of shares between the village and the director, and then, when the director had enough cash, outright privatization – it was again marred by the incestuous relations between the local officials and the directors. Just like the small to medium TVEs, at the end of the day, when the large ones were privatized they were in the hands of the directors who had been placed there by the local officials, and in some cases in the hands of the local officials themselves.

As such, the fundamentals of the process of privatization did not rest on traditional capitalist values of free trade and open bidding, but was instead completely contained by the village clique. The process was locally based, taking on the characteristics of crony capitalism, in which an elite few establish a closed network for the imparting of wealth to each other for reciprocal favors, all at the expense of the state and the populous. It was not economic and not political but cliquish, where everything was organized and decided by a few actors within an insular locality. Each of the companies to be sold, for instance, not only had their assets devalued, but also had their shares owned by the collective devalued, sometimes by more than half, which favored the buyers at the expense of the collective. The differential polyester chip factory, for example, started out with over 39 billion yuan worth of shares in 1999, and ended up three years later with 18.9 billion yuan worth, two thirds of which were concentrated into the director's hands.

This was the same factory that Huang felt he held under the table shares. "I built that company and made it profitable," Huang says. "Then I gave Sun Xue the directorship for which he owes me a certain percentage of profits every year." To make sure that Sun did not cheat him out of the deal, Huang set up his wife as the company's chief accountant. In 2001, those close to Huang say, Sun Xue did not give as much as usual. Verve competition throughout the countryside had suppressed prices and increased manufacturing costs. Profits, Sun said, were down 300 percent year on year. It seems reasonable enough, and it seems fair enough that Huang's usual exuberant pile of hundred yuan notes would be more modest. Yet that New Year when Sun came into his home, Huang was all churlish, hurling the unassuming pile of bills on the floor and waving his finger in the face of Sun, "You think we don't know how much you make!"

The differential polyester chip factory was originally jointly owned by the township, the village and a state-owned corporation, as were the village's other large TVEs. This was a form of shareholding, to be sure, but only with a major role played by government entities. The process of privatization brought in the individual as a new shareholder, weaning him over the course of three years into the main shareholding position. The acrylic fiber plant, for example, started out with 7 million shares in 1999, which were divided between the township, the village, and the differential polyester chip factory. The director of the plant since 1995 was required to invest 1.5 million yuan to take an initial 21 percent stake. In 2001, total share price was devalued to 6.3 million at the expense of other investors. That same year the director increased his stake to 39 percent, and the next year was able to buy out the other shareholders completely.

Given the asset size of the companies, the complete privatization process took part rather quickly. Within three years, a company that had been under government control, and with tens of millions in assets, was turned over completely to a private shareholder. With political pressure bearing down on the local governments to expediently "transform the institutions," they were eager to divest no matter the cost.

This played all the better into the interested cadres' hands who pushed it through. Huang Wen's color master batch plant is a case in point.

It is purely a matter of speculation whether the Huang's machinated when they set up the color master batch factory in early 1998, only to begin to turn it over to Huang Wen – rather, give it away to Huang Wen – less than a month later. Neither Huang Wen nor Huang Song would ever admit to planning it as such, but the coincidence – indeed the timing – was adroit. With demand for raw synthetic silk material booming among a dearth of supply, the village knew that the first to set up a factory would be able to cash in on a few years of outrageously high returns. In late 1997, the Huang's had the village put in 1.1 million yuan, and the township 550,000 yuan, while securing a bank loan for 4.8 million yuan. Total initial investment was 6.45 million yuan. The factory was up and running at the beginning of 1998, then bargained away to Huang Wen in February that year. Huang put in an initial investment of 1.5 million yuan, securing, what amounted to after book cooking, a whopping 48 percent of the company. Despite the initial investment of over 6 million yuan just weeks before, the evaluation found the company only worth 3.15 million yuan. By 2002 the company would only be worth 2.1 million on the village books, allowing Huang Wen to then buy out the township and village completely for just another 600,000 yuan.

At the end of it all, Huang Wen took over the whole thing himself for the ridiculously low price of 2.1 million yuan. "I saved the village government," he says without a hint of malfeasance. "It was a money-losing industry and a burden to the government. I had to pay a good 2.1 million yuan for it."

By 2002, Shuang village's collective enterprises had all passed into the hands of their directors. They had become fully private, owned and operated by the individual with no theoretical connections to the state. Likewise, the enterprises' debt, that had vexed the local and central government, was now off the village's record. The village and township leaders, Huang and Huang, had done their bureaucratic obligation; they had met the political reality.

Of course there were more to follow. After privatization had reached its conclusion and passed from the political agenda, foreign investment quickly became the next assignment. Again it was one of financial necessity.

The local governments found that being free from debt also meant being free from revenue, for they could no longer rely on the TVEs to

Plate 4.5 Farmland waiting to be turned into an industrial park.

provide income. The fees collected from village enterprises were constant, to be sure, but they relied completely on the continued health of the said enterprises. Should their markets collapse and their business falter then no fees would be forthcoming. Or the directors might decide he no longer agreed with the terms of the contract and, one day, stop paying. There were no real legal means to uphold contracts, after all, and one could never be sure. Furthermore, the fees were not enough to cover village expenses nor provide a consistent guarantee of jobs for the local population.

Having sold out the enterprises, the new role now embodied by the local governments, by default, was that of administrator. The townships and village cadres were no longer owners and no longer managers, but administrators of the towns and villages; they were administrators of the people and the land. The village head was busy mediating in disputes among villagers; the village's party secretary supervised the construction project for an industrial park to attract private and foreign enterprises. As before, they were occupied by lunch treatments in the town's restaurants for visitors coming and going.

It was a new role for the local governments, one that they would need to get used to, but still a role that lacked the fundamental characteristics of a government in a modern civil society. The local governments could not just assume the position of administrators and perform executive functions for they still had the problem of finances. They had to provide basic services: water, electricity, gas. They had to provide education and health benefits. Most importantly, they had to keep everyone employed with a steady pay check. Where was the money to come from? Where were the resources? Taxes were leveled by the central government and went straight to Beijing. However, Beijing did not hand down adequate revenue to support the local governments, especially at the village level. Thus the local governments were not able to completely extricate themselves from doing business. That is, they still had to find their own means to generate revenue.

The solution was in the land. If the local governments had sold out the businesses, they still possessed the land for which they could sell, or rent, or exploit. Foreign investment, both from overseas and cross-province, was the best means to make use of the land. By encouraging foreign investors to set up shop in the localities it could not only bring a steady amount of capital to village coffers, in rent and fees, but also provide employment opportunities.

So the order was handed down by the Wujiang City government in early 2002 for the townships and villages to bring in foreign investment. It was such that Huang Song came to Taipei that October with the fervent ardor of a deer looking for a mate.

But there is more to the story than that, for the very people who make up the village collective have not benefited in the least from the transactions, nor very much from the calling of FDI. It is true that job opportunities may flourish and services increase, but the very enterprises that were sold off were supposed to be collective. The collective received none of their due shares. The transfer of ownership and the flow of money passed only through the hands of a moneyed elite – between the local officials and the directors. When shares were devalued, they were done so at the expense of the collective and for the benefit of the director. For the officials overseeing the process it was all the same – the same incestuous relationship in which they would still get paid. The people, on whose backs the industry was built, would receive nothing, save the hopeful reassurance that life would go on as before.

The problem, however, is that it might not. With the former collectives now in the hands of the directors who ran them, the oversight of the village, which has a responsibility to the people, has been distanced. The village no longer manages the factory. It can regulate who the factory hires, but no longer when and how many it will hire, nor if it can or cannot dismiss workers. The factory is now in the hands of individuals who have no responsibility to the people and are interested in one thing and one thing only – profit.

Likewise, foreign investment offers less for the peasants than it does for the cadres. Short-term jobs, yes. But long-term stability is another question. FDI is a party affair, transacted and operated in close connection

Plate 4.6 Peasant home in Shuang.

with the local cadres. Should an FDI enterprise be successful, then nothing is stopping it from going national or multinational, moving its operations elsewhere at the behest of local officials who have been transferred or have connections elsewhere.

But even before that could happen, the possibility looms of being too reliant on FDI and not attracting any FDI. Industrial parks in the cities of Shanghai, Suzhou and Wujiang also vie for investment. Why should a foreign investor pick one Podunk village over another, or even a Podunk village over a renowned city? The strategy of every village, township and city in Sunan today is to attract foreign investment. Not all of them will be able to. What then?

The villages have no contingent plan today. If all fails the villages might fail too. The cadres may lose their posts but their own bank accounts are sufficiently swollen to live comfortably in the worst of situations. The peasants, however, have nothing. Should all fail, they will go down hard, losing everything. Left jobless and hungry; victims of a rapacious few local officials and elites.

Part II
Southern Fujian property rights transformations

5 Southern Fujian under economic reforms

For three decades the southern coastal province of Fujian suffered under economic degradation. As the front-line in the ongoing conflict with Taiwan, just 130 kilometers offshore, Fujian had been designated as a military bastion. With Jinmen and Matsu, two islands under Taiwan's jurisdiction, and just a stone's throw from the Fujian shore, launching regular artillery attacks, the central Chinese government feared destruction on a large scale, and thus limited industrial investment projects in favor of more protected areas. In fact, since the establishment of the People's Republic of China in 1949, through the beginning of economic reforms in 1979, Fujian failed to get even one major investment project. Such factors made its economic development fall below the national average, and lag far behind other coastal provinces. During this period, Fujian received but 1.5 percent of the country's total capital investment, the fourth lowest among the 29 provinces. From 1957 to 1975, Fujian's contribution to the national income declined from 1.56 percent to 1.26 percent, remaining the poorest of China's coastal provinces (He 1991: 160; Shieh 2000).

The sparse industrial investment that did come to Fujian was located away from coastal areas. Despite their traditional prosperity, the frontline cities of Xiamen and Quanzhou were starved of industrial investment from the 1950s through the 1970s. The richest and most industrialized city in 1978 in Fujian, in terms of industrial output per capita and rural income per capita, was Sanming, a western inland state-designated industrial center with the province's only integrated iron-and-steel complex and several chemical and machinery plants. To a considerable extent, over these three decades, Fujian was a lopsided planned economy, force-feeding the interior and starving the coast.

While military conflict retarded the province's industrial advancement, mountainous topography hindered its agriculture and transportation development. With 87 percent of total land area made up of mountains and highlands, industrial and commercial activities were concentrated in less than 10 percent of total land area, chiefly along the coast and plains. In 1978, cultivated area per capita in Fujian, was only 0.06 hectares, or half of the country's average of 0.12 hectares. Despite this, Fujian had remained an agrarian economy; in 1978, its agricultural output accounted for 30 percent of its total output, compared to 20 percent for the whole country (calculated from QGZH 1990: 8, 14, 439, 446).

The economic reforms of the late 1970s brought vast economic changes to Fujian, allowing it to take advantage of its coastal position to increase exports, as well as bring in necessary foreign investment and trade, from which overseas Chinese businesses were the first and most important target to approach. Also, China's Taiwan policy changed from military confrontation to economic integration and political conciliation in which Fujian, again, played a pioneer key role. In 1979, Fujian and nearby Guangdong were the two provinces selected for "special policies and flexible measures" in a wide range of economic affairs, particularly in attracting foreign investment and trade. Four Special Economic Zones – Xiamen, Shenzhen, Zhuhai, Shantou – were set up, granting tax breaks and various privileges to foreign investors. Fiscal relations with the central government also got a boost, giving the province a foxed subsidy of 100 million yuan from Beijing during the 1980–1984 period. More importantly, "special policies," including a favorable comprehensive responsibility system that institutionalized the province's autonomy for fiscal revenue and expenditure, and foreign trade earnings, were given to Fujian. Following the establishment of Xiamen as a Special Economic Zone, an "Open Area" encompassing eleven counties and cities in the southern Fujian was opened in 1985, and was later expanded to include 33 counties and cities.

These open-up policies paved the way for Fujian's rapid growth and dynamic development under reforms, particularly for the eastern coastal counties. Between 1978 and 2001, the gross domestic product (GDP) of Fujian grew at an average rate of 20 percent annually, significantly faster than the national average of 15 percent during the same period. This robust growth pushed Fujian toward the front ranks among China's provinces in terms of GDP per capita – from 22nd (among 29) in 1978, to 7th (among 30) as of 2001 (calculated from ZTN 1979, 2002). More than anywhere else in China, particularly compared with once pro-collective Jiangsu, growth in Fujian in the reform era came from trade, foreign investment, and the private sector. By 2001, the province had approved 29,414 foreign joint ventures, acquiring investment contracts of 69 billion yuan and actual investment of 38 billion yuan. Such figures made it the third largest province in the country (*Xinghua News* 9/7/2002). Lyons suggests that Fujian's economy during the 1980s and 1990s exhibited similar development patterns as that of the East Asian model. Over the two decades of 1976–1996, Fujian's growth by labor-intensive manufactured exports and foreign investment closely resembled Japan, Taiwan, and South Korea. Fujian's development strategy of export orientation and acquiring technological and business know-how from abroad, mostly through overseas-Chinese connections, also reflected the East Asian development pattern (Lyons 1998a).

Much like the entire country, whose interregional disparities are associated with differences between well-endowed coastal and deprived inland provinces, Fujian has seen a widening of disparities between its eastern coast and western inland. While the central government's military concerns molded a planned economy that retarded the province's development, the reforms in 1979 allowed free market forces to re-shape the provincial economy. Local governments were granted more leeway, which made them more willing and daring to take initiatives in economic affairs. This put the provincial government in control, allowing local officials to temper and twist central government policy to their interest and intentions. As a result the GDP and industrial output of Fujian's coastal counties, like Jinjiang and Nanan on the southeastern coast, accelerated dramatically, quickly outperforming their inland counterparts (Lyons 1998b, 2000; Tsai 2002). The regional distribution of foreign investment has also been highly uneven. More than 90 percent of foreign direct investment since 1979 has been concentrated on the coast – mainly in Fuzhou, Quanzhou, and Xiamen which received 75 percent of foreign direct investment in Fujian in 1979–1996 (Hu and Hu 2000).[1]

The preferential treatments and special policies enacted in Fujian may account for the opportunity structure that facilitated the fast-growing economy. However, without gauging the local institutional environment in which economic activities have been embedded, one may misread the qualitative differences in regional institutional arrangements. This chapter takes Jinjiang as a case study in order to explain its transitional trajectory in property rights arrangements that reflect a typical development pattern in southern Fujian. Jinjiang, the richest city in Fujian, falls under the jurisdiction of Quanzhou, a beautiful port city that was once one of the premier ports for international trade. Since the early reforms, its economy has developed in a full swing and achieved remarkable growth. Between 1991 and 2001, the GDP per capita in Fujian increased from 2,041 yuan to 12,362 yuan at an annual average growth rate of 20 percent, whereas the GDP per capita in Jinjiang accelerated from 2,069 yuan to 29,508 yuan, jumping ahead at an annual average growth of 30 percent (calculated from FTN 1992, 2002).

This chapter first illustrates property rights arrangement in Jinjiang's fast-growing rural economy, which originated from household handicraft industry in the pre-reform period and after two decades transformed into modern private enterprises and multinational joint ventures. Contrasted with transformations in the Yangtze Delta region whose local state system steered economic and social institutional transformation, Jinjiang's development appears to be rooted in indigenous local institutions upon which bureaucratic systems are also based. As it moves into the new century, the local political system is allowed greater latitude in decision making and resource generating. The lasting effect of this state-initiated institutional transformation has, ironically enough, undermined the center's direct command, but at the same time it has legitimized traditional grassroots authority structured upon clan networks and local identity.

Property rights in southern Fujian: the Jinjiang model

Since the 1970s, state-owned enterprises' share of industrial output in Jinjiang has declined sharply. In 1970 it stood at 38 percent, but by 1992 it had fallen to 2 percent. Replacing the state companies have been enterprises run by villages and joint-households or individuals. Over this same period, they have increased their share of industrial output from 36 percent in 1970, to 91 percent in 1993 (Table 5.1). In fact, state-owned enterprises in Jinjiang since the mid-1990s have been almost completely driven out of its industrial production. Equally important, official statistics indicate that rural enterprises are overwhelmingly under the ownership and administration of village governments or lower institutions (joint-household or household), with little contribution from county- or township-run enterprises.

As surprising as they are, the statistics tell only part of the story. Figures on property rights transformation in Jinjiang industry need to be interpreted with caution. It is clear that ownership of industrial assets have shifted downward in the hierarchy of government jurisdiction from county to village and household, but the actual property rights arrange-

Table 5.1 The ownership structure of industrial output in Jinjiang and Shishi, 1970–1993 (millions of yuan; % of total GVIO)

Year	GVIO (millions of yuan)	State-owned enterprises Amount	%	Township-run enterprises Amount	%	Village-run and below Amount	%
1970	45.9	17.4	38	12.2	27	16.30	36
1975	60.8	17.9	29	19.8	33	23.10	38
1980	189.6	40.1	21	58.8	31	90.80	48
1985	636.1	66.4	10	91.3	14	478.43	75
1990	2,341.2	–	–	–	–	1,891.50	81
1991	3,595.6	115.8[a]	3	–	–	3,054.60	85
1992	7,064.0	134.1[a]	2	221.2	3	5,499.80	78
1993	14,270.3	–	–	96.0	1	12,996.30	91

Sources: Calculated from data in JGTZ various issues; FJN 1991, 1992, 1993, 1994.

Notes
The data for 1970–1985 are in 1980 prices, and for 1990–1993 are in 1990 prices. After 1990, some types of ownership (e.g., foreign joint ventures) are not included in any of the three categories, and thus the sum would be less than the total GVIO.
a Shishi data is unavailable and not included.

ments in different rural enterprises – namely those registered as village-run (*cunban*), joint-household (*lianhu*), or individual – cannot be divined from official statistics. That is to say, does classification as "village-run" necessarily entail cadre involvement and government intervention? If not, how are the bundles of property rights arranged? Also, "fake collectives" (*jiajiti*) and "wearing red caps" (private enterprises with collective licenses) have been reported in other regions (Liu 1992; Parris 1993; Young 1995: 96–97), suggesting that the property rights of collective or "village-run" enterprises deserve closer examination.

In 2001, Jinjiang City had jurisdiction over 15 townships and 385 villages, and a population of 1.02 million, plus 0.5 million migrant workers who flocked to work from inland provinces. Nearby Shishi City governed 7 townships and 115 villages, with 296,000 residents plus 20,000 migrant workers. The prosperity of this area can be shown by a simple figure: in 2000, of the 385 villages in Jinjiang, 107 villages reported industrial output value higher than 100 million yuan (*Fujian Qiaobao* 7/13/2001).

Fieldwork for this chapter was mainly conducted in 1995–1996 and 1999–2002 in several villages and townships in Jinjiang and Shishi, including Yangcun and Pingcun villages of Chendai township, Jinjiang City, and Hancun village of Hanjiang township, Shishi City. With a small area of 36 square kilometers, Chendai is the richest township in Jinjiang, and one of the richest in the country. In 1984, Chendai became the first township to produce an industrial output of more than 100 million yuan. The township had a population of 73,000, divided into 26 administrative villages, of which seven with a population of 22,000 were recognized by the government as belonging to the Hui (Muslim) minority. Despite carrying "Chen" in its township name, the most popular surname in Chendai is Lin, not Chen. In 2000, the Hui minority accounted for 30 percent of the township's total population, but contributed 44 percent of the industrial output in Chendai, mainly by the 935 footwear related factories (Ding 2001).[2] Chendai became known as "China's shoe town." In 2001 it reported an amazing industrial output value of 6,600 million yuan, and GDP per capita of 41,493 yuan, 40 percent higher than the Jinjiang average (Chen 2002). The small township now sees a comprehensive production chain of shoe related industries, such as leather and tannery, machinery, hardware, rubber and plastics, paints and dyes, textiles, and shoe parts.

Within Chendai, Yangcun, with nearly 8,000 native residents in an area of 4.5 square kilometers, had more than 100 footwear factories in 2001. In 1991, Yangcun became the first "100 million yuan village" (*yiyuancun*) in Fujian, and in 1994, its production value topped 230 million yuan. In that year, Chendai's industrial production value grew to 2,516 million yuan; of the 26 villages, 10 had production values above 100 million yuan.[3] Although the production output of Pingcun village reached only 84 million yuan in 1994, its per capita industrial output (41,683 yuan) exceeded even Yangcun's (36,520 yuan). The most developed village in Shishi's Hanjiang township is Hancun village, about 25 kilometers from Chendai. Its production output grew rapidly from 18 million yuan in 1991 to 236 million yuan in 1994. Overall, Yangcun, Pingcun, and Hancun are among the most advanced and industrialized villages not only in Fujian, but in all of China. As of the mid-1990s, the per capita industrial output of these three villages was five to seven times as high as the country's average, indicating that they stood among the top tier of China's countryside (Table 5.2). The main features of the property rights in these villages are summarized below.

Private ownership from the outset

How have today's flourishing enterprises in Jinjiang developed over the past three decades? The answer can be traced back to the early 1970s, when a number of Jinjiang's household factories and partnerships resumed operation in the later period of the Cultural Revolution, meeting pent-up demand for household commodities among urban residents. Before reforms were officially launched Jinjiang already had 1,141 township and village enterprises, of which 143 were registered as township-owned, and 998 as village-owned (JSZ 1994: 306). The output value of the 998 village-run enterprises amounted to 31.3 million yuan, even higher than that of state-owned enterprises (29 million yuan) (ZGC 1992: 31). However, compared with its counterparts in coastal regions, Jinjiang was still at a low level of industrialization in the pre-reform era. In 1978, industry in Jinjiang accounted for 37 percent of its total social product, much lower than Suzhou's 65 percent (calculated from data in ZGC 1992: 50 and SUSJTZ 1986: 5). Similarly, the Yangtze Delta region's industrial output outperformed Jinjiang's. In 1975, for example, Jinjiang's per capita

Table 5.2 Basic data on field sites in southern Fujian, 1994

	Population	No. of industrial enterprises	GVIO (10,000 yuan)	GVIO per capita (yuan)
Jinjiang	1,245,500	–	2,297,822	18,449
Chendai township	72,050	2,118	251,566	34,915
Yangcun village	6,298	238	23,000	36,520
Pingcun village	2,008	103	8,370	41,683
Shishi	282,018	4,908	554,991	19,679
Hanjiang township	46,931	754	111,500	23,758
Hancun village	5,264	98	23,600	44,832
Fujian province	31,268,700	–	–	7,203
All China	1,198,500,000	–	–	6,417

Sources: Information from fieldwork; calculated from data in ZTN 1995, FTN 1995.

GVIO (69 yuan) equaled only 20 percent of that in Wujiang (343 yuan) and 14 percent of that in the Shanghai suburbs (478 yuan) (calculated from SJN 1994; SUSJTZ 1986; SUTN 1989; USZ 1994).

The ownership of Jinjiang's rural enterprises was collective in name but private in nature. With few exceptions, most of these enterprises either adopted the "leaned-on" (*guakao*) strategy, namely, obtaining a false collective registration for individual or partnership business, or operated as cooperatives (*hezuo jingying*), jointly managed by the collective and peasants. It was rare for enterprises to be established by collective funds and run by government officials (see also JSZ 1994: 304). At the time, private business was still gravely prohibited, and local entrepreneurs therefore had no choice but to operate under the umbrella of the collective (i.e., township or village government).

In the early 1970s, Shishi, a harbor township of Jinjiang, experienced a revival of small factories and petty private businesses. During the Cultural Revolution, more than 30 household hardware factories were engaged in producing Chairman Mao badges. Meanwhile having a Chairman Mao badge pinned to the chest was an overwhelming fashion nationwide; Mao badges were an integral part of the cult of Mao. As such the production of Mao badges, even by private factories masquerading as collectives, was thought patriotic and deserving of special treatment from the government.[4]

In 1974, there were 918 vendors and shops in this small town, selling various articles smuggled from Hong Kong and Taiwan (ZGC 1992: 31). Most of the factories and shops were independently or jointly run by different households, which obtained business licenses by "attaching" their businesses to the collectives. The booming market activities and household factories were attacked as the "restoration of the capitalist" (*ziben zhuyi fupi*), periodically provoking crackdowns by the government in Beijing. For example, in 1971, a work team from the provincial government was sent to Shishi to clean up "underground black factories," which then tore down twelve private factories and jailed five owner-proprietors. In 1975, Chen Yonggui, then the Vice-Premier, inspected Fujian and criticized the market activities of Shishi as showing "everything but a KMT flag." In 1977, in a national campaign to clean up "the restoration of capitalism," the factory production and commodity markets in Shishi experienced an unprecedented setback, when more than 150 private owner-proprietors were arrested and charged with "speculation" (*toujidaoba*) (Guo 1993: 10–70; ZGC 1992: 538–540).

After 1978, as the political climate improved, the local economy regained its momentum and the once repressed commercial activities in this small township were revived and expanded. Shishi was called "little Hong Kong," attracting many outside traders, merchants, retailers, and vendors from all over the country, who came for goods unavailable or in short supply elsewhere, including electrical appliances, pornographic material, and fancy clothes. The shops were surreptitiously run by individual households, either without any registration, or with collective licenses issued by the government.[5] In the early 1980s, a booming garment industry developed, further increasing the scale of local market transactions in Shishi.

Likewise, Chendai's Yangcun village also exhibited a strong private sector. The village had established private factories for agricultural machine repair, grain processing, straw weaving, and hardware processing in the mid-1970s, all under the guise of village-run enterprises. In fact, they were mostly individual or partnership enterprises run independently by villagers. Local cadres rarely participated or intervened in the day-to-day management of the firms. By the early 1980s, a large number of joint enterprises registered under collective licenses, and such registration became the major organizing principle for township and village enterprises in Jinjiang. In 1980, Chendai had 20 enterprise licenses but more than 190 "leaned-on" factories. From 1978 to 1983, Yangcun village registered seven enterprises with the township's Office of Enterprise, but by 1983, there were actually 80 "leaned-on" factories, in which a number of firms shared one license under the collective (ZGC 1992: 470). Most of these enterprises were, however, small in scale and hired a small number of villagers for regular and seasonal works.

In practice, the collectives (township and village governments) offered some conveniences to local enterprises. For example, Yangcun village implemented a "five uniform, six self-managed" (*wutongyi, liuzizhu*) policy, similar to the practices implemented in Wenzhou during the early reform period (see Liu 1992). The "five uniform" principle applied to uniformity in licensing, in invoices, in tax collection and administration fees, in seal-stamping administration, and in bank accounts. Since a single collective license was shared by ten or more factories, all the official documents, such as bank accounts, invoices, and stamps, were also shared. The "six self-managed" principle applied to investment and partnership, production and marketing, leadership, management, labor employment, and profit distribution. In general, the administrative fee was about 3 percent of gross income, of which 2 percent was paid to the village, and 1 percent to the township. Since the village government controlled access and use of bank accounts and invoices, it could monitor the businesses' cash flows, enabling it to assess management fees accurately. By 1990, each enterprise had received its own license, albeit a "fake collective" one, and the management fee then changed to a fixed annual remittance.

In 1984, a set of state regulations was announced for rural individual businesses employing no more than seven workers, although private enterprises employing more than seven workers were not granted legal status until 1988 after the passing of a constitutional amendment.[6] The 1984 regulations legitimized individual and private enterprises in the countryside. Nonetheless, this policy did not substantially change the collective registration of private enterprises in Jinjiang. According to the 1994 records of the Chendai township government, among the 2,118 industrial enterprises, 1,241 (59 percent) were registered as township- or village-run, 646 (31 percent) as private or individual, and 231 (11 percent) as joint ventures. In fact, the nominal category generally did not refer to any specific property rights arrangement, with the registration of enterprises as township- or village-run demonstrating conformity to older institutional arrangements. According to an enterprise manager in Chendai, when all village enterprises renewed their business licenses in 1992, despite the fact that all of the enterprises were privately run, higher-level authorities demanded that 60 percent of the enterprises be registered as collective and 40 percent as individual. "So," as the interviewed manager noted, "the township government grouped the enterprises with larger scope and assets as collective (township or village-run), and the smaller enterprises as individual or private."

Local officials and enterprise managers have no doubt that the enterprises are privately owned. In interviews, local entrepreneurs showed no hesitation in labeling their factories as privately run (*siying*) or private individual (*siren*). Only asking specific questions such as "Under which ownership type is this enterprise registered?" would reveal the nominal village-run ownership category. It was also unthinkable for the local government to claim any kind of property rights over these "collective" enterprises. Instead of propagandizing about the collective economy, the government's materials and reports like to use the term "people-run" (*minying*) enterprises to describe the booming economy of the region (e.g., Economic Bureau of Shishi City 1994: 81–85).

A good illustration of one of these people-run enterprises is Lin Shuipeng's factory in Shishi's Hancun. In 1982, Lin went into partnership with his nephew to establish his firm. They bought local seaweed and transported it to Guangdong for sale. The business was operated under the umbrella of the Hanjiang Township Sea Products Collection Station, which received an annual administrative fee of 2 percent of the sales income. In 1987, Lin's wife became a partner with two other housewives and started a garment factory. Three years later, the partnership broke up and Lin started a children's garment factory with a labor force of 20 to 30. It was licensed as a village-run enterprise.

Shareholding investment and family management

Although labeled as village- or township-run enterprises, the rural enterprises in Jinjiang were established with investments from individual residents, where collective investments and contributions from local governments were limited. Inasmuch as household savings were limited, partnerships and shareholding came into fashion in the 1970s and 1980s. The four factories in Yangcun village that were originally set up in 1976 all

136 *Southern Fujian property rights transformations*

obtained investments from and sold shares to villagers, who thus became the firms' shareholders. A firm's biggest shareholder usually served as the factory director. The shoe plant (originally a hardware-processing plant) was opened with an original investment of 20,000 yuan contributed by nineteen shareholders. On starting work at the factory, each worker also paid a deposit of 300 yuan, which was to be returned after one year of employment.

At the end of 1980, joint-household (*lianhu*) enterprises, along with township-run and village-run enterprises, became recognized as "non-private" enterprises by the county government. The central government did not officially approve new joint-household (*lianhu*) ownership forms until 1984, but the Jinjiang County government had issued a regulation mandating similar arrangements at the end of 1980. Two or more households could organize themselves and register as a joint-household enterprise. By maintaining the "cooperative" form, these enterprises avoided the danger of being tagged as "tails of capitalism." This type of enterprise subsequently mushroomed in Jinjiang. One source stated that in 1985 more than 34,600 households – 16 percent of all households in Jinjiang – were engaged in such enterprises (ZGC 1992: 390). In 1984, joint-household firms in Jinjiang accounted for 44 percent of the employment and 52 percent of the output value of total TVEs. In that year, the share of joint-household enterprises in the national TVEs sector accounted for only 10 percent of employment and 7 percent of output value. By 1992, this gap had significantly not shortened (Table 5.3).

In fact, village-run and joint-household enterprises had converged so that villagers individually or jointly invested in and managed their enterprises, periodically submitting management fees to the village. Joint-

Table 5.3 Ownership structure of rural enterprises in Jinjiang and China, 1984 and 1992 (%)

	1984		1992	
	Jinjiang	China	Jinjiang	China
Employment				
Township-run	21	36	8	25
Village-run	24	40	34	24
Joint-household	44	10	45	7
Individual	11	14	13	44
Output value				
Township-run	13	48	16	37
Village-run	25	38	38	30
Joint-household	52	7	41	6
Individual	10	7	5	27

Sources: JGTZ 1984; JSZ 1994: 307, 1434; ZXQN 1993: 143–147.

household management was intended to accumulate assets, particularly start-up capital, and to reduce risk. Over time, as assets increased, experience accumulated and differences emerged in management and distribution of profit, these joint-household enterprises tended to collapse and be replaced by individual enterprises or regrouped households. In the late 1980s, Chendai showed an annual failure rate of 20 percent of joint-household enterprises, and marginally more in the case of new start-ups. Since the early 1990s, as individual households accumulated assets, family enterprises have increasingly emerged.

A survey in 1995 reported that 76 percent of the village households in Jinjiang operated their own family businesses, of which 37 percent manufactured garments, 29 percent produced shoes, and 34 percent engaged in commerce or service.[7] About 29 percent of the sample enterprises involved partnership in investment and management, with cooperation primarily linked by kinship ties. In Yangcun village, which had 238 registered enterprises in 1994, one-third of them were run cooperatively by siblings. Equally important, often all members of the family are mobilized in the management of these enterprises. For a small scale family firm located in the household, with a labor force of less than 30, the typical division of labor was "man for outside; woman for inside." The husband would usually take charge of making deals with outside parties, seeking out raw materials and market channels, and building necessary business connections. The housewife was responsible for production processes, management on the shop floor, and accounting. A significant portion (81 percent) of village enterprises employed fewer than 30 workers and were usually located in the courtyards of the villagers' residences (Table 5.4).

Chendai Garment Company provides another model of shareholding management in Jinjiang. Originally the Yangcun Shoe and Hat Factory, the company was established in 1979 on a shareholding basis, licensed by Yangcun village. The original investment of 20,000 yuan comprised eleven local shares and another four shares from Hong Kong. The company hired eleven workers, all shareholders' relatives. In 1982, the village began to implement the household responsibility system in agricultural production. Some of the managers and workers were primarily occupied by their farm work. Subsequently, the factory's production efficiency decreased, even coming to a halt during the harvest. The factory eventually ceased operation, and all the assets were divided up among shareholders. The factory director, Lin Qiu, together with his brother, son, and son-in-law, then founded another factory. In 1984, with an investment of 60,000 yuan from the township government, which also provided the original license and appointed a cadre to help during the initial period, Lin's factory and three other village garment and leather factories combined to form a new Chendai Garment-Shoe-Hat Company, with Lin serving as "general representative" (*zong daibiao*). The company took the lead in negotiating with external parties for raw materials, in taking orders, and in handling

Table 5.4 Household enterprises in Jinjiang, 1995

	Pingcun Village		Shantou Village		Total	
	No.	%	No.	%	No.	%
Household factory						
Yes	39	78	37	74	76	76
No	11	22	13	26	24	24
n	50	–	50	–	100	–
Partnership						
Yes	15	38	7	19	22	29
No	24	62	30	81	54	71
n	39	–	37	–	76	–
Firm Size						
less than 10	14	36	22	59	36	47
11–20	7	18	5	14	12	16
21–30	10	26	4	11	14	18
more than 30	8	21	6	16	14	18
n	39	–	37	–	76	–
Product						
Garment	12	31	16	43	28	37
Shoes	22	56	0	0	22	29
Commerce and service	5	13	21	57	26	34
n	39	–	37	–	76	–

Source: Data calculated from survey, "Economic development and women's work in Jinjiang," conducted by Yu-hsia Lu, institute of Sociology, Academia Sinica, 1995.

financial matters. It also provided a business license, bank account, and seal for the subordinate factories, which operated independently and did their own accounting, while benefiting from the economies of scale provided by the amalgamation. By 1988, Lin Qiu's own factory was valued at 1,700,000 yuan. In 1990, Lin reorganized the company into the Dali Shoe Factory, with the other three factories contracted as its workshops, their original owners serving as managers and shareholders. So as to take advantage of reduced taxes for foreign investment, the new factory was registered as a foreign joint venture in the name of a relative of Lin's in Hong Kong.

The foregoing discussion of organizational features of Jinjiang's rural enterprises highlights the dynamism of partnership, shareholding, and household management. The collective registration of private enterprises, along with investment by partnership and shareholding, is one of the strategies of individual households and entrepreneurs for gaining economic advantage within state-determined constraints. Individual households and entrepreneurs have earned substantial profits and, more important, have secured significant property rights over their enterprise assets, despite different ownership labels (township-run, village-run, joint-household, and individual) adopted. These organizational configurations emerged as soon as reforms began, rather than evolving from preexisting collective ownership of local enterprises. There is no transfer of property rights in enterprise assets because the original owners (individuals, families, or joint-households) retain their control of and residual income from assets. In other words, there is no de facto privatization occurring in the course of Jinjiang's industrialization and development, partly because local governments had few collective enterprises available for contracting or leasing to individuals to start with.

From family businesses to enterprise groups

In the late 1990s, the extraordinary growth of Jinjiang and Shishi's local economy slowed down, paralleling the national trend. The country's per capita GDP had accelerated at an average growth of 24 percent in 1990–1995, before slowing down to 7 percent in 1995–2002. In the same period, taking Jinjiang and Shishi together, its per capita GDP had rocketed at an annual growth of 58 percent in 1990–1995, before cooling down to 11 percent in 1995–2002 (see Table 1.2). Similarly, the country's rural peasants' income increased by 18 percent annually in 1990–1995, yet slowed down to 7 percent in 1995–2001: Meanwhile rural peasant's income in Jinjiang and Shishi grew by 33 percent in 1990–1995, but only 6 percent in 1995–2001 (see Table 1.1). Despite the not-so-amazing growth rates post mid-1990s, the region's economic performance still led the national average and continued to maintain momentum. In 2002, for example, Jinjiang's agricultural output accounted for a slim 2 percent of total output. Nearly 80 percent of its labor force, plus 700,000 outside workers, were involved in industry and the service sector (*Xinghua News* 12/28/2002). Among all the cities and counties nationwide, Jinjiang's ranking in comprehensive strengths jumped ahead from 55th in 1991, to 13th in 2002. In the same year, Shishi's economy ranked 16th among the country's top 100 county-level cities.

Since the mid-1990s, continuing industrial growth in the Jinjiang region has created new local characteristics. One is the gradually expanding industrial scale from household factories toward large-scale privately owned enterprise groups that profit from exporting and nationwide markets. Despite being much smaller in scale than TVEs in southern Jiangsu, Jinjiang enterprises' scale has continued to grow through the 1990s. Its TVEs' average firm size increased from eleven employees in 1990, to thirteen in 1995, and then to eighteen in 2001 (calculated from FTN 1991, 1996, 2002).

The government's propaganda and gazette has continued to encourage large rural enterprise groups to achieve operations of scale. Like elsewhere in the country, official documents in the mid-1990s promoted "changing the institutions" (*gaizhi*), despite the fact that there was simply no collective enterprises that remained to be transformed in this region. Unlike in traditionally pro-collective regions where "changing the institutions" mainly referred to property rights rearrangements, the same label in Jinjiang first pointed to "changing the registration." In the early 2000s, Jinjiang City government announced several "opinions and steps" to "clarify" (*lishun*) enterprises' managements and their relations with governments. Among them, "taking off collective caps" (*zhaimao*) was the first step, particularly for those planning on becoming stock listed companies. As a result, 2,587 enterprises, or 79 percent of enterprises needing to be clarified, took off their collective registrations and transformed into private or shareholding companies (HDXW 11/25/2002). In addition, "changing the institution" in Jinjiang entailed business enlargement through merger and acquisition, also aiming high on turning enterprises into stock listed companies. In 2001, Jinjiang City government set up a task-force office for promoting stock-listed companies through business enlargement. At the front was the city's some 30 large enterprises with over 50 million yuan in asset. In 2001, Jinjiang's large-scale enterprises with more than 5-million-yuan annual sale income amounted to 1,334, accounting for a small 6 percent of total enterprises. Nevertheless they contributed 51 percent of Jinjiang's total industrial output value, becoming the driving force of local economy (HDXW 12/16/2002).[8] In Chendai township in 2002, 78 enterprises reported an annual production value of more than 10 million yuan, collectively accounting for 60 percent of the township's total production value (Chen 2002).

Meanwhile, profits generated from exports and international trade accelerated, particularly for large enterprises. From those embryonic years of family capital formation, this region has begun to see substantial and fully formed private corporations. Rural household processing factories learned to cope with global markets, developing into price-aggressive and technology-competitive ventures. As the local economy integrated itself with global markets, its performance leaned heavily on the health of the global economy. Quanzhou, the prefecture in which Jinjiang is located, manufactured more than 500 million pairs of shoes in 2002, one-fifth of the world's total consumption (*Xinhua News* 4/3/2003).[9] As of 2002, Chendai township has seen 21 of its local enterprises set up 45 sales offices in 25 countries; at least 432 of Chendai's enterprises put themselves accessible on the Internet from which their product information was constantly exposed to potential buyers around the world (Ding 2002). The Jinjiang government also took initiatives to extend international business opportunities for local enterprises, deploying exhibitions in the country's big cities and abroad. In March 1999, the first International Jinjiang Shoe Fair was held in Jinjiang's exhibition center, attracting thousands of buyers and agencies nationwide and abroad. In 2002, in a Shanghai-based "International Trade Fair for Sports Equipment," footwear enterprises from Quanzhou amounted to nearly 1,000 companies, close to one fourth of total participating enterprises. Also in 2002, Jinjiang's shoe enterprises have established over 200 sales agencies abroad, particularly in developing regions like Russia, Eastern Europe, the Middle East, and South Africa. In September 2002, Jinjiang government led an entrepreneur delegation visiting Hungary where both sides quickly contracted to designate a "shoe street" in the newly established Asia Center of Budapest, the largest wholesale and exhibition center in Europe. The aptly named "Jinjiang shoe street," occupying a floor area of 1,500 square meters in the Eastern European metropolis, took in dozens of Jinjiang's large shoe enterprises and further extended their retail routes into European hinterland.

Another trend in Jinjiang's post-reform development was a new wave of industrial park constructions, which began in the late 1990s. As of 2002, Fujian had seen 670 industrial parks developed in the province's 84 county-level units (county, city, and urban district), taking in more than 57,000 enterprises, among which nearly 10 percent were large enterprises with more than 10 million yuan investment. In Quanzhou prefecture, there had been 160 industrial parks, including 14 of provincial-level, developed by different levels of local governments. The firms in industrial parks amounted to 2,546 firms, contributing one fourth of all industrial output in the prefecture (QZWB 4/14/2002). In the early 2000s, more than 80 percent of newly established or expanded enterprises chose to settle in industrial parks (QZWB 12/24/2001). The provincial government announced that it would further develop 50 industrial parks, each with more than 1,000 mu (67 hectares) to attract more companies.

The whole act, could be reminiscent of the "zone fever" that swept through China in 1992–1993, where the national widespread copying of the development zone in 1992–1993 characterized an irrational and wasteful collective behavior by local governments to designate thousands of zones competing for cash inflow and foreign investments that would be granted with exemptions from regulatory constraints (Zweig 1999). That highlighted the local state's predatory strategy toward tax and resource accumulation, and thus became both cause and symptom of China's macroeconomic difficulties in 1993 (Yang 1997: 57). The zone fever was to a certain degree cooled down by the state's "soft landing" strategy in 1994–1996. Nevertheless, in the early 2000s, it appeared to be re-emerging and spreading across the country. In 2003, among the planned 2 million hectares of those some 900 state- and provincial-level development zones approved by the central government, only 14 percent went into construction and the remaining 86 percent was left unused and idle (QZWB 1/10/2003).

Whether the booming industrial parks in Fujian entail another wave of zone fever remains to be seen. Having said that, it should be noted that the development of industrial parks in Jinjiang since the late 1990s seem to carry less zone-fever symptom, and more of a sophisticated drafted regional development project which aims to reorganize land use and upgrade local infrastructure to take in more state-of-the-art advanced enterprises. As local industrial production keeps growing, demand for premises increases. In 1996, the Jinjiang government proposed to settle newly established enterprises together in development parks. Two years later the city government launched a development project to build three provincial-level industrial parks with a total planned area of 26 square kilometers, including Wuli high-tech industrial park, Jinnan export processing zone, and Anhai general industrial park. As of September 2002, 118 enterprises, including several stock listed companies, had been approved to move into the parks, bringing in a total investment of over 3,200 million yuan (QZWB 10/23/2002). At the same time, 26 township-level industrial parks were established in Jinjiang's fifteen townships, which aimed to attract more new or expanded firms.

Local social institutions: family coordination in practice

This section examines how Jinjiang's economic development and transformation relates to indigenous local institutions. The shortage of household commodities during the Cultural Revolution, caused by paralyzed state firms, provided a burgeoning market opportunity for rural factories. Yet this only explains the demand side, and cannot adequately explain what factors enabled these household and privately owned enterprises to develop and maintain healthy growth momentum. The organizational features of Jinjiang's rural economy were not mandated by state reform policies, nor were they anticipated by policy makers. Instead, the local social context and institutional environment shaped the growth of enterprises in Jinjiang.

What has propelled the development of the privately owned economy over the past two decades? What are the institutional forces underpinning these particular configurations of property rights (i.e., private; family-centered enterprises)? This study suggests that Jinjiang's economic organizations, dominated by household and partnership management and investment, are embedded in the local institutions of family and clan, with local governments playing a supportive role. Family and clan enforce norms and standards of conduct centered on kinship principles and community identity. Starved of upper government's financial support, local governments relaxed rules to encourage investment and streamlined bureaucracy to boost efficiency. Family institutions in local society and local government's laissez-faire policies characterized Jinjiang's development model. Such a local institution promotes and constrains certain features of social relations and economic activities. Although initially suppressed by the Chinese central state in the transitional process, they have survived and have borne fruits.

Lineage identity and kinship principles

For centuries, social order and community solidarity in rural China was based on lineage organization and ancestor worship. Fujian is known for its strong patrilineal kinship lineages, as seen in the prevalence of single-surname villages (Freedman 1966). However, in communist China, the lineage group was divested of its role as a corporate group benefiting members through jointly owned property (Potter 1972: 121–138; Watson 1982). Lineage organization, ancestor worship, and regional religious cults were denounced as "feudal superstition" and banned for decades. However, in the reform era, Jinjiang's indigenous kinship institutions have gradually revived and fused with local political and economic institutions. In fact, since the 1990s the lineage identity and kinship institutions have been revitalized and widely spreading to villages in southern Fujian (see also Feuchtwang and Wang 2001).

Since the late Qing dynasty, Hancun village has been divided geographically and socially into three neighborhoods, or "corners" (*jiaoluo*) – West Corner, East Corner, and Rear Corner. A number of *fang* (sub-lineage or lineage branches) occupy each "corner." In the West Corner, the major sub-lineages are four lines of the Lin surname, along with some other minority lineage groups, called *wei-cu-bian* in the local dialect (meaning "far behind the houses"). During the turmoil periods of the Great Leap Forward (1958–1960) and the Cultural Revolution (1966–1976), as elsewhere in rural China, a large number of Hanjiang's lineage halls and genealogies were destroyed. Some of them, however, were preserved. In the early 1960s, the brigade office was moved into Lin's lineage hall, preventing this ancestral shrine from being demolished. In the early 1980s, the ancestral shrine was refurbished for its original use again. One of Lin's preserved genealogies had been hidden by a sub-lineage member, then the father of the village party secretary. Since the 1980s, most of the ruined ancestral shrines in Hanjiang township have been rebuilt, and the tattered genealogies are being restored and revised, even cataloged and copied into microfiche and onto CD-ROMs.[10]

The quick revival of lineage identity and kinship principles in Hancun illustrates that, despite state suppression for three decades, these indigenous institutions are deeply rooted and were silently preserved. The kinship connections and lineage-centered social relations are most observable in social events such as weddings, the birth of children, birthday banquets, and funerals. In Hancun, these events are participated in jointly by relatives within the same sub-lineages and "corner" neighborhood. Kinship principles and lineage affiliation have resumed their former position as central to social norms and local institutions. They are now so deeply and widely practiced in the community that even young children are aware of the sub-lineage origin of each fellow villager.

Kinship networks and clan identity are particularly active and vivid in the seven Hui (Muslim) villages in Chendai. Overall, these Hui people were assimilated to southern Fujian culture as early as the Ming dynasty (1368–1644) and now no longer practice Islam or Muslim dietary restrictions or religious rituals (Zhuang 1993). But as verified by local genealogies and historical documents, they identify themselves as descendants of Muslims who arrived in Quanzhou – a Silk Road maritime port under the Yüan dynasty – in the thirteenth century. They organize their lineage affairs through a grassroots Hui Affairs Association. In fact, government recognition as a minority group offered the Hui community an advantageous position in consolidating its *lineage* identity (much more important than its *ethnic* identity) at no risk of political repercussion, and further mobilizing overseas resources through kinship connections. The Hui lineage successfully connected itself with overseas fellow lineage members in the Philippines, Indonesia, Singapore, and Taiwan. The mutual visits and communications between local and overseas lineage communities have been enthusiastically established and maintained.[11]

Overseas connections and homeward capital

Since opening its doors to outside investment in 1978, Chinese governments, from central to local, have worked hard to persuade the well-heeled among 30 million overseas Chinese to bring their money back home. The effort, along with the emotional tug to the homeland felt by many ethnic Chinese, has drawn millions of overseas compatriots with open wallets. This is particularly true for Jinjiang and Shishi that are among the major hometowns of overseas Chinese, particularly those in the Philippines, Indonesia, Malaysia, Singapore, and elsewhere in Southeast Asia. The massive emigration to Southeast Asia started under the Qing dynasty (1644–1912), and reached its peak in the 1930s and 1940s. According to a 1987 census on overseas Chinese, those who originated from Jinjiang number 944,500, of which 651,700 (70 percent) reside in the Philippines, 95,000 (10 percent) in Indonesia, 75,000 (8 percent) in Malaysia, and 45,000 (5 percent) in Singapore. Between the 1950s and the 1980s, about 270,000 people had emigrated from Jinjiang to Hong Kong. Also, more than a million Taiwanese residents are descendants of Jinjiang emigrants (JSZ 1994: 1184–1224), whose ancestors emigrated across the strait to avoid imperial meddling and unrelenting poverty in the 1700s and 1800s. According to an official survey conducted in 1990, among the population of 1.25 million in Jinjiang and Shishi, nearly 70 percent were classified as either "returned overseas Chinese" (*guiqiao*) or "overseas Chinese dependents" (*qiaojuan*). Their fellow countrypeople from Jinjiang and Shishi residing overseas (excluding Taiwan) numbered 1.5 million (QSHZ 1996: 295, 300).[12] In this region of southern Fujian, including Xiamen and Quanzhou, overseas connections are common in people's daily lives (see also Huang 1989: 25–40; Zhuang 2001b).

Channeled through clan origin and kinship networks, overseas Chinese capital has long been a driving force for Jinjiang's local development. The inflow of overseas capital comes in three different forms: endowments for public services, remittances for families, and direct investment in the setting up of joint ventures. Overseas Chinese of modest means often bring cash and gifts for their relatives, while wealthy businessmen underwrite schools, roads, and temples in their ancestral villages. Besides, the most enthusiastic and resourceful endowment draws from overseas Chinese associations, particularly clan and community associations. Among millions of Chinese immigrants, Jinjiang's compatriots are most committed to hometown affairs and establishing locality associations. In the late 1990s, for example, among the 4,000 overseas Chinese civic associations in the world, 20 percent were classified as clan and locality associations. However, for Jinjiang emigrants in the Philippines, of 445 civic associations, 278, or 62 percent, belonged to clan or community associations, implying an extraordinary enthusiasm and support to devote their resources and build networks centered on clan and locality identities (Zhuang 2001a).

Since the 1930s, overseas endowment has been a major financial source for Jinjiang's public services (e.g., education, infirmaries, libraries, nursing homes, charity affairs, etc.) and local infrastructure (e.g., roads and bridges, tap water, electricity and street lights, etc.). The statistics in 1935, when the Nationalist government was still in power, show that the educational expenditures of Jinjiang County government amounted to 474,000 yuan, of which only 30,000 (6 percent) was derived from government allocation with the rest from overseas endowment (ZGC 1992: 382). During times of political repression, such as the Anti-Rightist Campaign (1958–1961) and the Cultural Revolution (1966–1976), interactions between local residents and relatives abroad were limited, but foreign remittances (*qiaohui*) still continued. According to a statistical record, the foreign remittances from overseas Chinese to Jinjiang from 1950 to 1980 reached a low between 1959 and 1962. However, the lowest offering in 1962 still amounted to 20.73 million yuan, around one-third of those in the previous decade and one-fourth of those in the late 1970s and early 1980s (calculated from QSHZ 1996: 176). In Fujian, Jinjiang topped other counties in foreign remittances that in turn added to people's savings and dynamized local economy.

Overseas connections and support have been a consistent and important source for household livelihood and local charity throughout most periods in communist China. Even during the national famine of 1959–1962, thanks to ceaseless support from overseas relatives and fellow villagers, Jinjiang escaped the starvation that struck other rural regions across China. Most aid from abroad was delivered in the form of such foodstuffs as rice, wheat flour, and cooking oil. The reforms' open-door policies immediately saw a resurgence and quick growth of homeward-bound financial assistance and endowment. For instance, from 1950 to the early 1990s, endowments from overseas compatriots amounted to 230 million yuan, among which 170 million yuan was used in education, building schools and setting up fellowships. An overwhelming majority, 97 percent, of today's educational institutes in Jinjiang, including 43 middle schools, 367 elementary schools, and 289 kindergartens, were originally established or partially financed by overseas donations (QSHZ 1996: 295; JSZ 1994: 1209–1215). Amid each school's campus sits a number of memorial tablets on which the benevolence of donations from overseas fellow villagers is recorded and praised. Another source records that overseas donations Jinjiang received between 1979 and 1997 amounted to more than 1 billion yuan, of which the lion's share went to education. Between 1993 and 1995, for example, of all the overseas donations, 58 percent went to education, 20 percent to cultural and sanitary facilities and 13 percent to infrastructures like roads and bridges (Editorial committee of Jinjiang municipal gazetteer 1998: 276). Until recently, overseas capital injection in endowments has constantly grown; between 1994 and 1999, Jinjiang's annual average donations in public services have all exceeded 100 million yuan. Of Jinjiang's overseas compatriots, the largest group is from the Philippines, whose contributions account for 53 percent of all overseas donations in the period between 1949 and 1995 (Zhuang 2001a).

Besides the financial support of local public services and individual households, the reforms further opened the door for overseas involvement in expanding foreign trade and foreign investment in Jinjiang, which has made the most lasting impact. Since 1978, Jinjiang enterprises have actively engaged in "processing trade" and "compensation trade" in order to obtain overseas resources and business opportunities.[13] Between 1980 and 1987, more than 60 percent of local enterprises in Jinjiang had entered into sub-processing and assembly contracts with foreign businesses (ZGC 1992: 157). Most of these business opportunities were found through kinship or local connections with overseas fellow countrymen; contracts were signed by local government on behalf of the local enterprises.[14] In addition, between 1979 and 1987, 3,325 rural factories, accounting for 60 percent of 5,418 rural enterprises in Jinjiang, were operated by local "overseas Chinese dependents" through the investments of their overseas relatives (JSZ 1994: 1219; ZGC 1992: 384).

The early to mid-1980s saw a surge of local economic activities in processing and compensation trade, marking the first period of overseas participation in the local economic boom. From 1984 on, overseas capital began to make direct investments in the local economy by establishing joint ventures (*sanzi qiye*). In the first few years, from 1984 to 1988, for example, 154 joint ventures were established, yet none of them were wholly foreign-owned enterprises (JSZ 1994: 306). Again, most of the joint investment was linked by kinship. According to a survey of foreign-invested firms in southern China, foreign investment in Quanzhou, the prefecture in which Jinjiang is located, was overwhelmingly determined by local connections and kinship (East Asia Analytical Unit 1995: 219–227; Lever-Tracy *et al.* 1996: 131–178). In 1993, the survey found, around 99 percent of foreign investors in Quanzhou were Hokkien speakers (the regional dialect), 88 percent were of local origin, and 86 percent still had relatives in the area. Investors came mainly from Taiwan and Hong Kong, who were following their local origins and kin ties in making investments and building joint ventures in the PRC. For example, most Hong Kong investors, the largest foreign venture group in this region, were not Cantonese but southern Fujianese.[15] These findings imply that the overseas Chinese found that dialect, kinship, a common origin in a clan, a village, or (if necessary) a county gave a sure footing of trust for an investment or business deal to be conducted. Hsing's study in Guangdong and Fujian also finds that the cultural affinity between the Taiwanese investors and their local Chinese agents, including local cadres and workers, contributed to a much faster and smoother process of cross-border capital flows, and consequently created a local–global coalition of economic development (Hsing 1998).

Overseas connections also benefit local enterprises by offering access to establishing joint ventures, even without any foreign investment. As with the collective registration of private enterprises, a number of local enterprises obtained the title of joint ventures through a nominal joint investment from overseas relatives. Such a title allowed the enterprises to take advantage of tax and other privileges accorded to foreign joint ventures. For example, the Chendai Garment-Shoe-Hat Company in Yangcun village changed from a township-run enterprise to a joint venture in 1990, while actually there was no foreign capital invested. Overseas relatives merely provided the necessary documents for processing registration as a foreign joint venture.

In sum, family ties and kinship principles have formed the core axes of local institutions in Jinjiang, particularly in the post-Mao era as state suppression has gradually loosened. Local family coordination is distinct from bureaucratic and market coordination. It shapes social relations while also coordinating economic activities in the community.

The role of government in local coordination

As discussed in previous chapters, the Yangtze Delta region had seen its local governments establish corporate forms of economic growth and dominated economic decision makings. But Jinjiang's local government has acted less like an arbitrary corporate authority and more like a provider of administrative services, and for a certain period, a political shelter. During the early reform period, rather than intervening in day-to-day management, local government sheltered and created a more favorable environment for privately run (household and joint-household)

148 Southern Fujian property rights transformations

businesses, which were still severely constrained by central government policies. In the mid-1990s, Shishi City's government proudly called its development strategy, "small government, big society" (*xiao zhenfu, da shehui*), which advocated less involvement by cash strapped governments and more by society. After the state policies recognized and approved individual and private businesses, political shelter was less necessary, but local government's role in providing infrastructure and social welfare became the imperative.

Local policy initiatives and central repercussions

As we have seen, in this locality, household and joint-household factories began to emerge as early as the mid-1970s, reflecting market opportunities due to demand in household commodities among urban residents. Since then, local governments deliberately ignored the central government's regulations and tacitly recognized non-farm activities and businesses. The shift of local bureaucracy's policies and attitudes partially was the result of a government reshuffle in the later Cultural Revolution when the native "gray camp" beat northern "red camp." The gray camp, also called "old district faction" (*lao qu pai*), was led by native-born cadres who had joined the local Communist Party or guerrillas before 1949. The red camp, led by cadres who were veterans of Mao's Red Army in north China before taking key positions in the new communist local authority in 1949. In the following years the red camp cadres closely followed Mao's commands in a series of political campaigns, from the Great Leap Forward, the Socialist Education Campaign, to the Four Cleanups Campaign. It wasn't until 1970, two decades after liberation, that the posts of Jinjiang county's Communist Party secretary and mayor were occupied by Jinjiang natives. The native gray camp won the power struggle and then subtly moved away from a doctrinal hatred of capitalism toward tolerance and neglect for local market-oriented economic activities.

Before the reforms and open policies were officially launched to "legalize" household and joint-household factories with characteristics of private ownership, local governments in Jinjiang sidestepped state policy by designating these factories as township- or village-run enterprises. The township authorities in Chendai, which were said to be very much "mentally emancipated" (*sixiang jiefang*), took the initiative in the early 1970s to mobilize villagers' savings to invest in household factories (ZGC 1992: 31, 393). In nearby Shishi, whose streets were filled with vendors and shops with smuggled commodities, the township government also issued a number of temporary regulations to license small shops and tax the commerce (Guo 1993: 25–27).

Jinjiang County authorities, observing practices in Chendai and Shishi, decided to take extraordinary measures and to institutionalize local economic activities without support from the central government. In 1980, without requesting permission from above, the county's government declared specific regulations about the rural economy. The regulations allowed villagers to establish joint-stock household enterprises and partnerships, to employ wage workers, to hire sales personnel engaging in cross-county trade, and to earn dividends according to the number of shares held. The government would no longer intervened in peasants' sideline productions but instead would open local markets for their free trade (JSZ 1994: 304; Guo 1993: 41–44). At the time, the measure was unprecedented and considered drastic. Not until 1984, three years later, did the central government approve joint-stock investment and partnerships among rural households.[16] As a result, during 1980–1981, the number of joint-household enterprises in Jinjiang increased by more than 500, and the investment value increased by more than one million yuan, contributing one third of the county's production output (ZGC 1992: 393–394). Between 1981 and 1984, the central government always declared a No. 1 document about rural policies, signaling its ultimate significance. However, according to a local retired cadre, whenever there were any new measures declared, they were actually already implemented in Jinjiang. The upper-level officials surprisingly commented "you Jinjiang people lead the central government by one step in the reforms' road" (Field interview; also see He 1999).

During the early reform period, the administrative assistance and protection offered by local governments also helped local enterprises to make deals with outside parties, particularly with state enterprises and government agencies. To cope with the hostility toward private and small rural enterprises, hundreds of Jinjiang's sales agents (*gongxiao*) had been traveling on the mainland, seeking market channels for local products. They carried official introduction letters, identification cards, and official invoice books issued by local governments. This army of sales staff, under the protection of the collective's umbrella, was vital for the success of local enterprises, particularly during the period of poor transportation and limited market information. Relying on social connections (*guanxi*), banquets, gifts, and, more importantly, bribery, they successfully found buyers in the bureaucratic system as well as in the free market.

The measures of the Open Policy promulgated in the late 1970s and early 1980s, particularly the "special policies and flexible measures" authorized by the central government for the foreign economic relations of Fujian and Guangdong, also greatly benefited Jinjiang's economic development. In the late 1970s and early 1980s, the earnings of foreign trade in Jinjiang were mainly derived from processing trade and compensation trade, which were regulated and channeled by local governments. In most cases, local governments took orders and signed contracts with foreign parties on behalf of local factories, and transmitted part of the foreign remittances to the local producers.[17] Unlike their counterparts in southern Jiangsu and Shanghai where revenue came mainly from profits and taxes collected on government run enterprises, Jinjiang's local governments in the early reforms received the lion's share of revenue from foreign remittances earned from processing and compensation trade.

Case study: a crackdown on "practicing capitalism" in Jinjiang

The policy initiatives and efforts by Jinjiang's local governments to "legitimize" and support local economies were impressive and attracted attention nationwide. But it paid a price for fame. In 1985, a crackdown on "practicing capitalism" in Jinjiang was initiated from the central government in Beijing and propagated nationwide. The crackdown implied a policy fight between pro-market and pro-socialism cliques in the national leadership. Jinjiang, among a few coastal go-ahead places, was scapegoated to make a case. This event showed how local governments worked together with local enterprises in "crossing the river by feeling each stone" during China's reform courses.

In the early 1980s, a time of uncertainty and limited guidelines as to what was the best "model" or course for rural enterprises, Jinjiang's practicing capitalism had started to develop rapidly. Ironically, the vagueness of state policies gave local governments more latitude in manipulating local strategies. In this situation, the endorsement of big political figures became critical in legitimizing the development strategies. During his premiership in 1983, Zhao Ziyang was brought to Chendai for an official visit. In January and May of 1985, Wan Li, then the Chairman of the National People's Congress, and Yao Yilin, then the Vice-Premier, also visited Chendai to inspect its prosperous rural economy. The recognition Jinjiang earned from top-ranking national leaders strongly encouraged the local government and promoted an atmosphere of confidence and optimism in the local society. According to a local official,

> During that period [the early 1980s], we, Jinjiang people, had nothing but the courage and bravery to rush ahead (*gan chong*). To compete with state-owned enterprises, our sales staff used smuggled watches, record-players, and surely red envelopes (*hongbao*, red envelopes containing cash) to seize market channels. Our rural economy gained prosperity but some outside people began to feel red eyes and sour grapes, and had managed to hurt us.
>
> (Author's field interview, April 1995)

In the early 1980s, one of the most popular products manufactured by Jinjiang's rural factories was instant canned consumables of which the most popular was *yin er* (silver ear), a type of semi-transparent white fungus believed to be highly nutritious. Some enterprises labeled the products "medicine for lowering blood pressure," or "cold-relief drug." The purpose of labeling this way was to open the door to medical institutions (e.g., hospitals, infirmaries, clinics) whose clients could receive these "medicines" fully subsidized by the state's medical care system. Within months, this marketing tactic bore great fruit across the country, and consequently many more local enterprises enthusiastically joined in the same business.

On July 13, 1985, less than two months of Wan Li's visit, a crackdown on "practicing capitalism" in Jinjiang was ignited by the central government and immediately publicized nationwide. The evening news report of the Chinese Central TV Station broadcast an open letter from the Central Committee Discipline Inspection Commission of CCP, addressed to the Jinjiang Prefectural CCP Committee and the Jinjiang Administrative Office. This open letter, which the nation's newspapers reprinted the next day, condemned the Jinjiang government harshly for ignoring and permitting the production of large quantities of "counterfeit drugs" by local enterprises.

> As leading party and government organs, you, the Jinjiang Prefectural CCP Committee and the Jinjiang Administrative Office, as well as the Jinjiang Discipline Inspection Commission, have actually been ignoring such phenomena and permitting them [local enterprises] to go unchecked; you even have commended the townships and towns that have manufactured large quantities of counterfeit drugs to harm the people. You must therefore seriously examine your leadership and the heavy responsibilities for such a serious situation.
> (*Renmin Ribao*, *Fujian Ribao* 7/14/1985)

Understandably, this open letter from Beijing seriously shook the Jinjiang government and local residents. It cast a heavy shadow on the local society. In this situation, according to the rules of the game in Chinese politics, the Jinjiang model and its development strategy seemed doomed. The next day, Jinjiang county authorities announced a public reply to the open letter, stating that they had made several decisions, including sending a work team to Chendai where the manufacturing of counterfeit drugs was concentrated to make a thorough investigation. Also, the Jinjiang government announced that it would organize party members, cadres, and local residents to "study seriously the open letter and educate all cadres in observing law and discipline and upholding social ethics" (*Fujian Ribao* 7/15/1985). In the same month, articles issued by Xinhua News Agency and People's Daily newspaper continued to criticize the "vicious act" of the Jinjiang government and enterprises for mass-producing "counterfeit drugs" and, through bribery, opening market channels in the country.

According to an investigation report, among the 57 enterprises charged with producing "counterfeit drugs," 45 enterprises were located in Chendai. During 1983–1984, the output value of "counterfeit drugs" in

Chendai amounted to 20 million yuan. Another source reported that more than 200 enterprises were shut down in the aftermath of the crackdown (ZGC 1992: 395). After the clean up, eighteen local officials and enterprise managers in Chendai township, including its party secretary, mayor, and the director of Industry-Commerce Bureau, as well as local cadres in the villages, were jailed with sentences ranging from one to eight years. In addition, the party secretary of Fujian Province, Xiang Nan, lost his position and was transferred to Beijing.

Discussing the "counterfeit drug event" still remains taboo in Jinjiang, even after more than ten years. Local officials and residents implicitly interpret the event as a political penalty, instead of a legal case, in which Jinjiang was a victim of the political struggle between the reformist and conservative groups in Beijing. The dismissal of Xiang Nan, the provincial party secretary who was a disciple of the reformist leader Hu Yaobang, represented a hit from the conservative group led by Chen Yun (Wu 2000). Despite the elite's strife at the party's summit, local society had its own understanding and the way of making a living. Those jailed cadres and enterprise managers in this "counterfeit drugs" event were treated as heroes in the neighborhood and received enthusiastic receptions when they were released from jail.

The "counterfeit drugs" episode of 1985 reflects the fact that despite its limited intervention in day-to-day economic management, local government's interests are still tightly interwoven with local enterprises. Local government and local enterprises often form a coalition and coordinate their efforts to obtain resources and to bargain and negotiate with, and sometimes to conceal information from, the central state.

The mutual dependence of local governments and entrepreneurs

Since the 1990s the domestic political environment has grown more permissive, allowing local enterprises more latitude in production and market transactions. Although political protection is less necessary, the role of local government in promoting local infrastructure and public expenditure strengthened. Because local governments (particularly township and village governments) are not adequately funded by higher jurisdictions, they can play a significant role in rural development only if they have sufficient revenues. Local enterprises and related economic activities have become the principal sources of these revenues.

Table 5.5 shows that villages in Jinjiang extracted sizable revenues from village enterprises by collecting enterprise remittances and land-contracting payment. In 1994, household factories in Hancun village that employed fewer than twenty workers, and registered as village-run, paid annual management fees ranging from 100 to 500 yuan. Medium-sized and large enterprises, whether registered as joint ventures or village-run, paid significantly higher fees for land use (ranging from 2,000 to 20,000

Table 5.5 Receipts and expenditures of village governments in Jinjiang (yuan)

	Hancun village Hanjiang township, 1995	Yangcun village Chendai township, 1994
Receipts	4,036,357	3,293,336
Township allocation	38,315	–
Village enterprise remittances	16,700	1,084,450
Agricultural land contract payment	–	220,000
Village collective enterprise profit	–	102,522
Village management income	3,712,562	1,834,138
Factory land and buildings	1,126,125	–
Residential land	2,152,404	–
Other land income	434,033	–
Other revenues	268,780	52,226
Expenditure	619,225	3,563,435
Special construction project	–	1,593,777
Infrastructure	44,757	35,000
Tap water	1,717	–
Seaside dike	38,498	–
Tree planting	4,542	–
Public restroom construction	–	35,000
Village administration costs	98,385	235,000
Cadre wages	42,800	165,600
Official travel	4,080	–
Official reception and treat	51,505	–
Welfare, culture, and education	402,691	451,000
Pension payments	183,450	–
Public safety	31,483	145,000
Sanitation	44,062	130,000
Village elementary school	6,580	150,000
Family planning	36,168	12,000
Subsidies for military dependents	21,841	–
Remittances to town government	0	605,690
Others	52,584	642,968
Village assets	869,447	9,560,231
Real estate	–	6,988,220
Cash and bank deposit	–	791,824
Other	–	1,780,187
Funds from overseas donations	4,355,080	1,500,000

Source: Author's fieldwork, 1996.

yuan), based on their occupation of more land than the maximum allowed for a village household.[18] In order to satisfy an increasing land demand for private residences and factory buildings, the Hancun village administration redrew the village's land plan in 1993, converting half of its farmland to industrial and housing uses. At the same time, the village government built 150 residential and commercial units and sold them to the villagers, for a total net profit of nearly 3,500,000 yuan. With the development of the local economy and a corresponding rise in villagers' expectations, there have also been fresh demands for housing and factory land. Between 1999 and 2002, Hancun mobilized 11 million yuan to build an ocean dike reclaiming a six-hectare swampy ground. The project received a small portion of funding from the governments, a total amount of 1,420,000 yuan or 14 percent of total expenses. The village administration itself took charge in locating the rest of the funds needed by collecting fees from potential land users. By 2002 some 170 villagers' villa-style houses stood on the reclaimed land, called "New Village" in the locality. Next to the New Village the village administration set up a small industrial park in which the village would sell land rights for 25 to 50 years to companies wishing to invest. As a result, since the early 1990s the Hancun village government has used its control of village lands to act as a real estate and land-contracting company and so far has obtained a substantial fund from this source for the village coffers.[19]

In Yangcun village, the primary sources of revenue also came from enterprise remittances and asset management fees.[20] In 1992–1993, the village government raised 3,200,000 yuan by "selling" lands to the villagers for housing and factory buildings.[21] As of 1994, Yangcun village collected more than 1,000,000 yuan from enterprise management fees for license registration, land use, and public services. The village government also built and leased commercial buildings to villager-merchants, making an annual profit of more than 1,000,000 yuan.

Revenues collected in the villages are used for village infrastructure (e.g., road and bridge construction, tap water, farmland irrigation, etc.), the administration of village governments (e.g., cadres' salaries, hospitality, etc.), and social services (e.g., pensions, education, sanitation, public safety, family planning, etc.) (Table 5.5). These two rich villages spent considerable sums on infrastructure and social services. In 1994, Yangcun village spent 1,563,435 yuan to replace tap water pipelines connected to each village house. In 1992–1993, it spent 3,700,000 yuan paving a village road and building 30 public rest rooms. Between 1982 and 1992, Yangcun invested more than 5,000,000 yuan in constructing village school buildings and hiring more teachers. It is also interesting to note that part of Yangcun's income was turned over to the township[22]. In contrast, Hancun obtained financial support from the township government that also shared part of the expenditure on the infrastructure maintenance (e.g., roads, parks, and street lights). Finally, both villages hold large sums of village funds received from overseas villagers' donations for social services.[23]

This self-reliance in village affairs emphasizes the centrality of village government in supplying social services and infrastructure construction to the community, using financial resources drawn from village enterprises and related rent payments, as well as donations by overseas villagers. Village governments can profit considerably by transferring use rights over land and buildings to entrepreneurs in return for rents. Consequently, a "secondary market" in use rights and rights to income over productive assets is created (see also Walder 1994: 59).

Gaining authority through democracy: clan power in action

As the local economy prospers, the role of village government as collective property manager and provider of administrative services continues to expand. The establishment of democratic institutions at the village level in the late 1980s has since had profound effects on village politics. It changed the relationship between state and peasants, or to be specific, between the township government and the village administration. The village administration no longer served as a subordinate division to the township government. The power, authority, and legitimacy of the village leadership had no longer been granted from the township government, but resided in grassroots popular support and recognition. At the same time clan powers and kinship networks came into play a critical role in village leadership that gained its autonomy and authority through grassroots democracy.

Since the late 1990s, in many places in rural China, the village elections and self-government applied not only in villagers' committees, but also in village party branches (Li 1999; Unger 2002). This reflects another fundamental change in village politics because for past few decades, and even for the present, village party branches, instead of villagers' committees, have acted as the "core of the village leadership," and been entitled to "lead the community," the role reconfirmed in China's Organic Law of Villagers' Committees. In many places where village elections have been practiced since the 1980s, tensions arouse between village party branches and villagers' committees for both were empowered to manage public affairs in the community (Li and O'Brien 1999; Guo and Bernstein forthcoming; Li 2003; Wang 2000). While villagers' committees claimed their popular support through elections, party cadres became subject to more stringent performance monitoring and feedback from the local populace. As a result, some kind of election institutions had been introduced into the organization of the party branch to strengthen its legitimacy and authority. Therefore, the village's party secretary would also need to be equipped with a new power base derived from the legitimacy of the election process. The implication is that finally the village boss, the party secretary, may represent the villagers' interest far more than that of the party from above. Such a typical trend had also occurred in villages in this chapter in southern Fujian.

Hancun's experience illustrates how the locus of power extended from the government-appointed party secretary to civil associations and villagers' committee, and back to party branch again. To a certain extent it appeared to depend on who the person is on the leadership post, but underlying the power shift clan networks and lineage identity play a key role. No matter how the locus of power is the party secretary or villagers' committee, as it turns into the early 2000s, both seek their legitimacy from popular support of ordinary villagers, rather than party bosses from above. Democratic institutions imposed from above interweaved with grassroots kinship institutions to shape the nature and configuration of local politics.

Like millions of its counterparts in rural China, Hancun's ultimate power rests with the one-man rule of the village party secretary who occupied the same post for 18 years – from 1979 to 1997 – despite his deteriorating reputation. Villagers openly criticized his siphoning of money into his own pocket. His own house continued to get bigger and higher dwarfing everything else around.

Hancun went through a revival of pre-revolutionary lineage identity and kinship associations in the 1990s. As the appointed party secretary lost his popularity, clan leaders took the lead in organizing village affairs. For example, in 1988, a highly respected village gentry who just retired from the post of Quanzhou deputy mayor, Mr. Lin Qiang, organized a dozen educated elders committed to village cultural and lineage affairs. They collected chronological materials and records, and published a 12-volume series of the history of the village. They also founded an elder association, and took charge of several overseas-donated funds for the elders, elementary education, and farmland irrigations. Instead of giving directly to the village administration, overseas fellow compatriots channeled funds into the village's non-official elder association with the intention of preventing their donations ending up in the cadres' pockets. Also, the executive committee of the elder association deliberately consisted of prestigious representatives from each sub-lineage in the village, making its decision makings and resource distributions satisfying the common good of the community. For example, in the 1990s when a booming economy enriched many villagers, celebrations and funerals became embellished for show, giving too many treats and drinks. Villagers felt pressure and obligation to spend on big gatherings. To counter this embellishment, in 1995 Hancun's elder association announced a declaration to set up an expense ceiling for social events such as funerals, and wedding and birthday banquets. This action bore no governmental sanction from above but the association's authority and legitimacy embedded in the village's kinship networks enabled its execution. In this respect, the locus of decision making extended to a civil association.

The next change came with the popular elections of villagers' committees. Following Fujian's implementation of village elections, Hancun saw its first competitive election of a villagers' committee in 1991, which required more than one candidate for each post and any electees garnering over 50 percent of the vote in order to take office. Villagers, many of them private entrepreneurs without party affiliation, saw election to the villagers' committees as a viable way of countering the power of the party secretary. It turned out that sub-lineages in the village nominated their own people and split the vote, which left the offices of villagers' committee chairman and deputy chairman vacant. Only one candidate, Lin Wei, won the vote of confidence to get elected onto the villagers' committee of seven members. In the next election in 1994, again Wei garnered over 50 percent of the vote to get elected as deputy chairman of the villagers' committee along with one other candidate. The chairman's post, however, remained vacant and that year no one else was elected to the villagers' committee. Apparently voters with different sub-lineages each wound up voting simply for candidates from their own clans. To resolve the power vacuum and the broken village administration, the township government intervened and set up a provisional villagers' committee, filling the vacant posts by including the party branch cadres such as party village secretary, deputy party secretary, and other party branch executive members. Meanwhile, Wei, the only one who won a majority support in elections and the son of the village's widely respected clan leader, won most villagers' trust and support. In 1997, Wei was appointed as the village party secretary.

In 2000, Hancun followed a "two-vote system" for choosing the village party secretary in which all villagers voted to nominate party-member candidates for the party secretary and then the village's party members gathered to elect the party secretary. Thus, the village party secretary would have to gain support from both party members and ordinary villagers, but not from above as before.

In the post-reform era, Hancun's party branch still oversees its grassroots politics and village affairs, including big infrastructure projects involving 5 million yuan. The only element different, and the most important, is the party branch's power base is now drawn from below and no longer from above.

There has been democratically elected villagers' committees, to be sure. This innovation does not deserve as much fanfare as it has been getting because the villagers' committee director in Hancun, like elsewhere in rural China, is still subordinate to the village party secretary. An individual's competence and morality is key to his popularity for winning election. But underlying the democratic arrangements, kinship ties are also a significant factor in election campaigns. These kinship groups operate more like local voter constituencies and information networks, rather than corrupt institutions. As experienced in Hancun, large local families are the country's only institutional form of political pluralism.

Conclusions: property rights and local institutions in the villages

This analysis of economic development and local institutions in Jinjiang suggests an evolving process of change in property rights. In the course of development, the main actors in property rights arrangements – local governments, private entrepreneurs, and overseas investors – hold various rights. There has been literally no privatization in which assets previously owned by communes or brigades were transferred to individuals. Early in the reforms, local government's chief asset was bureaucratic facilitation (e.g., license registration, provision of official business documents, and transaction services, such as banking and invoicing), which enabled local enterprises to participate in direct production and market transactions. Meanwhile, foreign relatives and fellow villagers offered their financial resources, information, and technology to their families and clan members. With these facilities and resources, local entrepreneurs and households established individual or joint-household firms, with property rights to these enterprise assets under their control.

As reform proceeds and the local economy expands, the property rights arrangements in local society also change. As the local economy prospers, local government benefits from the growing revenue base. The local government can draw income by controlling access to the most valued productive asset, land, thereby improving its capacity to offer services and resources to the community. Local enterprises have participated in direct production with limited intervention from governments. They rely on the infrastructure facilities and administrative services provided by the local government.

It is worth emphasizing that property rights arrangements in Jinjiang have been rooted in a local environment in which family ties and kinship principles play the core role. This points to the importance of local history and indigenous institutions. Owing to its location on the front-line in any potential conflict with Taiwan, Jinjiang was earlier starved of central government investment and, consequently, had only a modest industrial base. Kinship principles and clan consciousness survive to this day and provide a basis for the expansion of the local economy. This family and clan coordination also constrains the operations of local government, which has enabled but not directed the development of the economy. In this sense, the "entrepreneurial familism" at the grassroots society in southern Fujian plays a critical role in its economic surge in the reforms era. It echoes the view that "Chinese familism will fuel the motor of development" once predatory and irrational policies of political authorities and other external constraints are removed (Wong 1988b). It supports the argument that the contributions of China's family system are part of the explanation for China's economic success in the reform era (Whyte 1995). The local geopolitical legacies, kinship institutions and clan loyalties have differentiated southern Fujian from other fast developing regions in rural China and help to explain its development performance, path, and transformations.

State policies and market penetration may account for some aspects of the reform process, but local institutions shape the local economy's organizational features and power structure. While the Jinjiang model is not typical of the Chinese countryside, it does illustrate how local family coordination (displayed in clan identity, community solidarity, kinship networking, etc.) provides a foundation for economic organization and property rights.

More intriguing, and more critical to China's local governance, is the effect that kinship networks and local families have on grassroots politics. The village self-governance and village elections implemented in the past decade, and its consequent arrangement in choosing party leaders, have altered the power base of village leaders from township government to villagers' popular support at the grassroots level. Cadres chosen in popular elections certainly are more responsive to their constituents, at least in southern Fujian, and as a result more independent in their decision makings.

It is reasonable to speculate that more diverse and heterogeneous variations of property rights arrangements and local politics will develop in the future. Such variations, this study has argued, result from variations in local social structure and institutions. Research documenting such variation and change will continue to provide valuable data and inform theoretical analyses of the ongoing transformation of China's society and economy.

6 Hancun village
The case study

The case study of the town of Shihshi in Fujian serves as a prime example of the distinct nature of property right development in this corner of China. An exploration of the town, and the individuals and families that make it, bring into sharp focus the role of lineages in the local economy, and how the small business model grew.

Shishi before the reforms

The city of Shishi sits on the focal point of a stout peninsula jutting off of Fujian into the Taiwan Strait. From its imperial days of bustling trade with other coastal cities and overseas Chinese communities, to its streets today overflowing with goods from around the world, Shishi has always displayed a natural tendency toward trade and commercial markets. Before the 1949 revolution, Shishi was known as the little Hong Kong, with vendors relying on overseas connections to import foreign goods and pedal them on the thriving local markets. Everything from toothpaste to milk powder and pens traded freely in those days. Over half of the goods were stamped with a "made in the USA" label.

Shishi in the socialist period

The 1949 revolution changed all this of course, or at least it tried. Between the mid-1950s and early 1970s – the period of Anti-Rightist movement and commune system – imports were banned and all goods produced had to be planned and distributed by the government. In 1953, for instance, Shishi followed the national trend of practicing the "socialist correction" (*shehui zhuyi gaizao*) over individual businesses and private commerce. This meant all industry and business was brought into the cooperative system in which products were bought and sold through the bureaucracy instead of free market mechanisms. Naturally, commercial activities disappeared for some time.

However, in Shishi, commercial activities were concealed and found a way to survive. Despite the crackdown, Shishi constantly tested the limits and sought ways to deceive authorities. In 1970, for instance, 33 companies sprung up manufacturing Mao Zedong buttons and other paraphernalia, a crackdown upon which would be seen as un-politically correct. It took advantage of the breakdown of production among the state firms during the Cultural Revolution, which had led to a shortage of household commodities and thus an increased demand. Following the button manufacturer's lead, companies making screws and bolts and other hardware began to emerge. Yet without political insurance they were easy to catch, and in 1971 twelve factories were shut down and confiscated and five proprietors jailed as capitalist roadsters.

It did little to dissuade others, for by 1974 the Shishi market, pedaling goods and commodities in short supply, again revived. "Shishi is capitalism's rebound," bellowed Vice Premier Chen Yonggui in 1975, "the only thing it lacks is a KMT flag!" The next year, a documentary, *"Tiezheng Rushan,"* (iron proof like a mountain) on this rebound of capitalism was circulated around the country, much of which picked out Shishi as model of anti-socialist values. The crackdowns intensified, and in 1977 318 stores in Shishi were caught selling products in defiance of the government system. Over 300 local salespersons were sent to "education camps" (*xuexiban*).

This all did a fine job stagnating growth in the city and its surrounding area. Due to investment by overseas Chinese, the peninsula supported modern infrastructure at one time. In the 1930s schools were built and public hospitals and clinics opened. Roads from coastal villages connected the ports to Shishi, providing healthy communication links. During the periods of crackdown, between the mid-1950s and mid-1970s, however, roads fell into disrepair, infrastructure provisions ceased, factories and shops shut down, overseas Chinese bank accounts were censored and remittances controlled, and a shortage of commodities sent prices shooting upwards.

Yet even through the hardest of times, the support of the overseas Chinese communities stood as the cornerstone of life in Shishi and its peninsula. From the days of the Qing dynasty and through the Cultural Revolution continuing on to today the overseas community has allowed Shishi's markets to bustle, its towns to flourish, and industry to grow. While much of China starved in the famine of 1959–1961 and the Cultural Revolution of 1966–1976, overseas Chinese from the Philippines and other Southeast Asian countries provided rice, oil and other necessities to the peninsula's residents. The profession of second hand clothing vendors selling pawned items from overseas Chinese and their families originated in the 1940s and further developed in the shortage period of the Cultural Revolution. At its height in communist China there were more than 200 vendors selling second hand necessities brought in by overseas Chinese. These second hand clothing vendors were the preliminary model that later developed into the cloth market in Shishi. During the Cultural

Revolution period, hundreds of "unlicensed vendors" filled up Shishi's streets. This market flourished to a peak in 1975 with more than 1,000 individual vendors doing business on Shishi's streets, selling agricultural products and products from state firms and from abroad. It stopped in 1977 with a giant crackdown in which street vendors were sent to educational camps or slapped with harsher penalties.

Shishi in the reform era

With the reform in the 1980s, overseas support came to define Shishi's economic characteristics. Visits to Fujian in the early 1980s by Premier Zhao Ziyang and Wan Li, then the Chairman of the National People's Congress, as well as other national political figures gave Shishi the green light to open up its markets, to produce goods, and for overseas Chinese to come home and help develop the motherland. At the same time, overseas Chinese provided capital injections into the local economy, giving rise to small home-based manufacturing facilities. Because of the sudden demand for clothing and the inability of the state-owned factories to meet this demand, many of the small private factories springing up in Fujian concentrated in this industry, producing clothes, shoes, and hats. Overseas funded ventures mainly undertook processing works with materials imported from abroad. In 1981, Shishi had 69 enterprises funded or established directly by overseas fellow villagers. Between 1979 and 1981, output value increased from 2.3 million yuan to 11 million yuan.

The Shishi market provided a natural outlet for these goods. Clothing manufactured in a family's living room by a handful of family members could be taken to the Shishi market and sold to buyers arriving from all over China. Although private manufacturing was still prohibited by the central government throughout the 1980s, local governments and public organs would provide the necessary titles, legitimate property rights and paperwork to certify private factories to make and sell goods. Usually government organs such as the village government or the township or city governments, acted as the owner and operator of private factories, stores, or even sales teams providing them with business licenses, bank accounts, seals, and the certifying documents required for businesses dealings and transactions necessary during the period of the planned economy. In return, these governmental, or collective organs, obtained administrative fees amounting to around 3–5 percent of the sales income from enterprises or stores which used their official titles. Such practices became very common in Zhejiang and Fujiang during the reforms, and these businesses earned the name "fake collectives" or "wearing red caps."

The overseas connection

The overseas Chinese community with links to the villages provided a tremendous capital injection in the early days. The Taiwanese businessman, Lin Weixing, is a prime example of the influence of overseas Chinese in the village. Weixin's grandfather ran a commission agency in the village's harbor in the early 1900s, buying and selling commodities like foodstuff, tea, cigarettes, and wines. His father became an import–export merchant plying between Fujian and Taiwan. In 1949, as a ten-year-old kid, Weixin was taken to Taiwan by his family, and became one of the village's 6,000 overseas fellow villagers. In 1988, he returned to Hancun village setting up a small twenty-worker garment factory and participated in village affairs with great enthusiasm. In 1993, Weixin further invested 3 million yuan to start a Sino-Taiwanese joint venture, manufacturing garments and umbrellas. Weixin has also contributed large donations for lineage affairs and public services: 90,000 yuan to renovate a village temple in 1988; 80,000 yuan contributed to edit the village annals and to revise the lineage genealogy; 300,000 yuan to establish a fellowship endowment in the village primary school; 200,000 yuan for facilities for a village library and an entertainment room for the elderly. In 1996, in the rebuilding of the Lin lineage ancestral hall, Weixin promised an

Plate 6.1 Hancun village lineage hall.

unlimited donation for the completion of the project. In the end he contributed 500,000 yuan. "This is my home. I earned lots of money. I just want to contribute to the village and the Lin's lineage. I am nobody in Taipei, but here I feel good when I walk along the village roads and everyone knows me and respects me," he said.

The micro-entrepreneur Lin Shuipeng in Hancun village

As markets opened and demand at Shishi increased, the fever to produce spread. In the surrounding villages, private individuals rushed to build full factories to make goods to peddle on the market. Hancun village is one such village. Up the coast, just seven kilometers from Shishi, Hancun is one of Shishi's 30-odd satellite villages. On a plain of five square kilometers Hancun village has 1,486 households and a population of 5,336 natives and some 4,000 outsider workers. In the 1980s, there were some 100 family factories being operated by the locals. Over the past two decades, some of the family factories grew into medium-sized enterprises; some of them moved to nearby Shishi, and some of them closed. In the early 2000s, Hancun village already had 23 medium- and large-sized enterprises – each employing more than 100 employees – and some twenty family factories. Lin Shuipeng, a peasant from Hancun village, illustrates the career path for a peasant entrepreneur in this region. With only his black mop of curly hair on his head and seaweed in his hands, Lin began a climb to success through China's economic reforms and southern Fujian's own distinctive developments.

Born into a poor peasant family in a sparsely populated Hancun village, Lin lived through the hardships of peasant life. Suffering early from malnutrition in China's more desperate times, Lin was left standing at a mere 155 centimeters. His rotting teeth and blackened face are the scars of this past – now another lifetime behind him – ones that contrast sharply with the 500,000 yuan van he now drives, and the Western suit sporting a designer label on the sleeve.

It could be called success worked hard for. When the economic reforms came and peasants were allowed more freedom and autonomy in agricultural activities, Lin was quick to act. With no capital but an understanding of markets and agriculture Lin took advantage of the lay of the land. Hancun village, located on the sea and possessed of limited farming land, has traditionally specialized in sea-related products such as seaweed, clams, oysters, and crabs. Beginning in 1982, Lin and his nephew took to harvesting and buying seaweed from local growers, and selling it down the coast to Shantou in Guangdong province. He transported the raw seaweed to processing factories in Shantou before exporting it to Hong Kong.

In the early reforms, products could not be sold across provincial boundaries and private enterprises could still not sell on the market. But the townships and villages in Shishi, wanting to encourage entrepreneurship, and the central government having somewhat backed off, took to issuing permits in the name of state agencies or collectives for private businesses. Such was the practice of Lin's seaweed business. It operated under the umbrella of the township sea products collection station, which received an annual administrative fee of 2 percent of the sales income.

Lin's success on the back of these developments encouraged his wife, Xiaoling, to begin her own business. In her mid-30s at the time, Xiaoling watched household factories mushroom in the area and realized the way to get ahead was to run a factory. In 1987, taking a chunk of the capital that Lin had accumulated from his seaweed sales, she and two other partners – both housewives in the village – each put down an initial investment of 10,000 yuan for the establishment of a children's clothing manufacturing factory.

The factory was a roaring success. It earned a net profit of around 10,000 yuan per year. In 1990, the factory's fourth year of operation, the partnership broke up, partners taking back their initial investment plus profits and went their separate ways, making new investments.

Such developments had become a typical pattern in the coastal southern Fujian area. Family factories such as the Lin's obtained a village-run license from Hancun village to which they paid a lump sum administrative fee for using its name, or red cap. In order to share initial investment costs, as well as maintain the front of a collective, partnerships were widely adopted. As the partnership-firm grew and gained in profits, it became possible for individual investors to break off and start their own individual businesses. "Coordination among friends or relatives take time and consume energy," Lin Shuipeng said. "It's much simpler and straightforward to have one's own family business involving only one's own family members."

Yet while many others failed in carrying on a profitable family factory, Lin succeeded. After the separation, Lin and his daughter Jing, joined Lin's wife at the factory. Fresh out of junior high school and only sixteen years old, Jing took strait to factory work choosing to forgo senior high school. "Studying has no use for me and gives me no practical knowledge. I'd rather help my mother in the cloth business," she said.

It had become a full family affair. Xiaoling, the natural manager stayed on the factory grounds, overseeing the workforce, which, by the early 1990s had grown to twenty workers cramped in their living room over sewing machines stitching together shirts. She managed the books and bargained fiercely over prices. Like other traditional Chinese women, Xiaoling had limited education and was subordinate to her husband, particularly in front of guests or business partners. She also took care of all family affairs. She was equipped with a good sense of market orientation and possessed a talent of management and accounting. Although Lin retained the authority to make any call about selling prices and production processes, he always listened to his wife's opinions, as if she were the puppet master.

Jing completed her mother's managerial skills with her natural inclination to design and draw patterns, which she deftly put to use in creating new clothes. Hong Kong and Taiwan's children's clothes catalogues acted as the main medium for her to learn and copy from in designing new styles.

Lin ran the markets, spending much of his time wandering around the clothes bazaars in Shishi and Guangzhou, the major distribution centers of clothes in China in the early reforms. Given the market dynamics, the clothes bazaars provide a platform for sales and information exchange, as well as a means for gaining a reputation. Producers come to market with a collection of their products and samples for buyers to choose from. Prices, quantity, and turnaround time are discussed, addresses exchanged and orders taken. The manufacturer will produce the desired goods and ship them to the buyer. Business is conducted relying on personal ties and trust, and no one demands any legal proceedings in transactions.

Lin would bring goods to nearby Shishi to sell or take a twenty-hour train southbound to Guangzhou noting new styles, demand, or searching for customers. One of his most demanding duties was to travel all over the country to collect payments. At that time, there was no legal guarantee for any market transactions and "dead" receivables were quite common, particularly during the recession period of 1994–1995. Collecting debts in person was the only way to reduce costs; the collector was forced to personally seek out the debtor despite the fact that the efforts were in many times in vain.

By the mid-1990s, Lin had grown in reputation. He had established good relationships with buyers around the country who would shout orders at each other in broken Mandarin across the phone lines, often having to repeat the thick accent for the listener. These phone transactions provided an efficient and trustworthy way to do business, with payments following through direct wire transfer. Lin also started to gain new orders from first-time buyers who, pleased with the quality or design of a shirt, would call his number printed on the label.

Given such practices, and the abundance of orders, Lin's trips around the country to the clothes bazaars could cease. By 1995, Lin's factory was bringing in an income of 100,000 yuan a month. It allowed Lin to move into downtown Shishi, spending over one million yuan to buy the top four floors of a five story building, three of which he uses for his factory, which has increased 300 percent to 60 workers. The Lins have over 2 million yuan in assets today.

Today, Lin stays at home and takes orders, sitting in front of a large screen LCD TV watching Taiwanese soap operas between calls. "Life is much more relaxed now," he says chain smoking through nicotine stained lips. "That LCD TV costs upward of 30,000 yuan," he likes to boast.

"Am I now living like a Taiwanese across the strait?" he asked.

"You are among the highest society in Taiwan," I flattered him and Lin smiled.

The work habits of the family remain the same through all this; Xiaoling manages the factory and Jing continues to produce new designs and fashions. Lin's twenty-year-old son married a capable woman in 2001 who now shares much of the management work. Lin plans to have his talented daughter marry a local young man and live together with the family so that the factory's management and division of labor will not be affected.

A "speculator entrepreneur" in Shishi

One of the most legendary garment entrepreneurs is Song Taiping. In 2002, the Ministry of Agriculture awarded Song with one of the most glorious honors in the reformed land making him a National Entrepreneur Model of rural enterprises. In politics, Song is the deputy chairman of the People's Political Consultative Conference in Shishi, and a representative to the National People's Congress of Quanzhou City, as well as Fujian People's Political Consultative Conference. He owns two profitable enterprises, Shishi Sanxie Electric Automobile Company and Aihua Underwear Company, both of which are among the top tax payers in Shishi. His

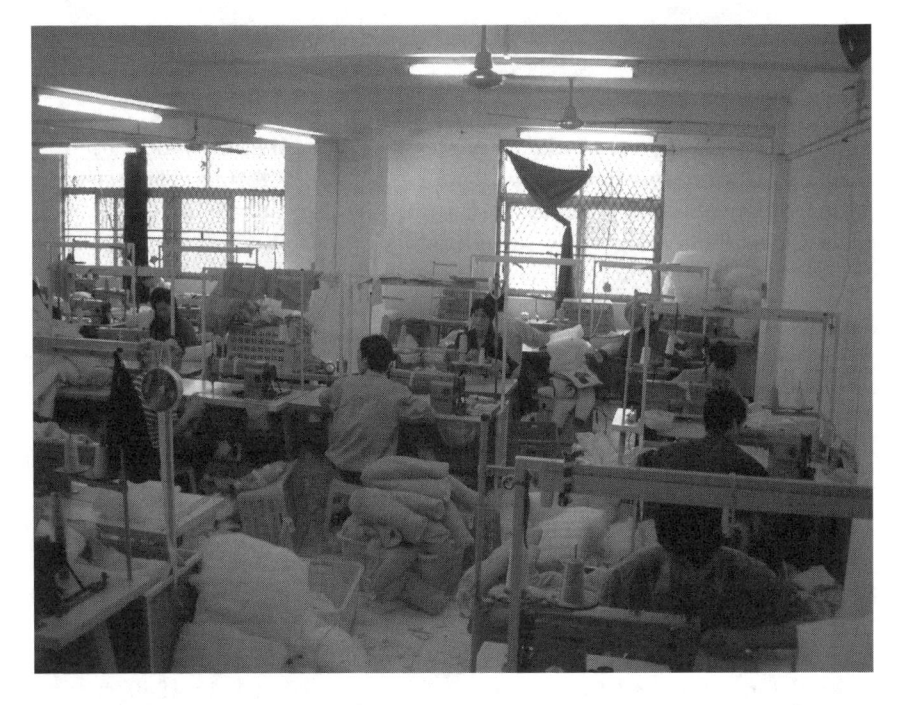

Plate 6.2 Garment factory in Shishi employing out-of-province workers.

Plate 6.3 A Hancun village entrepreneur at home with a 30,000-yuan large-screen LCD TV behind him.

automobile company manufactures electrical tractors now widely used in China's airports and harbors, and well received in foreign markets. His Aihua brassieres and pajamas have won over 300 awards in China, and played a leading design role in industry. Compared with Song's brilliant achievements today, his past is even more than a romance.

Born in 1945 into a poor working class family, Song had to earn his own living as a worker after he graduated from elementary school. He found jobs as a bee breeder and then a sales agent for a village-run agricultural machinery plant. In 1975, Song started his business career by establishing an individual hardware processing plant, mainly producing screws and iron nails. Within two years the plant started to turn over big profits, earning Song the name "Screw King" (*luosi dawang*) in the local society. In 1977, Song became one of the targets for a national rectification campaign aimed at cracking down on the emergence of capitalism in Shishi. Along with several other private proprietor-owners, he was attacked as the "tail of capitalism," charged with "speculation" and "running underground factories." He was sentenced to seven years re-education.

As the tides turned for Shishi, so did they for Song. In 1980, he was released from jail and recovered his reputation by an open visit and praise from Jinjiang's county authorities. Song decided to step into manufacturing brassieres, which were in a high demand in the re-opening Chinese society. He had much faith in the consumer-driven market mechanism, and invested a great deal of time and money into studying literature and designing attractive products. Relying on samples and product catalogues from abroad, Song designed many kinds of brassieres and started mass production with the brand name "flower lover" (*ai hua*) in 1983. The factory, initially co-invested by Song and four of his friends and relatives, started off with a workforce of 50 and a rental workshop of 100 square meters. Song claimed his invention of a new kind of brassiere that could adjust its cup size according to the body temperature. He obtained patents for it in countries around the globe. Within one year of its establishment, the marketing channels were successfully extended to Shanghai and other big cities, and production output and profits skyrocketed.

The fleet owner Lin Xiuyan

In the same way that local garment factories mushroomed in Shishi under the economic reforms, the shipping industry transformed itself from an inefficient cooperative to a privately owned and invested profit-making business. Like the story of Lin Shuipeng who seized on markets and opportunity to accumulate small amounts of capital to invest in his own business, so too did another Lin lineage villager come to embody the progress of the shipping industry.

Today, Lin Xiuyan is the principal owner of the shareholding Shishi Shipping Company and the richest man in Hancun village. He keeps at least 5 million yuan in cash on hand, part of which he uses to indulge in his gambling obsession. In 2002, his company boasted some 58 ships with a cargo capacity of 60,000 tons and over 120 million yuan in assets.

It wasn't always like this, however. Born in 1931, Xiuyan grew up as the old China fell and the new China was coming of age. His family had long been engaged in shipping and transportation which flourished in southern Fujian in Imperial and Republican China. The local economy in pre-1949 China was of shipping and fishing, which was anchored by families as the core business organization. When Xiuyan's great grandfather died in a shipwreck, his grandfather continued the trade and moved to Taiwan to open a shipping commission agency. His father then ran a cargo ship between Taiwan and Fujian throughout the 1940s. Xiuyan helped out his family by selling trinkets and other consumer products as a kid on the street. Later, along with the national campaign for forming cooperatives in the 1950s, he became an accountant for the village's shipping cooperative.

The shipping cooperative itself had just gone through the process of collectivization. In 1956, the national government ordered the establishment of producers' cooperatives. Hancun village organized the village's ships to form a shipping cooperative, involving over 100 villagers and thirteen ships with 650 tonnage shipping capacity.

Two years later Hancun village's shipping cooperative was incorporated into the state run Jinjiang County Shipping Company as part of central government policy establishing the People's Communes in which all of the peasants' production instruments, including land, tools, and animals were turned into public property. In 1958, with the new policy of "Ending Down" (*Tizhi xiafang*), the cooperative was designated as the third shipping team of the Jinjiang County Shipping Company.

Despite frequent changes of its business affiliation and bureaucratic jurisdiction, the ownership and organization of the village's shipping team had essentially retained the company's traditional characteristics. During the period of cooperatives between the 1950s and 1960s, although all property was seized by the state, making the ships legal property of the collective, the original individual owners still retained partial rights to the ship. The system allowed the original owner to collect 25 percent of the profits the ship made, although the owner could not sell the ship.

The company shipped wood, stone, and steel up and down the coast, and far up the Yangtze River. Profits would be divided in a way in which the owner of the ship received 25 percent, and the sailors and workers also taking 25 percent among themselves and dividing it according to their family size. The remaining 50 percent went back into the Jinjiang county-owned company.

With the reforms of the late 1970s and early 1980s, the shipping cooperative went through an overhaul of property rights arrangements. In accordance with the national trend, farmers in Hancun village underwent collective farming and adopted a production responsibility system. They even redistributed land and productive property among themselves. The winds of change were strong and infectious, as the partition of Hancun's brigade collective swiftly hit owners and sailors of the shipping cooperative. They blamed the cooperative system for their falling bonuses, and called for "working from reality and liberating minds." In 1984, the cooperative liquidated itself; its ships were worth 680,000 yuan, of which it owed the bank 150,000 yuan and had to pay out the owners of the previous ships. The remaining capital was split among the cooperative's 180 members. Each taking home 2,380 yuan.

But the cooperative was not finished; it just reorganized. Some 100 of the original members chose to remain and re-invest in what became the Shishi Shipping Company. They pooled their capital to buy new ships, and invited other investors to become partial owners of the ships too. In this way, the company had shares in each of the ships, though perhaps not the majority, which it shared with other investors and sailors. Each ship had its own shares and shareholders, including the company itself. Independent accounting was maintained for each boat and for the company. The company was responsible for shore activities such as finding merchandise and other linkages, as well as obtaining bank loans on behalf of the ships. Some shareholders gradually bowed out, and by the 1990s the company had three big shareholders along with about 150 small ones, of which some 100 were Hancun villagers. Xiuyan was the biggest shareholder of the company and played the dominant leadership role. Despite its private ownership, the company registered itself as a "collective" under the jurisdiction of Shishi City government.

One could say that it was Lin's love of dice and obsession to gambling that got him there. Everyday, all day, Lin sits around the table with four or five other ship owners throwing dice into a bowl in a game of Southern Chinese craps; large sums of money flow freely. Every hour he leaves the table to wander into an adjacent room filled with radio equipment to call out to his ships and monitor their positions. The constant crackle of the radio, voices calling out sea coordinates between bursts of static, is Lin's biggest pay off. While others feared the central government would bring the economic reforms to a crashing end, which might once again result in a brutal crackdown, Xiuyan felt they would last. His partners slowly got out of the business, selling off their shares to Xiuyan who borrowed capital to continue to invest. He mobilized his relatives and sub-lineage villagers to purchase shares from withdrawn shareholders, putting greater portions of the company in his control. "The trend toward free market was not at all

Plate 6.4 A ship from Lin Xuiyan's fleet.

clear in the 1980s. But still, peasants are nearsighted as chicken. They backed off when the winds changed direction. The winds did change, but then blew back again in the same direction in the end. I just had a vision that the reforms would continue, that the government would let it go on and one would prosper if he had enough guts," Xiuyan said.

In less than a decade and a half Xiuyan instilled tremendous growth in the company. In 1983, for example, it had some nine ships, employed around 100 people and made gross revenues of 460,000 yuan. In 1987, the company employed 510 sailors and staff, operated 38 ships and made gross revenues of 4,700,000 yuan. In 1998, it boasted 54 ships and made 26 million yuan. It had become the largest shipping company in Shishi, and the largest "city-owned" shipping company in Fujian.

The party secretary Lin Wei

Lin Wei is an unlikely character to serve as the village party secretary, the highest-ranking village-level official in the locality. A successful businessman with a strong sense of family, he practices everything the party scorned during the darker years. He never joined the Communist Party until the mid-1990s, and even then only at the urging and persuasion of township officials. He commonly practices the scorned habit among officials of speaking one's mind directly. In fact he has few nice words for local state officials ("Fuck their mothers, the rotten bastards!") or even for the party itself ("Shit, the CCP is more corrupt than the old KMT!"), opinions he does not keep to himself. Yet in maintaining control over the countryside here, people like Wei, born in the 1950s, and bread on the ground, have become an important characteristic of the southern Fujian countryside, not least because they are respected in their villages. As he put it years later, with over a decade of experience dealing with the party, "in the countryside you need only two things, money and a family power base."

As the reforms began, Wei went into partnership with Lin Shuipeng, his maternal uncle, pedaling their seaweed to Guangdong. In 1987, while Shuipeng joined his wife's clothes factory with the profits earned from their seaweed business, Wei took to manufacturing men's pants, counterfeiting brand names to sell on Hangzhou and Shanghai markets. By the late 1980s he was making 80,000 yuan a year in profits. "If there was a crackdown and investigations for counterfeiting practices, my lineage relative in the township government would warn me first and allow me to cover up in time," he says. In 1995, Wei partnered with his friend, pooling 1 million yuan to open a KTV in downtown Shishi. The three-story KTV attracted salesmen and merchants who would frequent it to entertain their buyers and government officials whose expenses would be reimbursed in full. Thanks to his large circle of connections, Wei's KTV was a hot business and made quick money, returning his initial investment within six months.

In addition to his own talent, Wei had the authority and prestige of his family. His father, Qiang, returned to the village in 1985 after retiring from the post of deputy mayor in Quanzhou City, and commanded the respect of a village elder. In fact, with his past experiences, and outside connections and commitment to community affairs, Qiang was the moral voice and opinion leader of the village. In this way he took up the leading role to lay down the social rules and regulations in the village. While such authority is usually designated from the top down, and more often than not from the government, the village party apparatus had lost its moral authority. Qiang and other village elders took over the village's civil affairs, loosening political control of the economy, revitalizing traditional social rituals and customs previously prohibited – such as weddings, births, birthdays and funerals.

An example of Qiang's influence in the community is illustrated by his initiative to regulate funeral rites. Funeral rites had become an extravagant spending practice that burdened every family, putting them under tremendous social pressure to spend as much or more than others. Qiang called the village elders together to settle upon guidelines for a simpler practice which would limit spending and ritual – no dinner treatments, except simple night snacks during the funeral period; funeral band size would be limited to be under ten people; no wreaths; no gambling; and no opera shows. The guidelines were posted on a village bulletin board, and came much to the relief of villagers who suddenly found themselves alleviated from social norms. In fact, these guidelines were such a success that neighboring villages also adopted them.

Qiang also played the role of fundraiser, soliciting 2 million yuan to build an ancestral temple together with a revised genealogy written in elegant calligraphy, and to be opened with a three-day festival. Overseas donation amounted to nearly 1 million, drawn from lineage members in the Philippines and Taiwan. Local contributions, including a donation of 500,000 yuan from Xiuyan, amounted to another million. "I felt I have done my duty as a village's elder leader." Qiang said upon the completion of the ancestral temple in 1998. "We don't intend to do things against the government, but we do need to keep a good record of our lineage development and connect well with our lineage members, particularly those abroad so that we feel proud of what we have done for our ancestors."

Aging but still full of life and vigor, in 1988, the 67-year-old Qiang organized the educated village elders to begin collection on the village history. They published a twelve-volume series of the history of Hancun village. Qiang held the role of moral administrator of the village, while his son Wei played the executive role in various community and lineage projects. In 1988, Lin's family brought together sub-lineage delegates and organized a series of celebrations in lieu of the anniversary of the first officially recognized crossing in history between China and Taiwan – in 1784,

100 years after the Qing government obtained Taiwan by defeating the Zheng family on the island, the imperial government chose Hancun village as the harbor in which to navigate with Taiwan's Lugang harbor. To be the first site for cross-strait traffic brought much sentiment and pride for Hancun's villagers.

Even without government funding and bureaucratic support, the festival brought villagers together in dragon boat races, puppet shows, lamp riddles, and basketball competitions, as well as huge feasts. As the general executive of the festival, Wei's popularity and reputation soared.

That same year the first village elections for officials of the villagers' committee, including villagers' committee chairman and deputy chairman took place. The Fujian provincial government had been making efforts to practice free and fair village elections, however, rules of the contest stipulated that candidates had to garner over 50 percent of the vote in order to take office. It turned out that in Hancun village, sub-lineages unofficially nominated their own people and split the vote which left the offices of villagers' committee chairman and deputy chairman vacant. Wei won the vote of confidence to get elected onto the villagers' committee of seven members.

In the next election three years later, Wei garnered over 50 percent of the vote to get elected as deputy chairman of the villagers' committee along with one other candidate. The chairman's post, however, remained vacant and that year no one else was elected to the villagers' committee. When the outcome was repeated in 1994, leaving only two deputy chairmen in charge of the people's government, the township officials told them to set up a temporary villagers' committee, filling the vacant posts by including party branch cadres – such as village party secretary, deputy party secretary, and other party branch executive members.

The party here found itself in a precarious position. The incumbent village party secretary was, in the words of local villagers, "a rotten bastard whose grandchildren would have no penis." First appointed in 1980, he had served as the party secretary for eighteen years siphoning money into his own pocket and letting local infrastructure decay. "With all political and economic power concentrated in the hands of the village party secretary, he could use his authority to channel public funds," one village cadre noted. His own house continued to get bigger and wider, dwarfing everything else around. His corruption was outrageous. When Wei took over as the village's deputy party secretary in 1996, he opened the books and discovered that the party secretary had 500,000 yuan which was unaccounted for, and for which he had to admit to "borrowing" from the village. Yet that was a trifling amount given that the village treasury had over 10 million yuan in 1991, which had mysteriously become 30,000 yuan five years later without any significant public infrastructure built.

For such reasons the party was shunned by locals and not viewed as a command center one would be willing to listen to. "Fuck your mother!"

Lin could be heard crying in 1996 when first asked to join the party, "No way. I ain't joining those bastards. I earn my money with my own hands. Damn him! Only a corrupt coward needs to make a living by becoming a party member."

Here is an interesting study of why the township authorities wanted Wei to join the party in the first place. He did not have good relations with the township officials – as his constant curses flung their way stand testimony to – and given such strong opinions, it comes as no surprise that he did not give higher local officials gifts or pay customary respect. Most villagers were not welcome into the party ranks or even treated kindly by party officials. The party secretary's contempt for the village played itself out to rotten extremes through neglect and horde tactics. However, this only isolated him, and thus the party, leaving the central government only two choices: either let the village fall apart by continuing to use someone incapable, corrupt, but obedient to the party, or find someone trusted and respected by the village who can get things done but is not necessarily obedient to party policy. In fact, in 2002, such a decision had found its way to the highest office in the land and soon came to express itself in the newest official slogans as the "Three Represents," which was supposed to mean that the Chinese Communist Party would represent three key forces in society: advanced production, advanced culture, and the interests of the majority. However, these points essentially boil down to one thing: letting businessmen join the party.

In Hancun village, the real ability of the party was strictly undermined by the people's lack of trust. In 1984–1985, for example, the village's overseas Chinese community in the Philippines donated 350,000 yuan to the village to build new school buildings, and 450,000 yuan for an academic scholarship fund. The catch however, was that they did not want to give the funds to the village administration. Fearing the notorious village party secretary would pocket it, they demanded that separate civil committees be set up to oversee spending for local infrastructure projects and welfare programs. Thus the retirement fund was controlled by a committee of elders, which included delegates from each sub-lineage. "They were not foolish enough to let the government handle any of it," said a village elder. "Everything must be in the hands of the people."

Facing a dilemma of effective governance or a paralyzed administration, the township government decided to put Lin in the position of village party secretary and needed him to become a party member. In early 1996, Lin received a notice to pay a visit to the township party secretary, who was in charge of overseeing the fulfillment of leadership positions under him, including that of the village party secretary.

Black leather sofas suspended against clean tile floors with the crass voices of cadres shouting obscenities at each other in local dialects bouncing off the empty white walls. They drank strong green tea and smoked incessantly.

"Here's an application to join the party. Fill it out," the township party secretary said pushing the form at Wei.

"Fuck your mother, I don't want to join."

It wouldn't be the last time the township authorities told him to join. Over the next several months, when the opportunity arose, at a villager's wedding, at a passing in the sun filled street, again over tea and cigarettes, the township party secretary and other officials would press Wei, and in the end, although Wei would never consent, they filled out the form for him making Lin a party member by default. It led directly to Wei becoming the village's deputy party secretary and then, a year later, to the post which holds all the power in the village: the village party secretary.

Although Wei passively accepted the appointment, he actively made the decision not to resist. It was partially a matter of face to turn it down – the party as corrupt and incompetent as it was, and Wei not sparing any scurrilous remarks in discussing it – but also a matter of prestige to accept. He would gain honor and respect as the party secretary, which would greatly elevate his status and pride. Furthermore, with both political and popular support it would put the ability to enact local policy in the village into his hands. The old party secretary was also weighing on the village. Not a day passed without curses all around about the level of corruption and the diabolic man.

Plate 6.5 Villagers' residences in Hancun's New Village area.

Plate 6.6 Ocean dike around Hancun village built by Lin Wei.

So it was that Lin became the village party secretary. Lin's greatest success in the role has been to create "New Village," a reclaimed area of 90 mu (6 hectares) that the sea had once swallowed. Lin built an ocean dike and moved a graveyard to level off the area and set up plots. In 2002, some 170 houses stood on the land. Next to New Village, Lin set up a small industrial park in which the village would sell land rights for 25–50 years to companies wishing to invest. Seven companies have built factories there including those of Taiwanese and Philippine investors.

7 Conclusion
Local institutions and the future of China

Lin Wei, the former seaweed salesman and business entrepreneur, is today a government official. He serves as the Hancun village party secretary in charge of all village affairs and bureaucratic procedures. He rides his 125cc motor scooter around the village, blue rubber flip-flops hanging over the edge, eyes squinting into the sun and wind. "Fuck your mother, I spend too much time dealing with village affairs!" he complains. "But my appointment as village party secretary has reduced internal factional rivalries in our village. The younger generations all listen to my words. Fuck your mother! Without me, the village would turn into a chaos."

Huang Wen, the former Red Army foot soldier and Shuang village party secretary, is today the owner and CEO of the color master batch factory. It is a business he built up himself under the role of government official before relinquishing his bureaucratic post to take full control of the company under the privatization scheme. The irony is that just as a popular private entrepreneur like Lin Wei was really the only one in Hancun who could become the party secretary, a former village party secretary was the only one who could become the owner and entrepreneur of the private companies in Shuang.

Local institutions, by constraining and promoting certain economic organizational features (i.e., property rights arrangements) have made such a phenomenon possible. In two prosperous yet disparately diverse regions of rural China, anomalous economic and social developments have occurred. The focus of this study has mapped the distinctive regional strategies of business and management in each region, charted the diverse paths which have led away from state socialism, examined regional differences in the network patterns of entrepreneurial activities, and explored how different local institutional configurations have promoted or impeded local authority and entrepreneurs in the pursuit of economic development.

The dramatic differences in the nature of property rights arrangements between the lower Yangtze Delta region and southern Fujian give all indication that the organizational features of rural enterprises, characterized by their distinctive configurations of property rights, cannot be reduced to the old dualisms of market/plan, public/private, or capitalism/socialism. Such a finding echoes the views of other scholarship on transitional economy in post-communist countries (e.g., Selden 1998; Lin 1995; Stark and Bruszt 1998).

The preceding chapters have provided a window into the social and economic consequences of the shift of economic activity away from the command system in communist and once-communist countries. This concluding chapter offers a summary and final reflection on the questions posed at the beginning of the study, which concern regional variations of local institutional arrangements and consequential property rights transformations and social implications in China's prosperous rural villages. This chapter emphasizes that the incorporation of local institutions, particularly the configurations of social networks and local social institutions, holds the key to understanding regional variations in the rural economy and future development of China.

Local institutions as the explanation

The empirical findings on the property rights transformation in rural economies in the Yangtze Delta region and southern Fujian provide more adequate clues to extend and modify both current theoretical perspectives and the relevant literature about China's transformation. The market transition accounts assume that the existence of well-defined private property rights is a basic precondition to the proper functioning of a market economy, and it also suggests that the Chinese reforms have been moving toward a market system coordinated by horizontal linkage and open market transaction rather than by bureaucratic vertical command. This study shows that in Shanghai suburbs and southern Jiangsu, one of China's successful coastal development models, there had been a collective period without moving toward privatization. Market transition theory does appear to offer a logical explanation for private economy in southern Fujian. However, its theoretical assumption needs to be considered with caution. The organizational configurations of private business in southern Fujian emerged as soon as reforms began, and did not evolve from collective ownership of local enterprises. There was no transfer of property rights of enterprise assets, because the original owners (individuals, families, or joint-households) retained their control and residual income of assets as soon as they set up the businesses. As privatization refers to the process of transferring property rights of enterprise assets held by the local state, there was no de facto privatization occurring in the course of the industrialization and development of local economy in this region. Literally, there was no market transition *per se* away from command system in the reform era. It was not until the late 1990s and early 2000s in the Yangtze Delta when some sort of privatization occurred in the rural economy.

Stressing the continuity of cadre power and the community corporate structure, the arguments of local state corporatism seems to be supported by the organizational features of rural enterprises in the Yangtze Delta region. The perspective of local state corporatism assumes, however, that the institutional bases of cadre power derive from and depend on the state bureaucratic system from which local cadres receive their appointment and resources. As reform proceeded, local cadres indeed further consolidated their power bases. However, such a power consolidation is based on their ability both to strengthen their leadership in accelerating local economy and to coordinate their network resources rather than on their political positions or vertical allocations within the state bureaucratic system. In this sense, market transition theory can hold its ground by arguing that the continuity of cadre power has shifted its power base onto the market institution rather than continuing its reliance on the political command system. Even the role of the local state in the local economy of southern Fujian does not necessarily contradict the assumptions of local state corporatism, for local governments, while not the principal actors, did play the roles of political shelter and administrative service provider while also interweaving their interests with the local enterprises. This study shows local public bureaucrats in state socialist societies, under certain incentive arrangements, may behave as efficiently as private entrepreneurs in a market economy. As such, property rights reform in socialist countries should not be equated with privatization; property transformation can occur without conventional privatization.

The literature on China's transformation often focuses on the consequences of changes in economic institutions. Likewise, economists are more interested in the outcomes of property rights transformation than the social conditions in which the transformation process is situated. This study suggests a different focus: it examines the social mechanisms that produce relationships between local institutions and economic transformations. After analyzing the recent transformation features of property rights relations in these two coastal regions, this study emphasizes that institutions bounded by the locality play a key role in enabling certain types of property rights arrangements to emerge and be sustained. This leads to the argument that *it is the variation of social and political institutions in each locality that dictates variations in economic organizations and property rights relations.*

In the Yangtze Delta region, an area historically rich in resources, local governments in the reform era have long been controlling sufficient resources for local expenditures and cadres have maintained tight and efficient control over local enterprises. In the early reform era local officials suppressed the private sector and established themselves as the core nodes in the local networks of economic activities. As a result, economic institutions – such as property rights relations and enterprise organizations – became embedded in local bureaucratic coordination characterized by patron–client ties and vertical social relations in the command system.

In southern Fujian, on the other hand, an area of scarce resources, cadres tried to encourage more revenue-generating activities in non-state sector, and thus cadre control of local economic affairs has been inherently weak. Consequently, the private economy thrived under the protection and support of local governments, relying on the resources mobilized through family and clan networks, often extending to overseas kinship and clan communities.

The emphasis on locality actually reflects that before the major policy shift pronounced by the Third Plenum of the Eleventh Communist Party of China's Central Committee in December 1978, much of the coastal region – including the Yangtze Delta and southern Fujian – had already initiated their own reforms in mounting enterprises and re-organizing their production institutions. The TVEs in these coastal regions came into being under the initiatives of local elites and the collusion between local cadres, entrepreneurs, villagers, and social networks extending into urban bureaucracies and firms, or foreign factories or families. The implication clearly is that, contrary to official and popular proclamation, the impetus for rural reform in the late 1970s was provided by local initiatives engineered by local cadres in the Yangtze Delta and individual entrepreneurs in southern Fujian who both sought a path to revive the economy by mobilizing local resources and social connections available to them. The reform policy that followed simply reflected the political recognition and acceptance of this local impetus.

To extend the current theoretical perspectives that highlight political institutions and market institutions respectively, this study argues that local social institutions play a vital role in explaining the regional variations of property rights arrangements in rural China. Political institutions in the localities set the contextual condition that constrains and facilitates both the arrangement and operation of social institutions, which in turn characterize the features of economic institutions. Local social institutions, represented by bureaucratic coordination in the Yangtze Delta region and the kinship coordination in southern Fujian, are found to be a major explanatory mechanism in understanding the reforms' social and economic transformation.

Social embeddedness and path dependence of economic transitions

This study draws on the idea of social embeddedness to explain economic action, its outcomes and institutions in Chinese reforms. The basic premise is that the proper analytic unit, because it is the actual economic unit, is not the isolated firm but rather the networks in a locality that link firms and connect persons. This study shifts the research and analytic focus from the attributes and motivations of individual personalities to the properties of the localities and networks in which entrepreneurial activity is embedded and reproduced. Embeddedness is used to refer to the fact that economic activity and outcomes are affected by actors' dyadic relations and by "the structure of the overall network of relations" (Granovetter 1992: 33). How do these networks of interpersonal relationships that develop within local institutionalized environments influence economic organization and economic performance? Quite a number of recent studies in Chinese transformations have focused on this issue, which also hold that social forces, social relationships and connections, and networks play a key role in shaping the political economy and market activities in China's reforms and post-reform trajectory (Keister 2002; Wank 1999, 2002; Bian 2002; Boisot and Child 1996; Lin 2002). This study of rural China suggests that embedded networks set up affinities for certain types of organizational configurations. When economic actors reproduce these affinities in order to achieve specific goals in a context of economic action, economic organizations also take on systematic transformations. As such, this conceptualization leads to the idea of "path dependence," meaning that history and institutions matter, and past institutional legacies significantly influence the path of transformation.

This study counters traditional diagnoses and prescriptions for postsocialist economies that present a dichotomous choice of reforms directed by state agencies versus reforming via market forces. It argues instead for the possibility of alternative coordinating mechanisms governed neither by hierarchy nor by markets, but by social institutions in the localities. The particular local institutions across regions that have come into being under Chinese reforms push entrepreneurs to take a route to achieve economic competitiveness different from the routes seemingly favored by the conventional wisdom of neoclassical economists. The selection of these different organizational strategies means that efficiency and effectiveness are not only relative but are also socially constructed in each organizational context. This perspective thus challenges the neoclassical economic view that assumes economic efficiency will be maximized only through the implementation of privatization and marketization.

This study also draws attention to the theoretical implications of the locality issue. Economists are likely to assume localities to be irrelevant in constructing transition strategies. Analyses of the post-socialist transformations typically center at the level of the individual firm, or focus on policies and institutions at the level of the national economy such as enterprise reform, legal frameworks, and open policies. This study, by contrast, brings localities into focus as sites of economic action. Localities are not simply compartments separating subpopulations of the same species of organization, but are social complexes in which different behavioral patterns, social rules, routines, and practices interweave and involve not only business transactions but political, community, and social activities. As the new economic sociology suggests, globalization does not displace the properties of localities but makes them all the more salient.

Some recent research in the fast-growing field of post-socialist transformations in Eastern Europe and China also focus on local initiative utilizing a network-oriented approach. Like the views stressed in this study, they also point out that a typical post-socialist economy was never as monolithic as it appeared to be. Rather, a post-socialist transformation was fueled by a vast network of personal ties, reciprocal favors, and capital-enhancing strategies that fostered networking skills and entrepreneurial spirit indispensable for post-socialist transformation (Grabher and Stark 1997; Tsai 2002). Local legacies, both economic and social in nature, inherited from the past have had created variation in local governments' attitudes toward entrepreneurs and in the ability of the local entrepreneurs to mobilize local and outside resources. An extraordinary range and elasticity in local state and entrepreneurs' activities have been reflected in the efforts by local authorities to cope with conflicts with national policies and by local entrepreneurs' innovative institutional modifications under uncertain and adverse conditions (Blecher and Shue 1996; Whiting 2001).

This study presents a picture of economic transformations characterized by the different local institutional paths of extrication from centrally planned command. It counters the view based on an economic paradigm of free-market capitalism and universal efficiency principle which tends to treat politics and society as realms separate from a transitional economy. The factors that neoclassical economics assume to be universal traits of the human condition are mostly drawn from the development experience of the modern West. Western institutions are embodiments of beliefs in individual autonomy and economic rationality; market institutions based on price mechanisms and private property rights have "worked well." This paradigm cannot be taken for granted in explaining the post-socialist transformations in East European and Chinese economies that do not share the West's institutional heritage. Therefore, in order to understand the social reality and social mechanisms in a fast changing country like China, explanations based on an attempt to apply a theory rooted in Western experience to an alien institutional arena need to be taken cautiously and tested with solid empirical evidence. A study of social institutions in the localities allows us to understand how and why locally embedded social institutions embody economic activities and facilitate and constrain certain types of economic development paths. Incorporating such local social elements in analyzing economic transformation and the global market may lead to a set of well-grounded arguments and powerful explanations in the field of China studies and economic sociology.

Local institutions in China's rural transformation

The Yangtze Delta property rights transformation

In Shanghai suburbs and southern Jiangsu, local governments played a pivotal role in initiating and developing rural enterprises throughout the reforms – some of them could be traced back to the collectivism period of the early 1970s. In the early reform period, property rights relations were relatively well-defined, where local governments operated as if they were the sole owners of township- and village-run enterprises, and, in practice, they fully controlled the variety of property rights pertaining to enterprises. That is, local governments and cadres maintained the right to use an enterprise asset, to appropriate the returns from assets, and to transfer assets to others. The privatization thrust since the mid-1990s gradually changed the collective-oriented property rights arrangements, separating village administrations and once collective enterprises. What remains unchanged, however, is the local power structure and elite networks that have long controlled the politics and resources at the grassroots level.

In the two decades between the 1980s and the 1990s, the party secretary and local cadres in the Yangtze Delta region moved to shore up all the key components of enterprise property rights. They endowed themselves with the right to appoint and dismiss managers, and even assume direct control if necessary; to control and distribute residual income earned from the assets; and to dispose of assets as they saw fit. More importantly, the political apparatus (the party branch and the village government) and economic organizations (the firms or the village corporations) were merged under the popular arrangement of village corporations and "collective unified management" (*jiti tongyi jingying*). The local cadres took on dual roles as "players and referees" concurrently, establishing and running the collective enterprises relying on their political authority and bureaucratic resources, and entitling themselves to the use and income rights of the enterprises.

During this collective period, collective (township- and village-run) enterprise assets were non-saleable, non-transferable, and non-inheritable both for the community residents and for the executive owner (the community government). Since the early 1990s, however, the shareholding arrangement in some successful enterprises in the Yangtze Delta region made a gradual and quiet shift of property rights away from local governments into the hands of local cadres and local elites. Such tactics used in the transfer of the asset rights were not unique. In fact, quite a few rich "model" villages across the country lost their collective characteristics and underwent the same process of transformation (see Lin and Chen 1999; Lin and Ye 1998; Li and Rozelle 2000; Fong 1999; Vermeer 1999; Clegg 1998). As delineated in the case studies in this book, up to the mid-1990s, many successful collective enterprises in Shanghai suburbs and southern Jiangsu had been converted from village-collectives into shareholding enterprises. The shares of these enterprises were held mainly by three groups: the community, the enterprises, and individuals (mainly local elites, e.g., managers, workers, and local residents). Since local cadres took on the dual roles as chief executives of the village corporation and as representatives of the local government, they retained solid control over the property rights of collective enterprises, and at the same time received a disproportionate share of the profits generated from these assets.

In the privatization era of the late 1990s, the Yangtze Delta countryside fazed out its collective enterprises. On the face of it, the localities sold off their once-booming township- and village-run enterprises to the free market, and rid themselves of the role of state capitalists. The truth of the matter, however, was that the traditional local elites kept control of most of the wealth. The situation was not one of free market competition, but instead local elite networking. The transfer of property rights was designed and enacted by local cliques working for their own interests, so that the new owners of the factories and companies were actually the old bureaucrats and factory directors, or their kins. All those new entrepreneurs touted in the state's propaganda and foreign media, such as the accolade of Outstanding Peasant Entrepreneurs, were in fact the same locally hand picked cadres who ran the industries before. At the end of it, almost all the same people who were in control prior to the great privatization drive are the same people who are in control today, even if it is under the new guise of open competition and market reforms. The same cliques who benefited before, reaping profits and piling up wealth, are the same ones who continue to dominate politics and enjoy the fruits of the grassroots villages in China's post-reform era.

The demeanors of village administrations and cadres carried continuity and change in the post-reform era. The locality has moved away from a planned economy, and even if the emerging economic order is still a far cry from a conventional Western capitalist economy, the local governments in the Yangtze Delta have taken on a new role in economic affairs. From owner of the collective enterprises, privatization turned the village administrations into an "infrastructure developer" in the village economy. The local bureaucrats sell land, charge fees, and work hard to bring in more private and foreign investment. They have become a key player in infrastructure construction in the local economy. Likewise, in public affairs the village administration's role in social services and infrastructure still remains. Villagers in this region continually receive collective services in medical support, education allowance, utilities, and pension from the village administrations – a situation in sharp contrast to their counterparts in inland poor regions and also in other prosperous coastal regions like Fujian and Zhejiang.

The southern Fujian property rights transformations

In southern Fujian, conversely, the configurations of property rights and local institutions in rural economies throughout the reform and post-reform era differ dramatically from those in the Yangtze Delta. Despite the nominal registration of collective enterprises as "village-run" or "joint-household," private businesses have been the backbone of the local economy since it was revived in the early and mid-1970s. Individual household or joint-household management, as well as partnership investment, have long been the major organizational forms. Local governments have acted less like a predominant corporate authority and more like an administrative service provider, and – for a certain period in the early reforms – a political shelter. Property rights relations are clearly perceived and well-defined in local society, despite the fact that private enterprises carried collective licenses and were categorized as "public assets" in legal terms and official statistics. In practice, individual households and private entrepreneurs have secured complete property rights over their enterprise assets since the local businesses and economy recovered from the Cultural Revolution in the mid-1970s.

Likewise, power, authority, and legitimacy in Fujian came from the grassroots level, where clan powers and kinship networks play a critical role. Instead of being appointed from above, the village authorities are elected from below. In 2000, Hancun followed a "two-vote system" for choosing the village party secretary in which all villagers voted to nominate party-member candidates for the party secretary and then the village's party members gathered to elect the party secretary. Thus, the village party secretary would have to gain support from both party members and ordinary villagers, but not from above as before.

In the post-reform era, Hancun's party branch still oversees its grassroots politics and village affairs, including big infrastructure projects involving as much as five million yuan. The only element different, and the most important, is the party branch's power base now drawn from below and no longer from above.

Underlying the democratic arrangements, kinship ties are also a significant factor in election campaigns. These kinship groups operate more like local voter constituencies and information networks, rather than corrupt institutions. As experienced in Hancun, large local families are the country's only institutional form of political pluralism.

Local institutions and the future of China

Which brings us to China today. While newspapers and commentators like to talk about China as a plenary state with uniform policies, the reality is a very diverse country with different policies and practices. Although authorities in Beijing may hand down a set of rules by which local governments from the South China Sea to the northern steppe plains must carry out – whether it be privatization or village elections – when central policy filters down to the different localities it takes on different forms according to local conditions. The anteceding chapters have illustrated how the single policy of shareholding or privatization turned into disparate economic developments in different areas of China. Likewise, in the future, nothing indicates that a study of state policy without taking locality issues into account will yield an understanding of China's economic or political development.

Throughout China, from the shores of Fujian to the farthest reaches of Xinjiang, local institutions exhibit certain patterns which mold central policy to local conditions. This study has detailed the patterns of two local institutions in two diverse areas. Each of these local institutions show consistent and logical developments and progress, not only facilitating an understanding in their development through an era of economic reforms, but also allowing the ability to predict how they might develop tomorrow. Should one expect, for example, large industry to succeed in Fujian? Or for village elections in Shanghai to really be free of domination by local cliques? The unlikelihood of such developments should be considered not only in academic analysis but also in policy discussions about China's current development.

The Beijing government now faces one of the largest tests of the day in tackling development in the countryside. It will do little good for policy makers to think in macro terms and hope that development can and will spread westward. China's diverse local institutions are sure to bring unexpected, and possibly adverse, excrescence – just as they have in Fujian and Sunan. The influence and importance of local institutions must be taken into consideration.

Notes

1 Explaining property rights transformations

1 To protect the anonymity of the villages and interviewees, this study has changed the names of the villages and people mentioned in this book. Real names are used for administrative divisions above the village level (e.g., township and county) and for public figures at the national level.
2 Approximately 4 million overseas Chinese, one fifth of the total overseas Chinese population, trace their origins to southern Fujian Province.
3 During the Great Leap Forward, CBEs were called on to produce industrial goods needed by agriculture. The major guidelines in this period included "self-reliance" (communes should rely on their own resources to develop CBEs), and "three locals," i.e., CBEs should use local raw materials, process them locally, and distribute the products locally. During the Cultural Revolution decade, between the early 1960s and early 1970s, some rural enterprises were set up at the commune and brigade levels but were restricted in the "five small industries," i.e., locally operated small- and medium-scale enterprises that use intermediate technology to produce iron and steel, cement, energy (coal and hydroelectricity), chemical fertilizers, and agricultural machinery. However, grain production was emphasized at the expense of other rural activities (Mo 1987; Wong 1982).

2 The Yangtze Delta in the reform era

1 There has been an extensive literature on the Sunan model. Detailed historical background and case studies about its TVEs development in the reform era can be found in Byrd and Lin (1990); Fei (1984, 1989); Wong *et al.* (1995); Ma *et al.* (1994); Ho (1994); Kung (1999); Hook (1998); Whiting (2001); Tao (1988); Song (1994); Zhou and Zhang (1991); Wei (2000).
2 In China, different bureaucracies and government departments (for example, the statistics bureau and agricultural bureau) compiled statistics and usually report disagreeing sets of statistics.
3 The principal coordinator of this research project was Nan Lin, who collaborated with Lu Hanlong at the Shanghai Academy of Social Sciences. I participated in the design of questionnaire, joined, and supervised the survey in Shanghai suburbs during the summers of 1993 and 1994, and independently conducted several rounds of in-depth interviews in the following years in some of the survey's sampled villages.
4 The questionnaire inquired into a wide range of detailed information about the village and the village's enterprises, as well as information about property rights arrangements and the background of key personnel. In addition, the

research members wrote up village reports based on in-depth interviews, covering qualitative information on such matters as the village's economic development history, the leadership and power structure, the development of property rights arrangements, the incentive system and profit allocation and distribution, and the economic and social relations with other units.

5 In practice, these two terms "collective unified management" (*jiti tongyi jingying*) and "collective contracting management" (*jiti chengbao jingying*) were favored in Shanghai and Suzhou respectively, but indeed referred to similar ownership relations and contractual structure. Their basic tendency is to retain the involvement of the "collective" (*jiti*) in the village-run enterprises, so as to be distinguishable from individual contracting (*geren chengbao*) under which the collective has limited discretionary power over the contracted enterprises.

6 For the evolution and variations of shareholding systems in rural Chinese enterprises, see Lin and Chen (1999); Ma (1998, 1999); and Vermeer (1999).

7 The production team, changed to "villagers' small group" after 1984, was a community group organized for collective agriculture under the brigade level. It lost most of its administrative functions as a result of the abandonment of the collective system and the implementation of the household responsibility system in agriculture in the early 1980s.

8 The firm leadership of township in the highly integrated economy in southern Jiangsu was partially due to the institutional background during the period of planned redistribution system. For a long time, the resource-rich localities in southern Jiangsu were under pressure to fulfill high agricultural production targets and high government grain purchasing quotas. To ensure that these requirements were met, the county banned production teams from engaging in non-farm activities so that most labor and resources could be devoted to grain production (Luo 1990: 139).

9 The "cadre" category refers to political cadres who hold political authority, such as party branch secretaries, party branch leaders, brigade (village) head, and production team leaders. It does not include those employed as civil servants such as school teachers and clerks.

10 Many of the old rural enterprises were originally set up to serve agriculture and to be an integral part of the planned economy, without much rational economic consideration. Although many villages in this area operated small factories dating back to the 1950s or 1960s, here the survey defines the starting time of the village enterprise as it first aimed at market- and profit-oriented activities, which distinguish themselves from the production activities in the agricultural collective period.

11 Around 1962, more than 60,000 urban workers and staff were sent down from Shanghai, Beijing, and Anhui to the countryside of Jiangsu. Again, during the "period of difficult national economy" (1961–1965), more than 1,530,000 city residents in Jiangsu were sent down to the countryside. The late 1960s saw another wave of massive intra-provincial migration by sent-down youth and urban workers, totaling nearly one million people in Jiangsu (Du 1987: 146–151).

12 Before the establishment of the Area, it was Chuansha county of suburban Shanghai. The Pudong New Area had been developed on partly-reclaimed land across the Huangpu River (the Yangtze's final tributary on which the port is built) from the main city area, and bigger than the country's four old Special Economic Zones (in Fujian and Guangdong) put together.

190 *Notes*

3 The Yangtze Delta in the post-reform era

1 1990 constant price, calculated from (SUTN 1995: 199, 1997: 134)
2 In his speech at the 15th Communist Party Congress on September 12, 1997, President Jiang Zemin enlarged the definition of "public ownership" to encompass the mushrooming collective and "mixed" collective-private sectors of the economy. Calling the non-public sector "an important component part of China's socialist market economy," Jiang argued that this sector should have its "legitimate rights and interests protected by law." Jiang also proclaimed "we shall also quicken the pace in relaxing control over small state-owned enterprises and invigorating them by way of reorganization, association, merger, leasing, contract operation, joint stock partnership or sell-off."
3 Namely, *yishou bugu* (selling over shareholding), *yigu buzu* (shareholding over renting), *yizu bubao* (renting over contracting), *yitui buliu* (withdrawing over maintaining), and *yisi bubao* (closing over protecting).
4 To name a few, Daqiuzhouang in Tianjin, Huaxi village in Jiangyin in Jiangsu, and Nanjie village in Zhengzhou in Henan were all renowned collective models and famous for their one-man rule by a charismatic village strongman. For Daqiuzhouang, see Lin (1995); Lin and Chen (1999); Lin and Ye (1998); Gilley (2001). For Huaxi village, see Li, J. (1998); For Nanjie, see Cao (2000); Deng *et al.* (1996). Also, for a typical one-man ruled village in Shandong, see Huang and Odend'hal (1998).
5 Shuang's income spread between directors and workers might be larger than its counterparts in nearby Wuxi, comparing the ratio of 4:1 and less than 3:1 in 1994 when a village survey was conducted in Wuxi (Kung 1999).
6 For a report on rising income inequality in rural China, see World Bank (1997); Rozelle (1994). For wage determination and income distribution between directors and workers in southern Jiangsu in the early reform period, see Wu, Wang and Xu (1990).
7 As of 2001, Jiangsu had 1,404 parks developed by various levels of governments in which 1,071 or 76 percent were operated by township governments. Village-run parks are not common and not officially counted (Jiangsu Provincial Government 2001).
8 For discussions on the role of village authorities in land rights, see Rozelle and Li (1998); Ho (2001); Cartier (2001).
9 Throughout the reforms, TVEs in southern Jiangsu had been specializing in capital-needed industry such as chemicals, machine building, textiles, and metallurgy with relatively high entry barriers, whereas TVEs in southern Fujian concentrated on low-value products with low entry barriers such as garments, foodstuffs, and footwear (Byrd and Zhu 1990; Chen 1999, 2001a, 2001b).
10 In the privatization of state-owned firms, there have also been reports and concerns regarding an increasing serious drainage of state property into private hands channeled through various malpractices (see You 1998: 186–189).

5 Southern Fujian under economic reforms

1 Tsai's study on China's informal finance shows that even within a single province like Fujian, which has similar macro-policy conditions, different developmental paths are still discernible. She highlights the orientation of the local government toward the private sector in explaining the private sector development and financial institutional diversity (Tsai 2002).
2 For a study on the prosperous economy and ethnic revitalization in Chendai's Hui community, see Gladney (1991: 261–292, 1995: 242–266).

3 Of the ten villages with production values exceeding 100 million yuan, five are Hui villages and the rest, including Yangcun, are Han Chinese villages.
4 It was estimated that, in 1969, over 90 percent of Chinese people wore Mao badges (Bishop 1996; see also Gao 1995: 299–301).
5 The 3rd Plenum of the Eleventh Central Committee of the CCP held in 1978 announced that products from sideline activities could be sold directly to end-users. In effect, with this change, local government gave official sanction to the return of individual entrepreneurship and of private production and commerce. The central government did not permit rural residents to transport and sell selected goods until 1984.
6 For the laws and regulations regarding individual and private enterprises in the reforms, see ZSJN (1994: 1–42); Kraus (1991: 16–24); Young (1995: 105–111).
7 The data, drawn from the survey on "Economic Development and Women's Work in Jinjiang," were kindly provided by Yu-hsia Lu, Institute of Sociology, Academia Sinica. The survey was conducted in two villages in Jinjiang in August 1995. The author was serving as a survey supervisor in the field. This research employed a systematic sampling method to select 50 households each from one village in Chendai township and one village in Jinjing township. The questionnaire was used to interview housewives regarding their family members' working conditions, family businesses (if any), share of housework, and personal background.
8 Another source reports that the output value of large-scale enterprises accounted for 32 percent of the total output. (HDXW 12/12/2002)
9 Among Quanzhou's exports, the Middle East market emerges as the major destination and contributes one third of Quanzhou's footwear exports. For example, the Iraq war in 2003 immediately cast a shadow on footwear exports in Quanzhou, causing the first decline in the spring of 2003 since 1999 (*Xinhua News* 2003).
10 The Quanzhou Maritime Museum has been collecting and compiling local genealogies in southern Fujian since the late 1980s. A research fellow confirmed that most of the genealogies were burned during various campaigns, but on the other hand quite a few were concealed and successfully preserved. Most of these recovered genealogies were maintained by old local gentry or retired cadres, whose social prestige and political position enabled them to conceal their lineage genealogies, despite some risks involved.
11 In August 1995, a lineage delegation from Taixi, a small and poor town on the west coast of Taiwan, visited its ancestral hometown for the first time since 1949. This lineage delegation, which the author joined, received such an enthusiastic reception in Chendai that a number of members burst into tears. According to one Taiwanese lineage member, "The reception was so intense and honorable that it could only happen to Lee Teng-hui [the president] in Taiwan."
12 These statistics on overseas Chinese include those living in Hong Kong and Macao, but exclude those in Taiwan.
13 In September 1979, the State Council formally promulgated the "Regulations on External Processing and Assembling and Small- and Medium-Sized Compensatory Trade." The processing and compensation trade are called *sanlai yibu* ("three comings-in and one compensation"), referring to the processing of imported materials (*lailiao jiagong*), the processing and assembling of supplied materials, parts, and components provided by overseas firms (*laiyang jiagong* and *laijian zhuangpei*), and the compensation trade (*buchang maoyi*), in which the foreign investors provide equipment, technology, and management support in return for exported output. The materials, parts, and production

equipment imported into China, and the finished goods exported, are free from duties.
14 All special trade arrangements required government approval, but a division of control over foreign trade and investment had been delegated to the local authorities, particularly in Fujian and Guangdong. Local governments sometimes took orders and subcontracted the businesses to local enterprises. In most cases, the business was first acquired by local enterprises through their social ties. Then local governments would sign the contracts with foreign parties on behalf of local enterprises and transmitted the foreign remittances to the local producers in Chinese yuan. Through their mediating role, local governments were entitled to receive a fixed amount of compensation and were able to control foreign exchange.
15 Approximately a slim 2 percent of Hong Kong's residents are Hokkien, and 90 percent are Cantonese, with their ancestral origins in Fujian's neighboring Guangdong Province.
16 In the Center No. 1 of 1984, the government openly approved new ownership forms such as joint-household enterprises (*lianhu*) and joint ownership by different administrative units (*lianyin*). It stated that governments at all levels should encourage collectives and peasants to pool their funds and jointly establish various kinds of enterprises based on voluntary participation and mutual benefit (see the Circular of the Central Committee of the CCP on agricultural work during 1984, in ZNN 1984: 2).
17 All special trade arrangements required government approval, but a division of control over foreign trade and investment had been decentralized to the local authorities.
18 The management fee could be seen as payment for use of the village label. But the underlying norm is that each firm has to contribute to the village, and the amount of the remittance is primarily determined by the firm's scale rather than its registration title. The fee is collected once or twice a year, generally as a lump-sum payment. For bureaucratic convenience, the payments from large firms were categorized as land and building fees, not management fees.
19 Basically, the terms and treatment of land contracting discriminates between villagers (including overseas villagers and relatives) and outsiders. But village cadres retain the power to make the final decision over the terms of the contract. The village can retain all the income from residential land but has to share the rent payment of industrial land with the township government. In an earlier work, Oi points out that the reforms up to the mid-1980s have transformed the primary function of village government from implementing government policies and managing agricultural production to being the general contractor of collective property (Oi 1986).
20 Yangcun combined management fee with land rent for enterprises registered as village-run. The basic terms were similar to those in Hancun, although Hancun categorized the land rent as village management income rather than enterprise remittances. The charge for a household factory was relatively low (say 500 yuan per year), but once the factory exceeded the land quota of a household, it was asked to contribute a much higher rent for land use.
21 According to law, land belongs to the state, and what the villagers purchased was actually the "use right" (*shiyonquan*). But in practice, local residents used the term "sell" for the transaction. The land purchased is allowed to be traded to other villagers, but not outsiders, at a mutually agreed price.
22 The income shared with the township mainly derives from payments of village enterprises (including 35 enterprises entitled joint venture). Since Yangcun village developed early and has a large number of enterprises, it has maintained the "custom" of sharing part of its enterprise remittance with the town-

ship. The flow of money between township and village governments should not be seen as part of the revenue-sharing system between higher levels of government. Villages are not part of the national fiscal system and do not receive any allocation from the national budget.
23 Hancun village has overseas-donated funds for the elders (1,500,000 yuan), for education (250,000 yuan), for farmland irrigation (2,500,000 yuan), and for party members (100,000 yuan). In 1993, Yangcun established an endowment of 1,500,000 yuan to subsidize the wages of school teachers.

Bibliography

Alchian, A. A. and Demsetz, H. (1972) "Production, information costs, and economic organization," *American Economic Review*, 62: 777–795.

Baker, W. (1990) "Market networks and corporate behavior," *American Journal of Sociology*, 96: 589–625.

Berger, P. and Luckmann, T. (1966) *The Social Construction of Reality*, Garden City: Doubleday.

Bian, Y. (2002) "Institutional holes and job mobility process: Guanxi mechanisms in China's emerging labor markets," in T. Gold, D. Guthrie and D. Wank (eds) *Social Connections in China: Institutions, Culture, and the Changing Nature of Guanxi*, Cambridge: Cambridge University Press, pp. 117–136.

Biggart, N. W. and Hamilton, G. G. (1990) "Explaining Asian business success: theory No. 4," *Business and Economic Review*, 5: 13–15.

Bishop, B. (1996) "Badges of chairman Mao Zedong." Online. Available HTTP: http://museums.cnd.org/CR/old/maobadge/ (accessed October 31, 2003).

Blecher, M. and Shue, V. (1996) *Tethered Deer: Government and Economy in a Chinese County*, Stanford, CA: Stanford University Press.

—— (2001) "Into leather: state-led development and the private sector in Xinji," *The China Quarterly*, 166: 368–393.

Boisot, M. and Child, J. (1996) "From fiefs to clans and network capitalism: explaining China's emerging economic order," *Administrative Science Quarterly*, 41: 600–628.

Bradach, J. L. and Eccles, R. G. (1989) "Price, authority, and trust: from ideal types to Plural forms," *Annual Review of Sociology*, 15: 97–118.

Byrd, W. A. and Gelb, A. (1990) "Why industrialize? the incentives for rural community governments," in W. A. Byrd and Q. Lin (eds) *China's Rural Industry: Structure, Development, and Reform*, Oxford: Oxford University Press, pp. 358–388.

Byrd, W. A. and Lin, Q. (eds) (1990) *China's Rural Industry: Structure, Development, and Reform*, Oxford: Oxford University Press.

—— (1990) "China's rural industry: an introduction," in W. A. Byrd and Q. Lin (eds) *China's Rural Industry: Structure, Development, and Reform*, Oxford: Oxford University Press, pp. 3–18.

Byrd, W. A. and Zhu, N. (1990) "Market interactions and industrial structure," in W. A. Byrd and Q. Lin (eds) *China's Rural Industry: Structure, Development, and Reform*, Oxford: Oxford University Press, pp. 85–111.

Caijing (Finance magazine) (2001) Sunan yuyan (Sunan fable), no. 38: 5, May issue.

Cao, J. (2000) *Huanghe bian de zhongguo: Yige xuezhe dui xiangcun shehui de guancha yu sikao* (China along the Yellow River: a scholar's observation and thinking of rural societies), Shanghai: Shanghai Wenyi, pp. 131–152.

Cartier, C. (2001) "'Zone Fever,' the arable land debate, and real estate speculation: China's evolving land use regime and its geographical contradictions," *Journal of Contemporary China*, 10(28): 445–469.

Chang, C. and Wang, Y. (1994) "The nature of the township – village enterprise," *Journal of Comparative Economics*, 19: 434–452.

Chen, C.-J. J. (1999) "Local institutions and the transformation of property rights in southern Fujian," in J. Oi and A. Walder (eds) *Property Rights and Economic Reform in China*, Stanford, CA: Stanford University Press, pp. 49–70.

—— (2001a) "Local institutions and property rights transformation: regional variations in Chinese rural reforms," in A. So, N. Lin, and D. Poston (eds) *The Chinese Triangle of Mainland-Taiwan-Hong Kong: A Comparative Institutional Analysis*, Westport CT: Greenwood Publishing Group, pp. 59–78.

—— (2001b) "Zhongguo dalu nongcun caichanquan bianqian de difang zhidu jichu: minnan yu sunan de diqu chayi" (Local institutions and the transformation of property rights in Chinese reforms: rural enterprises in southern Jiangsu and southern Fujian), *Taiwan Shehuixue* (Taiwanese Sociology), 2: 219–262.

Chen, J. (2002) "Dali kaichuang Chendai xiandaihua jianshe xinjumian" (Making efforts to create a new phase of modernization construction), the government report presented at the third plenum of the 13th People's Congress at Chendai Township, January 26.

Chen, W. X. (1998a) "The political economy of rural industrialization in China," *Modern China*, 24(1): 73–96.

—— (1998b) "Politics and paths of rural development in China: the village conglomerate in Shandong province," *Pacific Affairs*, 71(1): 25–39.

Clegg, J. (1998) "'Multi-stakeholder' cooperation in China – changing ownership and management of rural enterprises," in F. Christiansen and Z. Junzuo (eds) *Village Inc.: Chinese Rural Society in the 1990s*, Richmond, Surrey: Curzon, pp. 66–82.

Cohen, M. L. (1990) "Lineage organization in north China," *The Journal of Asian Studies*, 49: 509–534.

Deng, Y. and Xu, X. (1994) *Zhongguo nongcun jinrong de biange yu fazhan 1978–1990*, (The Transformation and Development of Chinese Rural Finance 1978–1990), Hong Kong: Oxford University Press.

Deng, Y., Miao, Z., and Cui, Z. (1996) "Nanjiecun jingyan de sikao" (A thinking on Nanjiecun's experience), *Zhanlue Yu Guanli* (Strategy and Management), no. 3, pp. 14–24.

Dengdai zhongguo de Jiangsu vol. 1 (Jiangsu in Modern China Book One) (1989), Beijing: Zhongguo shehui kexue chubanshe.

DiMaggio, P. J. and Powell, W. W. (1991a) "Introduction," in W. W. Powell and P. J. DiMaggio (eds) *The New Institutionalism in Organizational Analysis*, Chicago, IL: The University of Chicago Press, pp. 1–40.

—— (1991b) "The iron cage revisited: institutional isomorphism and collective rationality in organizational fields," in W. W. Powell and P. J. DiMaggio (eds) *The New Institutionalism in Organizational Analysis*, Chicago, IL: The University of Chicago Press, pp. 63–82.

Ding, Q. (2002) "Chendai – xiedou zhongzhen" (Chendai: an important shoe town), *Shidaichao* (Time's Current), no. 8.

Ding, X. (2001) "Zai haishang 'sichouzhilu' de qidian – jijinri Fujian Chendai Dingshi huizu" (The start point of silk road: a note on today's Ding Muslims in Chendai, Fujian), *Zhongguo Minzu Zazhi* (China Ethnicity), no. 3. Online. Available HTTP: http://www.56–china.com.cn (accessed October 31, 2003)

Dong, F. (2002) "Wenzhou moshi de jicheng yu tigao" (The inheritance and advance of the Wenzhou model), *Zhongguo Jingji shibao* (China Economic Times), January 8, 2002.

Du, W. (1987) *Zhongguo renkou: Jiangsu fence* (China's Population: Jiangsu Volume), Beijing: Zhongguo caizheng jingji chubanshe.

Durkheim, E. (1893) *The Division of Labor in Society*, trans. W. D. Halls (1984), New York: Free Press.

East Asia Analytical Unit (1995) *Overseas Chinese Business Networks in Asia*, Australia: East Asia Analytical Unit, Department of Foreign Affairs and Trade.

Economic Bureau of Shishi City (1994) *Shishi shi shehui jingji tongji nianjian 1994 (Statistical Yearbook of Social and Economic Statistics of Shishi City 1994)*, Shishi: Shishi City Government.

Economic Yearbook of Shanghai Editorial Board (1995) *Shanghai jingji nianjian 1995* (Economic Yearbook of Shanghai, pocket edition), Shanghai: Shanghai shehui kexueyuan.

Fei, H.-T. (Xiaotung) (1984) "Xiao chengzhen zai tansuo" (A further inquiry into small towns), in Jiangsu sheng xiao chengzhen yanjiu ketizu (ed.) *Xiao chengzhen da wenti* (Small Towns; Big Issues), Jiangsu: Jiangsu renmin chubanshe.

—— (1989) *Rural Development in China: Prospect and Retrospect*, Chicago, IL: University of Chicago Press.

Feuchtwang, S. and Wang, M. M. (2001) *Grassroots Charisma: Four Local Leaders in China*, London and New York: Routledge.

Fligstein, N. (1996) "The economic sociology of the transitions from socialism," *American Journal of Sociology*, 101: 1074–1081.

Fong, S.-C. (1999) "The shareholding system in a Shandong township: practice and impact," *Issues and Studies*, 35(4): 33–54.

Freedman, M. (1966) *Chinese Lineage and Society: Fukien and Kwangtung*, London: Athlone.

Fu, X. and Balasubramanyam, V. N. (2003) "Township and village enterprises in China," *Journal of Development Studies*, 39(4): 27–46.

Fujian jingji nianjian (Economic Yearbook of Fujian), various years, Fuzhou: Statistical Bureau of Fujian.

Fujian ribao (Fujian Daily) (1985) "Zhonggong zhongyang jiwei gei Jinjiang diwei Jinjiang xingshu de gongkaixing" (An open letter from the CCP central committee discipline inspection commission to the Jinjiang prefectual CCP committee and the Jinjiang administrative office), July 14.

—— (1985) "Jinjiang diwei Jinjiang xingshu gei zhonggong zhongyang jiwei de huifuxing" (A reply message to the CCP central committee discipline inspection commission by Jinjiang prefectual CCP committee and administrative office), July 15.

Fujian tongji nianjian (Statistical Yearbook of Fujian), various years, Beijing: Zhongguo tongji chubanshe.

Fujian tongji nianjian 2002 (Statistical Yearbook of Fujian 2002), Online. Available HTTP http://www.fjnj.net/fj/all119.htm (accessed October 27, 2003).

Fujian Qiaobao (Fujian Overseas Chinese News) (2001) "Fazhan tese zhuanyecun maixiang kangyu xiaokanglu – Jinjiang shi sancheng cun chanzhi chao yiyuan" (Developing characteristic specialized villages and moving toward well-to-do road: thirty percent of Jinjiang's villages achieve more than 100 million yuan in output value), July 13.

Gao, M. (ed.) (1995) *Shishi Shanggong Wenhua Yanjiu* (Research on the Commercial and Industrial Culture in Shishi), Xiamen: Xiamen daxue chubanshe.

Gilley, B. (2001) *Model Rebels: The Rise and Fall of China's Richest Village*, Berkeley, CA: University of California Press.

Gladney, D. C. (1991) *Muslim Chinese: Ethnic Nationalism in the People's Republic*, Cambridge, MA: Council on East Asian Studies, Harvard University.

—— (1995) "Economy and ethnicity: the revitalization of a Muslim minority in southeastern China," in A. G. Walder (ed.) *The Waning of the Communist State*, Berkeley and Los Angeles, CA: University of California Press, pp. 242–266.

Granovetter, M. (1985) "Economic action and social structure: the problem of embeddedness," *American Journal of Sociology*, 91: 481–510.

—— (1992) "Problems of explanation in economic sociology," in N. Norhria and R. Eccles (eds) *Networks and Organizations: Structure, Form, and Action*, Cambridge, MA: Harvard Business School Press, pp. 25–56.

—— (2002) "A theoretical agenda for economic sociology," in M. F. Guillen, R. C. Collins, P. England, and M. Meyer (eds) *The New Economic Sociology: Developments in an Emerging Field*, New York: Russell Sage Foundation, pp. 35–60.

Grabher, G. and Stark, D. (eds) (1997) *Restructuring Networks in Post-Socialism: Legacies, Linkages, and Localities*, New York: Oxford University Press.

Guillen, M. F., Collins, R. C., England, P., and Meyer, M. (eds) (2002) *The New Economic Sociology: Developments in an Emerging Field*, New York: Russell Sage Foundation.

Guo, B. (1993) *Shishi: Zhongguo minban tequ* (Shishi: A People-run Special Zone in China), Fuzhou: Fujian renmin chubanshe.

Guo, Z. L. and Bernstein, T. P. (forthcoming) "The impact of elections on the village structure of power: the relations between the village committees and the party branches," *Journal of Contemporary China*.

Hamilton, G. G. and Biggart, N. W. (1988) "Market, culture, and authority: a comparative analysis of management and organization in the Far East," *American Journal of Sociology*, 94(Suppl.): S52–S94.

He, D. (1999) "Difang zhengfou yujinjian mingying jingji de jueqi" (Local governments and the emergence of private economy in Jinjiang), *Nanyang Wenti Yanjiu* (Research on Southeast Asia), 97: 127–136.

He, R., Zhang, C., and Dai, J. (2000) "Jiangsu xuexi Zheijiang, Zhejiang zenmoban? – dui Jiangsu sheng xiangzhen qiye gaige han fazhan de kaocha" (Jiangsu learns from Zhejiang, and how will Zhejiang do? – an inspection on the development and reforms of Jiangsu's TVEs), *Zhejiang jingjibao* (*Zhejiang Economic News*), May 19.

He, S. (ed.) (1991) *Dengdai Zhongguo de Fujian* (Fujian in Modern China), Beijing: Dengdai zhongguo chubanshe.

Ho, P. (2001) "Who owns Chin's land? politics, property rights and deliberate institutional ambiguity," *China Quarterly*, 166: 394–421.

Ho, S. P. S. (1994) *Rural China in Transition: Non-Agricultural Development in Rural Jiangsu, 1978–1990*, New York: Oxford University Press.

Ho, S. P. S., Bowles, P., and Dong, X. (2003) "Letting go of the small: an analysis of the privatisation of rural enterprises in Jiangsu and Shandong," *Journal of Development Studies*, 39(4): 1–26.
Hook, B. (ed.) (1998) *Shanghai and the Yangtze Delta: A City Reborn*, Hong Kong and New York: Oxford University Press.
Hsing, Y.-T. (1998) *Making Capitalism in China: The Taiwan Connection*, New York: Oxford University Press.
Hsu, S.-C. (1999) "Two local regime types in China's rural industrialization: a comparative study of four townships in Fujian and Jiangsu," *Issues and Studies*, 35(1): 80–130.
Hu, X. and Hu, T. (2000) "Trends and patterns of foreign direct investment," in Y. M. Yeung and D. K. Y. Chu (eds) *Fujian: A Coastal Province in Transition and Transformation*, Hong Kong: Chinese University Press, pp. 211–230.
Huadong xinwen (Eastern China News of People's Daily) (2002) "Cong shuzi kan Jinjiang – laizi Fujian Jinjiang de baodao zhiwu" (Understanding Jinjiang from numbers: the fifth report from Jinjiang, Fujian), December 12.
Huang, P. C. C. (1990) *The Peasant Family and Rural Development in the Yangzi Delta 1350–1988*, Stanford, CA: Stanford University Press.
Huang, S.-M. (1989) *The Spiral Road: Change in a Chinese Village Through the Eyes of a Communist Party Leader*, Boulder, CO: Westview.
Huang, S.-M. and Odend'hal, S. (1998) "Fengjia: a village in transition," in A. G. Walder (ed.) *Zouping in Transition: the Process of Reform in Rural North China*, Cambridge, MA: Harvard University Press, pp. 86–114.
Jacobs, J. B. (1999) "Uneven development: prosperity and poverty in Jiangsu," in H. Hendrischke and F. Chongyi (eds) *The Political Economy of China's Provinces: Comparative and Competitive Advantage*, London: Routledge, pp. 113–154.
Jacobs, J. B. and Hong, L. (1994) "Shanghai and the lower Yangzi valley," in D. S. G. Goodman and G. Segal (eds) *China Deconstructs: Politics, Trade and Regionalism*, London: Routledge, pp. 224–252.
Jepperson, R. L. (1991) "Institutions, institutional effects, and institutionalism," in W. W. Powell and P. J. DiMaggio (eds) *The New Institutionalism in Organizational Analysis*, Chicago, IL: The University of Chicago Press, pp. 143–163.
Jiangsu CCP Committee and Provincial Government (1997) "Zhonggong Jiangsu shengwei Jiangsu sheng renmin zhengfu guanyu jinyibu shenhua xiangzhen qiye gaige de yijian" (An opinion of the Jiangsu CCP Committee and Provincial Government regarding further reforming township enterprises). Online. Available HTTP: http://www.syds.gov.cn/syds1/fgk/main.php# (accessed October 21, 2003).
Jiangsu Provincial Government (2001) "Xiangzhen qiye yuanqu fazhan qingkuang fenxi" (An analysis on the development of TVE park in 2001) Online. Available HTTP: http://61.155.107.237/ArticleDetailSearch.aspx?Article_ID=118 (accessed October 21, 2003).
Jiangsu sheng xiangzhen qiye tongji ziliao 1986 (Statistical material on rural enterprises, Jiangsu Province 1986) (1987) Nanjing: Jiangsu sheng xiangzhen qiye guanliju.
Jiangsu tongji nianjian (Statistical Yearbook of Jiangsu), various years, Jinjiang: Statistical Bureau of Jinjiang.
Jiangsu tongji nianjian 2002 (Statistical Yearbook of Jiangsu 2002) Online. Available HTTP: http://www.jssb.gov.cn/sjzl/sjzl.htm (accessed October 27, 2003).

Bibliography 199

Jingji ribao (Economic Daily) (2001) Sunan kan xiangqi tuotai huangu xingeju (A look at Sunan's township enterprises: a totally new situation), November 5.

Jinjiang nianjian 1996 (Jinjiang Almanac 1996) (1998) Editorial committee of Jinjiang municipal gazetteer, Beijing: Fangzhi chubanshe.

Jinjiang shi zhi (Jinjiang Annals) (1994), Shanghai: Sanlian Shudian.

Jinjiang xian guoming jingji tongji ziliao (Statistical Material on National Economy in Jinjiang County), various years, Jinjiang: Statistical Bureau of Jinjiang.

Ka, C.-M. (1993) *Taiwan dushi xiaoxing zhizaoye de chuangye jingying yu shengchan zuzhi: yi wufenpu chengyi zhizaoye wei anli de fenxi* (Market, Social Networks, and the Production Organization of Small-Scale Industry in Taiwan: The Garment Industries in Wufenpu), Taipei: Institute of Ethnology, Academia Sinica.

Keister, L. A. (2002) "Guanxi in business groups: social ties and the formation of economic relations," in T. Gold, D. Guthrie, and D. Wank (eds) *Social Connections in China: Institutions, Culture, and the Changing Nature of Guanxi*, Cambridge: Cambridge University Press, pp. 77–96.

Kornai, J. (1986) *Contradictions and Dilemmas: Studies on the Socialist Economy and Society*, Cambridge, MA: MIT Press.

—— (1992) *The Socialist System: The Political Economy of Communism*, Princeton, NJ: Princeton University Press.

Kraus, W. (1991) *Private Business in China*, London: Hurst & Company.

Kung, J. K.-S. (1999) "The evolution of property rights in village enterprises: the case of Wuxi County," in J. Oi and A. Walder (eds) *Property Rights and Economic Reform in China*, Stanford, CA: Stanford University Press, pp. 95–122.

Lever-Tracy, C., Ip, D., and Tracy, N. (1996) *The Chinese Diaspora and Mainland China: An Emerging Economic Synergy*, Houndmills, Basingstoke, Hampshire: Macmillan Press and New York: St. Martins Press.

Levi, M. (1990) "A logic of institutional change," in K. S. Cook and M. Levi (eds) *The Limits of Rationality*, Chicago, IL: The University of Chicago Press, pp. 402–418.

Li, A. (1998) "Sunan moshi de zaizao yu chanquan zhidu de chuangxin" (The rebuilding and innovation of property rights institutions of Sunan model), *Xiangzhen Qiye* (Township and village enterprise), no. 3, pp. 8–9.

Li, H. and Rozelle, S. (2000) "Saving or stripping rural industry: an analysis of privatization and efficiency in China," *Agricultural Economics*, 23: 241–252.

Li, J. (1998) *Huaxi village: Zhongguo mingcun jishi* (A record of China's famous villages), Zhengzhou: Zhongyu nongmin chubanshe. Online. Available HTTP: http://www.chinahuaxicun.com (accessed October 15, 2003).

Li, L. (1999) "The two-ballot system in Shanxi province: subjecting village party secretaries to a popular vote," *The China Journal*, 42: 103–118.

—— (2003) "The empowering effect of village elections in China," *Asian Survey*, 43(4): 648–662.

Li, L. and O'Brien, K. J. (1999) "The struggle over village elections," in M. Goldman and R. MacFarquhar (eds) *The Paradox of China's Post-Mao Reforms*, Cambridge, MA: Harvard University Press, pp. 129–144.

Lin, N. and Chen, C.-J. J. (1994) "Local initiative in institutional transformation: the nature and emergence of local market socialism in Jiangsu," paper presented at the Annual Meeting of the Association for Asian Studies, Boston, March 24–27.

—— (1999) "Local elites as officials and owners: shareholding and property rights in Daqiuzhuang," in J. Oi and A. Walder (eds) *Property Rights and Economic Reform in China*, Stanford, CA: Stanford University Press, pp. 145–170.

Lin, N. (1995) "Local market socialism: local corporatism in action in rural China," *Theory and Society*, 24: 301–360.

—— (2002) "Social forces: the powerful engine in transforming China," paper presented at the "The Political and Economic Reforms of Mainland China in A Changing Global Society" Conference, Taiwan National University, April 25–27.

Lin, N. and Ye, X. (1998) "Chinese rural enterprises in transformation: the end of the beginning," *Issues and Studies*, 34(11/12): 1–28.

Liu, Y.-L. (1992) "Reform from below: the private economy and local politics in the rural industrialization of Wenzhou," *The China Quarterly*, 130: 292–316.

—— (2001) "Qiangzhi wancheng de jingji siyouhua: Sunan Wujiang jingji xingshuai de lishi guocheng" (Privatization by force: the history of economic development in Wujian), *Taiwan Shehui Xuekan* (Taiwanese Journal of Sociology), 26: 1–54.

Long, S. (1994) "Regionalism in Fujian," in D. S. G. Goodman and G. Segal (eds) *China Deconstructs: Politics, Trade and Regionalism*, London: Routledge, pp. 202–223.

Luo, X. (1990) "Ownership and status stratification," in W. A. Byrd and L. Qingsong (eds) *China's Rural Industry: Structure, Development, and Reform*, Oxford: Oxford University Press, pp. 134–171.

Lyons, T. P. (1998a) "Fujian: challenge to the East Asian development model?," *American Asian Review*, 16(1): 35–99.

—— (1998b) "Intraprovincial disparities in China: Fujian province, 1978–1995," *Economic Geography*, 74(4): 405–432.

—— (2000) "Regional inequality," in Y. M. Yeung and D. K. Y. Chu (eds) *Fujian: A Coastal Province in Transition and Transformation*, Hong Kong: Chinese University Press, pp. 327–352.

Ma, R., Wang, H., and Liu, S. (eds) (1994), *Zhongguo Xiangchen qiye de fazhan lishi yu yuanxing jizhi* (The Development, History, and Operating Mechanism of China's Township and Village Enterprises), Beijing: Beijing University Press.

Ma, S. Y. (1998) "The Chinese route to privatization: the evolution of the shareholding system option," *Asian Survey*, 38(4): 379–397.

—— (1999) "The role of spontaneity and state initiative in China's shareholding system reform," *Communist and Post-Communist Studies*, 32: 319–337.

March, J. G. and Olsen, J. P. (1984) "The new institutionalism: organizational factors in political life," *American Political Science Review*, 78: 734–749.

Mo, Y. (1987) *Jiangsu xiangzhen gongye fazhan shi* (History of the Development of Rural Industry in Jiangsu), Nanjing: Nanjing gongxueyuan chubanshe.

Nee, V. (1989) "A theory of market transition: from redistribution to markets in state socialism," *American Sociological Review*, 54: 663–681.

—— (1991) "Social inequalities in reforming state socialism: between redistribution and markets in China," *American Sociological Review*, 56(3): 267–282.

—— (1996) "The emergence of a market society: changing mechanisms of stratification in China," *American Journal of Sociology*, 101: 908–949.

Nee, V. and Matthews, R. (1996) "Market transition and societal transformation in reforming state socialism," *Annual Review of Sociology*, 22: 401–435.

Nelson, R. and Winter, S. (1982) *An Evolutionary Theory of Economic Change*, Cambridge, MA: Harvard University Press.

Bibliography 201

Nolan, P. and Dong, F. (eds) (1990) *Market Forces in China: Competition and Small Business – The Wenzhou Debate*, London and Atlantic Highlands, N.J. New Jersey: Zed Books Ltd.

North, D. C. (1986) "The new institutional economics," *Journal of Institutional and Theoretical Economics*, 142: 230–237.

—— (1990) *Institutions, Institutional Change and Economic Performance*, New York: Cambridge University Press.

—— (1991) "A transaction cost approach to the historical development of polities and economics," in E. G. Furubotn and R. Richter, *The New Institutional Economics: A Collection of Articles from the Journal of Institutional and Theoretical Economics*, Houston, TX: Texas A&M University Press, pp. 253–260.

North, D. C. and Thomas, R. (1973) *The Rise of the Western World: A New Economic History*, New York: Cambridge University Press.

Oberschall, A. and Leifer, E. M. (1986) "Efficiency and social institutions: uses and misuses of economic reasoning in sociology," *Annual Review of Sociology*, 12: 233–253.

Oi, J. C. (1986) "Commercializing China's rural cadres," *Problems of Communism* 35: 1–27.

—— (1989) "Market reforms and corruption in rural China," *Studies in Comparative Communism*, 12: 221–233.

—— (1992) "Fiscal reform and the economic foundations of local state corporatism in China," *World Politics*, 45: 99–126.

—— (1995) "The role of the local state in China's transitional economy," *The China Quarterly*, 144: 1132–1149.

—— (1999) *Rural China Takes Off: Institutional Foundations of Economic Reform*, Berkeley, CA: University of California Press.

Oi, J. C. and Walder, A. G. (eds) (1999) *Property Rights and Economic Reform in China*, Stanford, CA: Stanford University Press.

Parish, W. L. (1994) "Rural industrialization: Fujian and Taiwan," in T. P. Lyons and V. Nee (eds) *The Economic Transformation of South China: Reform and Development in the Post-Mao Era*, Ithaca, NY: East Asia Program, Cornell University, pp. 119–140.

Parish, W. L. and Michelson, E. (1996) "Politics and markets: dual transformations," *American Journal of Sociology*, 101: 1042–1059.

Parris, K. (1993) "Local initiative and national reform: the Wenzhou model of development," *The China Quarterly*, 134: 242.

Peck, M. J. and Richardson, T. J. (eds) (1992) *What Is to be Done?: Proposals for the Soviet Transition to the Market*, New Haven, CN: Yale University Press.

Peng, Y. (2002) "*Zhongguo de cunzheng gongye gongsi: suoyouquan, gongsizhili yu shichangjidou*" (Chinese villages and townships as industrial corporations: ownership, governance, and market discipline), *Tsinghua Sociological Review*, 1: 39, December.

Perrow, C. (1986) *Complex Organizations: A Critical Essay*, 3rd edn, New York: Random House.

Potter, J. (1972) "Land and lineage in traditional China," in M. Freedman (ed.) *Family and Kinship in Chinese Society*, Stanford, CA: Stanford University Press, pp. 121–138.

Powell, W. W. and Smith-Doerr, L. (1994) "Networks and economic life," in N. J.

202 Bibliography

Smelser and R. Swedberg (eds) *The Handbook of Economic Sociology*, Princeton, NJ: Princeton University Press, pp. 368–402.

Powell, W. W. and DiMaggio, P. J. (1991) *The New Institutionalism in Organizational Analysis*, Chicago, IL: The University of Chicago Press.

Putterman, L. G. (1993) *Continuity and Change in China's Rural Development: Collective and Reform Eras in Perspective*, Oxford: Oxford University Press.

Quanguo gesheng zizhiqu zhixiashi lishi tongji ziliao huibian 1949–1989 (Historical Statistical Material on the Nation's Provinces, Autonomous Regions, and Municipalities, 1949–1989) (1990) Beijing: Zhongguo tongji chubanshe).

Quanzhou shi huaqiao zhi (Annals of Quanzhou's Overseas Chinese) (1996) Beijing: Zhongguo Shehui chubanshe.

Quanzhou shi xianzhen qiye zhi (The Annals of Quanzhou's Township and Village Enterprises) (1993) Quanzhou: Quanzhou wanbao.

Quanzhou wanbao (Quanzhou Evening News) (2001) "Xiangzhen qiye chengwei jinji fazhan zhuyao zengzhangyuan" (TVEs become the main source of economic development), December 24.

—— (2002) "Shengrenda diaoyanzu lai quan diaoyan xiangzhen gongye yuanqu" (The survey research team of provincial congress visits Quanzhou to investigate township industrial parks), April 14.

—— (2002) "Gongye yuanqu yinling chuangxin zhilu" (Industrial parks take the lead in innovation), October 23.

—— (2003) "Kaifaqu weihe cheng 'wei kaifa,'" (Why development zones become "undeveloped?"), January 10.

Redding, S. G. and Whitley, R. D. (1990) "Beyond bureaucracy: toward a comparative analysis of forms of economic resource co-ordination and control," in S. R. Clegg and S. G. Redding (eds) *Capitalism in Contrasting Cultures*, Berlin and New York: Walter de Gruyter, pp. 79–104.

Redding, S. G. (1990) *The Spirit of Chinese Capitalism*, Berlin and New York: Walter de Gruyter.

Renmin yibao (People's Daily) (1985) "Zhongguo zhongyang jiwei gei Jinjiang diwei Jinjiang xingshu de gongkaixing" (An open letter from the CCP central committee discipline inspection commission to the Jinjiang prefectural CCP committee and the Jinjiang administrative office), July 14.

Ronnas, P. (1993) "Economic diversification and growth in rural China: the anatomy of a 'socialist' success story," *The Journal of Communist Studies*, 9(3): 216–244.

Rozelle, S. (1994) "Rural industrialization and increasing inequality: emerging patterns in China's reforming economy," *Journal of Comparative Economics*, 19: 362–391.

Rozelle, S. and Li, G. (1998) "Village leaders and land-rights formation in China," *The American Economic Review*, 88(2): 433–438.

Sachs, J. (1993) *Poland's Jump to the Market Economy*, Cambridge, MA: MIT Press.

Scott, R. W. (1994) "Institutions and organizations: toward a theoretical synthesis," in W. R. Scott and J. W. Meyer (eds) *Institutional Environments and Organizations: Structural Complexity and Individualism*, New York: Sage Publications, pp. 55–80.

—— (1995) *Institutions and Organizations*, New York: Sage.

Sen, N. C. (1990) *Rural Economy and Development in China*, Beijing: Foreign Language Press.

Selden, M. (1998) "After collectivization: continuity and change in rural China," in L. Szelenyi (ed.) *Privatizing the Land: Rural Political Economy in Post-Communist Societies*, pp. 125–148.

Shanghai jiaoqu nianjian 1949–1992 (Almanac of Shanghai Suburbs 1949–1992) (1994) Shanghai: Shanghai renmin chubanshe.

—— various years, Shanghai: Shanghai renmin chubanshe.

Shanghai jiaoqu tongji nianjian (Statistical Yearbook of Shanghai Suburbs), various years, Shanghai: Shanghai Municipal Statistics Bureau.

Shanghai nongcun tongji nianjian (Statistical Yearbook of Rural Shanghai), various years, Shanghai: Shanghai Municipal Statistics Bureau.

Shanghai tongji nianjian (Statistical Yearbook of Shanghai), various years, Shanghai: Shanghai Municipal Statistics Bureau.

—— 2002 (Statistical Yearbook of Shanghai 2002) Online. Available HTTP: http://jiansuo.jfdaily.com (accessed October 27, 2003)

Shanghai Statistics Bureau 2003 (Shanghai Top 100 Comprehensive-Ability Villages). Online. Available HTTP: http://www.stats-sh.gov.cn and http://www.stats-sh.gov.cn/hygs/pmjb/bjc.htm (accessed October 10, 2003).

Shen, L. (ed.) (1991) *Xiangzhen qiye yu guoying qiye bijiao yanjiu* (Comparative Studies of Rural Enterprises and State Enterprises), Beijing: Zhongguo jingji chubanshe.

Shen, Y. and Tong, C. (1992) *Zhongguo renkou qianyi* (The Population Migration in China – Historical and Contemporary Perspectives), Beijing: Zhongguo tongji chubanshe.

Shieh, S. (2000) "Centre, province and locality in Fujian's reforms," in Y. M. Yeung and D. K. Y. Chu (eds) *Fujian: A Coastal Province in Transition and Transformation*, Hong Kong: Chinese University Press, pp. 83–118.

Shirley, M. and Galal, A. (eds) (1994) *Does Privatization Deliver?: Highlights from a World Bank Conference*, Washington, DC: World Bank.

Shishi shi jianshi yilai zhuyao jingji zhibiao (Main Economic Indicators of Shishi City Since its Establishment) Online. Available HTTP: http://stats.shishi.gov.cn/sj.asp?fg_id=3 (accessed October 10, 2003).

Shishi shi shehui jingji tongji nianjian (Statistical Yearbook of Social and Economic Statistics, Shishi City) (1994) Shishi: Economic Bureau of Shishi City.

Shishi shi zhuyao jingji zhibiao (Main Economic Indicators of Shishi City) Online. Available HTTP: http://stats.qz.fj.cn/qzhome/qztjsj/qx50/qzqx50.html#30 (accessed October 11, 2003).

Smelser, N. J. and Swedberg, R. (1994) "The sociological perspective on the economy," in N. J. Smelser and R. Swedberg (eds) *The Handbook of Economic Sociology*, Princeton, NJ: Princeton University Press, pp. 3–26.

Song, L. (1994) "Neifa xing zengzhang yu tidu zhuanyi" (Internal increment and resource transfer in southern Jiangsu), in Z. Tonghua and W. Kequan (eds) *Jinxiu Jiangnan de xiandaihua lantu* (The Modernization Blueprint of the Grand Jiangnan), Nanjing: Nanjing daxue chubanshe, pp. 27–44.

Stark, D. and Bruszt, L. (1998) *Postsocialist Pathways: Transforming Politics and Property in East Central Europe*, Cambridge and New York: Cambridge University Press.

Stark, D. and Nee, V. (1989) "Toward an institutional analysis of state socialism," in V. Nee and D. Stark (eds) *Remaking the Economic Institutions of Socialism: China and Eastern Europe*, Stanford, CA: Stanford University Press, pp. 1–31.

Su, X. (1994) "Jianshe you zhongguo tese de shehui zhuyi zai Sunan de chenggong shijian" (Constructing the successful practice of socialism with Chinese characteristics in Sunan), *Renmin ribao* (People's Daily), January 10, 1994.

Suzhou shi shehui jingji tongji ziliao, 1949–1985 (Statistical Material on Society and Economy, Suzhou City, 1949–1985) (1986) Suzhou: Statistical Bureau of Suzhou City.

Suzhou tongji nianjian (Statistical Yearbook of Suzhou), various years, Beijing: Zhongguo tongji chubanshe.

Svejnar, J. and Woo, Josephine (1990) "Development patterns in four counties," in W. A. Byrd and L. Qingsong (eds) *China's Rural Industry: Structure, Development, and Reform*, Oxford: Oxford University Press, pp. 63–84.

Swedberg, R. (1994) "Markets as social structure," in N. J. Smelser and R. Swedberg (eds) *The Handbook of Economic Sociology*, Princeton, NJ: Princeton University Press, pp. 255–282.

Swedberg, R. and Granovetter, M. (1992) "Introduction," in M. Granovetter and R. Swedberg (eds) *The Sociology of Economic Life*, Boulder, CO: Westview Press, pp. 1–28.

Szelenyi, I. (1978) "Social inequalities in state socialist redistributive economies," *International Journal of Comparative Sociology*, 19: 63–87.

Tao, Y. (1988) *Sunan moshi yu zhifu zhi dao* (The Sunan Model and Path to Prosperity), Shanghai: Shanghai shehui kexueyuan chubanshe.

Tsai, K. S. (2002) *Back-Alley Banking: Private Entrepreneurs in China*, Ithaca, NY and London: Cornell University Press.

Unger, J. (2002) "The kaleidoscopic politics of rural China," in J. Unger (ed.) *The Transformation of Rural China*, Armonk, NY: M. E. Sharpe, pp. 197–222.

Unger, J. and Chan, A. (1995) "China, corporatism, and the East Asian model," *The Australian Journal of Chinese Affairs*, 33: 29–53.

—— (1999) "Inheritors of the boom: private enterprise and the role of local government in a rural south China township," *The China Journal*, 42: 45–74.

Vermeer, E. B. (1996) "Development of the share-holding cooperative system and property rights in China," paper presented at the conference on "Property Rights in Transitional Economics: Insights from Research on China," Hong Kong, June 13–15.

—— (1999) "Shareholding cooperatives: a property rights analysis," in J. C. Oi and A. G. Walder (eds) *Property Rights and Economic Reform in China*, Stanford, CA: Stanford University Press, pp. 123–144.

Walder, A. G. (1986) *Communist Neo Traditionalism: Work and Authority in Chinese Industry*, Berkeley and Los Angeles, CA: University of California Press.

—— (1994) "Corporate organization and local government property rights in China," in V. Milor (ed.) *Changing Political Economies: Privatization in Post-Communist and Reforming Communist States*, Boulder, CO: Lynne Rienner, pp. 53–66.

—— (1995a) "Local government as industrial firms: an organizational analysis of China's transitional economy," *American Journal of Sociology*, 101: 263–301.

—— (1995b) "China's transitional economy: interpreting its significance," *The China Quarterly*, 144: 963–979.

—— (1996) "Markets and inequality in transitional economics: toward testable theories," American Journal of Sociology, 101: 1060–1073.

—— (2002) "Markets and income inequality in rural China: political advantage in an expanding economy," *American Sociological Review*, 67: 231–253.

Walder, A. G. and Oi, J. C. (1999) "Property rights in the Chinese economy: contours of the process of change," in J. C. Oi and A. G. Walder (eds) *Property Rights and Economic Reform in China*, Stanford, CA: Stanford University Press, pp. 1–24.

Wang, T., Yang, H. and Qiao, C. (1997) *Zhongguo gufen hezuo jingji – lilun, shijian yu duice* (China's Shareholding Cooperation Economy: Theory, Practice and Strategy), Beijing: Qiye Guanli chubanshe.

Wang, Z., Bai, G. and Wang, Z. (eds) (2000) *Zhongguo cunmin zizhi de qianyan* (The Leading Edge of Villagers' Self-government in China), Beijing: Zhongguo Shehui Kexue chubanshe.

Wank, D. L. (1999) *Commodifying Communism: Business, Trust, and Politics in a Chinese City*, Cambridge and New York: Cambridge University Press.

—— (2002) "Business–State clientelism in China: decline or evolution?," in T. Gold, D. Guthrie, and D. Wank (eds) *Social Connections in China: Institutions, Culture, and the Changing Nature of Guanxi*, Cambridge: Cambridge University Press, pp. 97–116.

Watson, J. L. (1982) "Chinese kinship reconsidered: anthropological perspective on historical research," *The China Quarterly*, 92: 589–622.

Wei, Y. D. (2000) *Regional Development in China: States, Globalization, and Inequality*, London and New York: Routledge.

Weitzman, M. and Xu, C. (1994) "Chinese township village enterprises as vaguely defined cooperatives," *Journal of Comparative Economics*, 2: 121–145.

Whiting, S. H. (2001) *Power and Wealth in Rural China: The Political Economy of Institutional Change*, Cambridge and New York: Cambridge University Press.

Whyte, M. K. (1995) "The social roots of China's economic development," *The China Quarterly*, 144: 999–1019.

Wong, C. P. W. (1982) "Rural industrialization in the people's republic of China: lessons from the cultural revolution decade," in U.S. Congress Joint Economic Committee (ed.) *China Under the Four Modernizations*, Washington, DC: U.S. Government Printing Office, pp. 394–417.

—— (1992) "Fiscal reform and local industrialization," *Modern China*, 18: 197–227.

Wong, J., Ma, R., and Yang, M. (eds) (1995) *China's Rural Entrepreneurs: Ten Case Studies*, Singapore: Times Academic Press.

Wong, S.-L. (1985) "The Chinese family firm: a model," *The British Journal of Sociology*, 36: 58–72.

—— (1988a) "The applicability of Asian family values to other sociocultural settings," in P. Berger and H. H. M. Hsiao (eds) *In Search of an East Asian Development Model*, New Brunswick, NJ: Transaction Books, pp. 134–152.

—— (1988b) *Emigrant Entrepreneurs: Shanghai Industrialists in Hong Kong*, Hong Kong and New York: Oxford University Press.

—— (1996) "Chinese entrepreneurs and business trust," in G. G. Hamilton (ed.) *Asian Business Network*, Berlin and New York: Walter de Gruyter, pp. 13–26.

Woo, W. T. (1999) "The real reasons for China's growth," *The China Journal*, 41: 115–137.

World Bank (1990) *China: Revenue Mobilization and Tax Policy*, Washington, DC: World Bank.

—— (1997) *Sharing Rising Incomes: Disparities in China*, Washington, DC: World Bank.

Wu, J.-M. (1998) "Zhongguo xiangcun kuaisu gongyehua de zhidu dongli: difang chanquan tizhi yu feizhengshi siyouhua" (Institutional dynamics of rapid industrial growth in rural China: local property rights regime and informal privatization), *Taiwan Zhengzhih Xuekan* (Taiwanese Political Science Review), 3: 3–63.

—— (2001) "State policy and Guanxi network adaptation in China: local bureaucratic rent-seeking," *Issues and Studies*, 37(1): 20–48.
Wu, J. X. (2000) "Jiang Zeming de huatielu?" (The Waterloo Battle of Jiang Zeming) Online. Available HTTP: http://www.ncn.org/zwgInfo/0011b/53-30b.htm (accessed October 25, 2003).
Wujiang tongji nianjian 1995 (Statistical Yearbook of Wujiang 1995), Wujiang: Wujiang tongji ju (Wujiang Statistics Bureau).
—— *2002* (Statistical Yearbook of Wujiang 2002) Online. Available HTTP: http://www.qsjournal.com.cn/qs/20030201/BIG5/qs%5E352%5E0%5E26.htm (accessed October 27, 2003).
Wu, Q., Wang, H. and Xu, X. (1990) "Noneconomic determinants of workers' incomes," in W. A. Byrd and Q. Lin (eds) *China's Rural Industry: Structure, Development, and Reform*, Oxford: Oxford University Press, pp. 323–338.
Xiangzhen Qiye Zhengce Fagui Xuanbian (Selected Laws and Regulations Concerning Township – Village Enterprise) (1987) Beijing: Xinhua chubanshe.
Xie, Z. and Ling, Y. (1994) *Xiangzhen Qiye Yunxing Jizhi Yanjiu* (Research on the Operating Mechanism of Township-Village Enterprises), Shanghai: Shanghai shehui kexueyuan chubanshe.
Xinhua News (2002) "Fujian maixiang waijingmao qiangsheng" (Fujian moving toward a strong province of foreign trade), September 7. Online. Available HTTP: http://big5.xinhuanet.com/gate/big5/news.xinhuanet.com/fortune/2002-09/07/content_553368.htm (accessed October 28, 2003).
Xinhua News (2003) "Zhanzheng yingxiang xielei chukou" (The war influenced shoes' export), April 3. Online. Available HTTP: http://big5.xinhuanet.com/gate/big5/news.xinhuanet.com/fortune/2003-04/03/content_813280.htm (accessed October 15, 2003).
Xinshanghai gongye tongji ziliao 1949–1990 (Statistical Yearbook of New Shanghai's Industry 1949–1990) (1992) Shanghai: Zhongguo tongji chubanshe.
Yang, D. L. (1997) *Beyond Beijing: Liberalization and the Regions in China*, London: Routledge.
You, Ji (1998) *China's Enterprise Reform: Changing State – Society Relations After Mao*, London and New York: Routledge.
Young, S. (1995) *Private Business and Economic Reform in China*, New York: M. E. Sharpe.
Zhongguo guoqing congshu: baixiangshi jingji shehui diaocha, jinjiang juan (A Series of China's National Information – One Hundred County and City Socioeconomic Survey: Jinjiang book part) (1992) Beijing: Zhongguo dabaike quanshu chubanshe.
Zhongguo nongye nianjian (Agricultural Yearbook of China), various years, Beijing: Nongye chubanshe.
Zhongguo siying jingji nianjian (Almanac of Chinese Private Economy) (1994) Hong Kong: Jingji daobaoshe.
Zhongguo tongji nianjian (Statistical Yearbook of China) various years, Beijing: Zhongguo tongji chubanshe.
Zhongguo xiangzhen qiye nianjian 1978–1987 (Yearbook of Chinese Township and Village Enterprises 1978–1987) (1988) Beijing: Nongye chubanshe.
Zhongguo xiangzhen qiye nianjian (Yearbook of Chinese Township and Village Enterprises) various years, Beijing: Nongye chubanshe).
Zhongguo xianyu jingjiwang (China County-level Economy Web) (2002) "Di er jie

zhongguo xianyu jingji jiben jingzhengli baiqiang xianshi mingdan" (2nd China county-level economy basic competitiveness top 100). Online. Available HTTP: http:// www.china-county.org/erjie/baiqiang.htm (accessed October 15, 2003).

Zhou, E. and Zhang, Y. (1991) *Chengxiang Xietiao Fazhan Yanjiu* (Research on the Urban Rural Coordination and Development), Nanjing: Jiangsu renmin chubanshe.

Zhou, X. G., Zhao, W., Li, Q., and Cai, H. (2003) "Embeddedness and contractual relationships in China's transitional economy," *American Sociological Review*, 68: 75–102.

Zhuang, G. (2001a) "Feihua jinjiangji shetuan de bianhua ji jinsanshinian yu zujidi de lianxi" (The change of Jinjiang's Chinese associations in the Philippines and their connections with their ancestral villages), *Nanyang Wenti Yanjiu* (Research on Southeast Asia), 105: 61–72.

—— (2001b) *Huaqiao huaren yu zhongguo de guanxi* (The Relationship of Overseas Chinese and China), Guangzhou: Guangdong gaoding jiaoyu chubanshe.

Zhuang, J. (1993) "Chendai dingshi huizu hanhua de yanjiu" (Research on Han assimilation of the Ding lineage in Chendai), *Haijiaoshi Yanjiu* (Research on Maritime History), 34: 93–107.

Zweig, D. (1999) *Distortions in the opening: "segmented deregulation" and weak property as explanations for China's "zone fever" of 1992–1993*, Hong Kong: Hong Kong Institute of Asia-Pacific Studies, Chinese University of Hong Kong.

Index

Locators following a modified main heading indicate references to extensive topics. Locators in brackets [ ] indicate charts or tables; locators followed by an asterisk (*) indicate pictures; locators with an n indicate endnotes.

15th Party Congress 72, 114, 190n2

Acer 103
Agricultural Bank 57, 81
Agricultural Bureau 35
Agricultural Supply Company 50, 51
Aihua Underwear Company 167–8
Anhui general industrial park 142
Anti-Rightist Campaign 145, 160
Australia 113

banks *see* financial institutions
Baoshan District 49
Beijing 128, 133, 151, 152, 186, 187
Bruszt 13
Budapest 141
Bureau of Agriculture of Jinshang County 54, 60
Bureau of Agriculture of Shanghai City 54, 60
Bureau of Light Industry in Shanghai 59

cadres *see* officials
capitalism 1, 7, 17, 118; *see also* free market
centrally controlled economy *see* planned economy
Chairman Mao 133; *see also* Mao Zedong
changing the system (*gaizhi*) 34, 72, 114, 139–40
chemical fiber market 110
Chen Yonggui 133, 161
Chen Yun 152
Chendai Garment Company 137, 147

Chendai township 131–2, 134, 137, 140, 144, 150–2; *see also* Jinjiang
clientelism 11
collective unified management (*jiti tongyi jingying*) 56, 68, 69, 184;
   definition of 27, 47, 82, 189n5
collectives; *see also* Sunan model:
   definition of 25, 106, 189n5; end of 34, 184–5; as private 27, 134; problems of 33; as shareholding system 48; *also mentioned* 11, 70, 188n3, 190n4
collectivization 18
command economy 1, 178
commune and brigade enterprises (CBE) 55, 56
Communist Youth League 75, 104
contract responsibility system 47, 81, 82, 83
corruption 5, 6, 174, 176
County Foreign Trade Bureau 67
Cultural Revolution:
   end of 75, 105; hardships of 68, 143, 161; industry during 56, 132, 133, 142, 161–2, 188n3; recovery from 186; regulations against industry 106, 161; *also mentioned* 4, 60, 104, 109, 143, 145, 148

Dakang Corporation 50, 51, 52
Dakang Real Estate Company 50
Dakang Taxi Company 50
Daqiuzhuang 52
Deng Xiaoping 48
Dupont 109, 110

Index 209

Durkheim 13

Eastern Europe 7, 13, 141, 183
economic growth 7, 33;
  difference 28; slowdown of 33, 139, 141; soft landing 35
economic policy: effects of 1
economic reforms 7;
  explanations of 8–13; government role 96; questions about 1, 8, 11, 70; role of local institutions 10, 184; secretes of 6; slow down of 65; social embeddedness explanation 16, 181
economic transformation 7, 14;
  difference 1, 3–4, 7, 12; role of institution 14, 15
emancipate the mind (*jiefang sixiang*) 55
embeddedness 16, 181–3
enterprises *see* township and village enterprises
entrepreneurs:
  government as 8; government ties 11; obstacles 133; private 5, 9, 166, 167; role of 157
Europe 141

Fei Hsiao-tung 65
financial institutions 57–8, 118
foreign investment:
  in 2000s 20; growth of 5, 35; in Yangtze Delta 66, 67–8
Four Cleanups Campaign 148
free market; *see also* capitalism:
  in countryside 101–2, 149; cronyism 118, 185; develops 1, 7; versus planned 9, 183
Fu Ya 86
Fujian; *see also* Jinjiang:
  compared with Jiangsu 98, 104; compared with Yangtze Delta 20, 48, 63–4, 129, 178, 186; economy 127, 128, 141–2, 162; enterprises 103, 134; income disparity of 129; local institutions of 181, 187; and overseas Chinese 162, 188n2; peasants 1, 3; private enterprises 13, 134–5, 162, 186; property rights 160, 186; shareholding system 48; weather 2

Gang of Four 54
Gao village 52, 67
Gao Xin 112

Gaonan Steel Rolling Factory 53
Giant 103
Glyn Cosmetics Company 50
government *see* local governments
Grand Hotel 100, 103
Great Leap Forward 27 107, 143, 148, 188n3
Guangdong 11, 103, 128, 135, 147, 164, 172
Guangzhou 166
guanxi 9, 149

Hancun village 176*, 177*;
  economy of 152–4, 164; enterprises of 132, 135, 164, 165; environment of 3, 5, 143; foreign investment in 163, 177; government of 155–7; lineages of 159–60, 163, 173, 193n23; local institutions of 156; *also mentioned* 1, 131
Hangzhou 103, 172
Hanjiang township 131, 143
Hanjiang Township Sea Products Collection Station 135
Hokkien 147
Hong Kong 133, 137, 138, 144, 147, 160, 164
Hu Yaobang 152
Huang Song:
  as authority 93–4, 110, 113, 114; background of 91; on foreign investment 102; on industry 107, 108; on privatization 114, 115; promoted 111, 112, 113; sells TVEs 118–20; in Taiwan 100, 103, 121; *also mentioned* 4, 6, 104
Huang Wen:
  background of 84–5, 91, 104; as capitalist 178; career of 91; as director of industries 112–13, 120; establishes industry 105, 107, 108; promoted 114; sells TVEs 119–20; as shareholder 89; *also mentioned* 75, 80, 93
Huaqiao village 53, 61
Huaxi 52, 190n4
Hui (Muslim) 131, 144, 190n2
Hui Affairs Association 144
Hungary 141

individual contracting (*geren chengbao*) 47
Indonesia 144
institution 14, 15

210 *Index*

Japan 128
Jiang Zemin 190n2
Jiangsu; *see also* Sunan:
  before reforms 104–5; compared with Fujian 98, 104; corporatist arrangements in 11, 13; enterprises of 52, 55, 114, 189n7; foreign investment in 66, 100; institutions of 55; manufacturing 105; privatization of 72, 81–91; successful villages 65; *also mentioned* 1, 3
Jimei 2
Jin Hairong 86
Jinan export processing zone 142
Jinjiang; *see also* Fujian 20, 131;
  compared with Yangtze Delta 132–3, 147–8, 149–50; crackdown against 150–2; economic wealth of 21–2, [23–4], [28], [153]; economy 129, 139, 140–2, 149; foreign investment 146–7; government role 147–8, 154, 186; industry [29], 132, 140; joint ventures 146; lineages of 143–4, 158–9, 186; local institutions in 142, 158; overseas networks 145–16; ownership structure [130], 133, [136], 139; practicing capitalism 150–1; private enterprises 134–5, 136–7, [138]; privatization 139, 140; property rights of 130, 158; reforms 149; shareholding 136–7, 140; state-owned enterprises of 130, 136; TVEs of 134, 135, 139
Jinjiang Shoe Fair 140
Jinjiang shoe street 141
Jinmen 1, 127
Jinshang County 54
Jinze 59
joint household (*lianu*) enterprises 136, 137, 149, 192n16
joint operation (*lianying*) 63, [64], 65
joint ventures 52–3, 67

Kang village 49–52
karaoke 4
KMT 133, 161
Kornai 8
KTV 103, 172lateral linkage (*hengxiang lianhe*) 63, 64

Li Dong:
  inventions of 110; moves to Shuang 108–9; *also mentioned* 5, 80
Lin, Nan 188n3

Lin Qiang 156
Lin Qiu 137–138
Lin Shuiping 168*;
  background of 164; career of 164–7; companies of 135, 172
Lin Shuiqiang: who is 1, 3
Lin Songfei 103
Lin Wei:
  background of 172; as entrepreneur 172; father of 173; as an official 176, 177, 178; on officials 172, 175, 176; popularity of 174
Lin Weixing 163–4
Lin Xiuyan 169–72, 171*, 173
lineages 1, 143–4, 158–9, 163, 173, 191n10–11
local governments:
  elections 155–7, 174; as enterprises 10; merge with enterprises 91, 98; financing industry 58; key role of 152, 155–6, 158, 184–5; sells land 121; weakened role of 19, 121
local institutions:
  change instigator 18, 19, 178, 181; development of 34; definition of 18; role in economy 13, 17–18, 34, 142, 178–9, 182; in Fujian 157–9, 181; importance of 179, 180, 181, 182, 186–7; in Jiangsu 55, 180–1; and networks 69, 99; in politics 159; power of 156, 159, 173; shaping reform 10, 12–13, 68, 182; *also mentioned* 7, 8
local state corporatism 10–11, 12, 98, 180
Lu Hanlong 188n3
Lugang harbor 174

Mao Zedong 161; *see also* Chairman Mao
Marco Polo 20
market reform *see* economic reform
market transition account 8–10, 12, 179
Matsu 127
Mei township 4, 100, 101, 103, 107
Meng Hailin 54, 60
Meng Jiang 93, 94
Middle East 141, 191n9
Ming Dynasty 1, 144
Ministry of Agriculture 167
Minnan 3, 21

Nanan 129

Nanhai County 61
Nanjing 4, 5
Nanjing University 65
Nee 8, 9
nepotism 6
New Village 154, 177, 177*
No. 3 Branch Factory of Shanghai Sewing-Machine Plant 65
North 14, 18

officials:
  benefit 99; as capitalists 5, 7, 10, 99, 175; control of resources 68, 69; corruption of 5, 6, 174, 176; engineering reforms 11, 33–4, 69, 184; as entrepreneurs 51–4, 180; as initiators 56, 58, 61–2
Oi, Jean 10, 11, 81, 96
overseas Chinese 144–7, 154, 161, 162, 163–164, 188n2

party officials *see* officials
party secretary *see* officials
peasants:
  employment of 35–6, 45, 48, 189n11; unemployment of 101
People's Daily 151
People's Republic of China 127
Philippines 144, 145, 146, 161, 173, 175, 177
Pingcun village 131–132
Pinwang 65
planned economy 7, 9, 127, 183
post-socialism 182, 183
private business 1, 8, 112; *see also* private enterprises
private enterprises; *see also* Jinjiang:
  birth of 34; growth of 10, 36, [38], 39, 45–7; hardships 111–12; importance of 8, 36
private entrepreneurs *see* entrepreneurs
private property *see* property rights
private sector *see* private enterprises
privatization; *see also* property rights, transformation:
  complete 74; contract for 116; elites benefit of 94, 98, 118, 122–3, 184–5, 190n10; government encouragement of 33, 72, 114, 115, 190; necessity of 114; opposition to 72, 114–15; process of 81, 140; in Sunan 73, 89; waves of 73, 74, 118; in Zhejiang 73, 162, 185; *also mentioned* 5, 10
property rights 8, 9, [26];

arrangement variations 25–7, 45, 81, 178–9; in local institutions 39, 157–8, 178, 180; obscured ownership 26; questions on 131; social consequences of 34, 185; transformation 26–7, 34, 72, 81, 157, 178–9, 185
Pudong 52, 61, 66, 189n12

Qiang 173, 174; *see also* Lin Wei
Qing dynasty 143, 144, 161
Qinghua University 65
Qingpu County 59
Quanzhou:
  industry 127, 140, 141; foreign investment 129, 146–7; overseas connections 144; *also mentioned* 3, 173
Quemoy 1, 127

rational choice 14
reforms *see* economic reforms
restoration of the capitalists (*ziben zhuyi fupi*) 133
rural China:
  structure of 19
Rural Credit Cooperatives 57
rural economy 7, 8
rural enterprises; *see also* township and village enterprises:
  as collectives 27, 70; growth of 35, [37–8]; pre-reforms 106, 189n10; success of 33
rural workers *see* peasants
Russia 141

Sanming 127
Science and Technology Commission for National Defense 65
Second Workshop of Shanghai Electric Plant 108;
Shandong 52, 99
Shanghai:
  economic wealth 21–2, [23–4], [28], 43; foreign investment in [66]; industry [29], 43, [44], [46] ; market 172; as shareholding system 48; successful villages of 49–55, 59–61; *also mentioned* 11, 20, 103
Shanghai Academy of Social Sciences 188n3
Shanghai Research Institute of Shipbuilding 61
Shanghai Statistics Bureau 35
Shanghai Welding Second Plant 61

212 Index

Shanghia Sifang Agriculture-Industry-Commerce Company 54
Shantou 128, 164
shareholding system 48–9, 52–4, 69, 71, 115, 189n6
Shenzhen 128
Shishi:
  as capitalist roadsters 161; as case study 131, 160; criticized by Beijing 133; development of 133–4; economy 139, 148, 160–1, 162; enterprises of 135; environment 160; government role 148, 165; and overseas Chinese 161, 163–4; in reform era 162; markets of 160, 161, 162, 164, 166; ownership structure [130]; private enterprises 162, 167*; also mentioned 1, 3, 20, 144
Shishi Sanxie Electric Automobile Company 167–8
Shishi Shipping Company 169–172, 171*
Shuang village 3, 6, 102*, 110, 113*, 117*, 120*;
  acrylic fiber plant 119; chemical fiber plant 110; chemical products factory 105, 106, 107; color master batch factory 119, 178; contract system of 82; differential polyester chip factory 109*, 118, 119; enterprise fees 97, 100; 116; enterprises in the reforms 75, 79–81, 96; environment 5; foreign investment in 121, 122; income gap of 94, [95], 190n5; location 74; money-losing enterprises 83, [85]; partnerships of 105; privatization of 74, 81–91, 93, 114–23; sale of TVEs 84, 116, 119; Second Workshop of Shanghai Electric Plant 108; shareholding 115; success of 112; TVEs of [76–8], [85], [87–8]; visits to 74; workers of 94, 104, 122*
Shuang village elites 91, [92];
  domination of 74–5, 81; power of 74, 114–15, 185; after privatization 74, 96, 184–5; before privatization 93, 114
Sifang Company 60
Singapore 144
social institutions see local institutions
social networks 9, 13, 16–17, 60–1, 69
Socialist Education Campaign 148
Song, Professor 4, 5
Song Taiping 167–9

Songjiang Agricultural Vocational School 54
Songjiang County 53, 72
Songjiang Enamel Factory 53, 61
South Africa 141
South China Sea 187
South Korea 128
Southeast Asia 161
Special Economic Zones 128
state enterprises 33, 35–6; see also township and village enterprises
state-owned firms see state enterprises
Sun Xue 90, 93, 119
Sunan:
  privatization 72–3; officials 56; silk industry 108; under reforms 71; also mentioned 3, 4, 187
Sunan model; see also collectives:
  definition of 33, 188n1; end of 34; growth of 33; institutional arrangement of 62; problems of 71; also mentioned 20
Suzhou:
  bank loans 57; financial capital of 58; foreign investment in [66], 103; TVEs 64; workers 60, 61; also mentioned 4, 39
Suzhou-Wuxi-Changzhou Spark Program 80–1, 112
Szelenyi 8

Taipei 100, 121
Taiwan:
  conflict with China 1, 127, 128; investors 6, 100–1, 103, 147, 163, 177; labor costs 103; lineage relations 144, 163, 173; also mentioned 3, 133
taking off collective caps (zhaimao)
Tangquio Township 65
Textile Ministry 80, 109
Tiananmen 65
Tianjin 1, 5, 11, 52, 108, 109
Tianjin Institute of Chemical Engineering 80, 109
Tianyi Garment Factory 67
township and village enterprises (TVE) 11, [39]; see also rural enterprises;
  capital for 56–9, 67–8, 135–6; collectives 71; development of 68, 69; disguised as 134; entrepreneurs of 34, 56; examples of 50; growth of 33, 35, 43–5, 71; human resources 60; importance of 36, 39, 56, 152, 154; in

reform era [63], 190n9; privatization of 9–10, 34; revenue generators 152; shareholding system 48, 72; state enterprises, compared to 35–6, 39, 110; state enterprises, cooperation with 65
Tuncun 4

USSR 7

Walder 81, 98
Wan Li 150, 162
Wang Hua 5, 80, 108–9, 110
Wang Jin 84, 86, 111–12, 116
Wenzhou 13
Wing Thye Woo 9
workers *see* peasants
Wujiang 39;
  City 4, 74; economic wealth 21–2, [23–4], [28]; industry [29], [40–2]; orders to privatize 114, 121
Wujiang Agricultural Machinery Plant 65
Wuli high-tech industrial park 142
Wuxi 52, 55, 65, 72, 190n5

Xiamen 2, 127, 128, 144
Xiang Nan 152
Xiaoling 165; *see also* Lin Shuiping
Xincun village 54
Xinguang Garment Factor 53
Xinguang General Company 52
Xinhua News Agency 151

Xinjiang 187
Xu Gen 93, 94
Xu Kun 89
Xunjiang village 61, 62

Yangcun Shoe and Hat Factory 137, 147
Yangcun village 131–2, 134, 147, 154, 193n23
Yangtze Delta:
  as case study 188–9; compared with Fujian 20, 48, 63–4, 129, 178, 186; compared with Jinjiang 132–3, 147–8, 149–50; foreign investment 66; industry growth 56–7; local institutions of 54, 180–1, 184–5; markets 20; property rights 34, 47, 72, 81, 184–5; as shareholding system 48–9
Yangzi Petrochemical Corporation 81, 90
Yao Yilin 150
Yixing 72, 114
Youth League 61

Zhang Guoming 52–3, 67
Zhao Ziyang 150, 162
Zhejiang 73, 162, 185
Zhou Min 84, 91, 93, 111–12, 115
Zhounan village 61, 62
Zhu Genrong 50–1
Zhu Liangcai 53, 61
Zhuhai 128

eBooks – at www.eBookstore.tandf.co.uk

A library at your fingertips!

eBooks are electronic versions of printed books. You can store them on your PC/laptop or browse them online.

They have advantages for anyone needing rapid access to a wide variety of published, copyright information.

eBooks can help your research by enabling you to bookmark chapters, annotate text and use instant searches to find specific words or phrases. Several eBook files would fit on even a small laptop or PDA.

NEW: Save money by eSubscribing: cheap, online access to any eBook for as long as you need it.

Annual subscription packages

We now offer special low-cost bulk subscriptions to packages of eBooks in certain subject areas. These are available to libraries or to individuals.

For more information please contact webmaster.ebooks@tandf.co.uk

We're continually developing the eBook concept, so keep up to date by visiting the website.

www.eBookstore.tandf.co.uk